SHADOW PLAY:

Philosophy and Psychology of the Modern Horror Film

SHADOW PLAY:

Philosophy and Psychology of the Modern Horror Film

by Willy Greer

Midnight Marquee Press, Inc.
Baltimore, Maryland, USA

Copyright © 2011 by Willy Greer
Interior layout and cover design by Susan Svehla
Copy Editing by Linda J. Walter
Tarot Illustrations by Liana Norton

Without limiting the rights under copyright reserved above, no part of this publication may be reproduced, stored in or introduced into a retrieval system, or transmitted, in any form, or by any means (electronic, mechanical, photocopying, recording or otherwise), without the prior written permission of the copyright owner or the publishers of the book.

ISBN 13: 978-1-936168-08-8
Library of Congress Catalog Card Number 2010938649
Manufactured in the United States of America

First Printing by Midnight Marquee Press, Inc., January 2011

Dedication

For my Mom and Dad, Nancy and Ed Greer,
who must be breathing a huge sigh of relief
that my morbid childhood obsessions culminated in something positive.
Thank you for supporting me in every creative endeavor I've ever undertaken,
and sorry if I worried you guys.

Acknowledgments

Thanks to Jeff Dean, my partner in geekdom, for booze-addled days spinning horror soundtracks and geeking out with me on pirate radio, and for making me feel like less of a freak by being as obsessed with horror movies as me; very special thanks to my grandfather, James T. Hayter, for his love and support during a dark time; warm thanks to Brian Johnson, Byrd MacDonald, and the Horror Movie Night Crew, for summer getaways watching slasher films out in the woods; thanks to Sarah Cormier for putting up with my endless days doing "research" in my underwear; thanks to Mark Halvorsen for invaluable critical feedback and assistance in putting together the proposal for this book; thanks to Isaac Munez for taking me to see R-rated horror movies when I was a kid; very grateful thanks to Grant Cogswell and Dan Gildark for having my back and believing in the book, and for bringing me out of my shell at a time when I was living in bitter, hopeless retail hell; very special thanks to Michele Rainier—my love, my best friend, and my ally; grateful thanks to Brian Sereda for helping me on my search for the perfect tarot archetypes; endless gratitude to Liana Norton for bringing the tarot cards to life in her wonderful illustrations; thanks to Aaron Santigian, for joining Brian Sereda and me in the horror soundtrack cover band Gargamel all those years ago, and for continuing to be an inspiring and supportive partner in art and music; and eternal thanks to Mr. Robert Bullwinkel, for more than I can possibly express.

Preface
About This Book

This is not a Leonard Maltin–style reference book. It is not a guide to what you should rent next—in fact, there are spoilers galore contained herein. Rather, this is a collection of essays and analyses that wallow, splash and swallow in the sweet, sweet brine of horror cinema. I'm trying to pinpoint for myself (and hopefully for somebody else out there) exactly why some horror films work and why others do not.

I'm attacking the subject matter from every imaginable angle, analyzing every facet of the horror genre—from the grindhouse freakouts to the artsy-fartsy existentialist pieces—in an effort to find some of the same primal matter that links them together. I'm also gonna be going back into my youth, to try to track down the origins of my own shadow, and why it craves the arcane, taboo imagery that it does.

The first two chapters deal with psychological aspects of the shadow, and the rest of the book dives headlong into the movies themselves. Uncomfortable moments in the author's childhood will be revealed, psychobabble will be spouted about Jung and various serial killers, and the endings of many films will be heartlessly given away. Let it be known at the outset that *Shadow Play* assumes that the reader has seen the films in question and will not be upset by spoilers.

Still here? Cool. Onward.

TABLE OF CONTENTS

13   Introduction:
      What is Shadow Play?
15   Chapter One:
      Shadows and Projections
26   Chapter Two:
      Me and My Shadow
36   Chapter Three:
      Defending a Mountain of Crap
90   Chapter Four:
      Art With Guts
116   Chapter Five:
      Visceral Horror
151   Chapter Six:
      The Bottom
166   Chapter Seven:
      Paranoid Horror
186   Chapter Eight:
      Fear in Cinema

One does not become enlightened by imagining figures of light,
but by making the darkness conscious.
—C.G. Jung

There are two types of violence: creative and destructive.
—Alejandro Jodorowsky

Carl Jung

Introduction: What is Shadow Play?

Unfortunately there can be no doubt that man is, on the whole, less good than he imagines himself to be. Everyone carries a shadow, and the less it is embodied in the individual's conscious life, the blacker and denser it is. If an inferiority is conscious, one always has a chance to correct it. Furthermore, it is constantly in contact with other interests, so that it is constantly subjected to modification. But if it is repressed and isolated from consciousness, it never gets corrected.

—C.G Jung, *Psychology and Religion*, 1938

Scholars of psychoanalytical pioneer Carl Gustav Jung are strong proponents of the process known as "shadow work," the goal of which is to integrate repressed elements of one's psyche into one's conscious self, heal old wounds, confront one's dark side, and ultimately live a fully authentic life. Doing this requires being aware of traits one dislikes in other people, turning one's gaze inward, and realizing that one possesses those very same traits but projects them onto others. Owning one's shadow in this way is, in my opinion, worthwhile work. But it is most definitely *work*, in the sense that it requires a great deal of effort and commitment on behalf of the subject. Emotionally it can be a grueling experience, and this may deter those who are starting out on the path to integration.

Thus, I believe, the human race invented "shadow play."

We explore the world of pain and scars with tattoos, piercing, branding, cutting and metal implants. These adornments are, more or less, fear-free, willingly received artistic injuries that result in beautiful scars. We ride roller coasters, we jump out of airplanes, we go out of our way to endanger our lives in the safest possible ways. BDSM (bondage and discipline/ sadism and masochism) is, of course, a fear-free, consensual, sexualized, and creative exploration of non-consensual, atrocious activities: kidnapping, torture, rape, etc.

Sports take the most globally detrimental urges in any society—the desire to compete against and dominate other teams/tribes/nations—and isolate them in *literal* arenas of fantasy. Not only are sporting events more or less make-believe wars, but also the setting (especially where boxing is concerned) is a direct symbolic link to the voyeuristic debauchery of the ancient Roman Coliseum. I won't be talking much about sports as shadow-therapy, because I've always been horrible at them and don't understand them. Ever last-picked for the kickball team in grade school, I dove into the arts to get away from sports. But I try to be man enough to look past my biases and tolerate sports as being as culturally important as the arts. And as far as I'm concerned, that's more than enough lip service paid to the fucking jocks.

And, of course, there are horror films and stories. And horror is what we'll be discussing here, as it's what I feel most qualified to analyze (I've been a horror geek since way before it was good for me).

In his own writings on the horror genre, Stephen King likens the primal mind to a river teeming with hungry gators, and posits that we crave horror because we've got to "keep the gators fed." While I think this is absolutely true, King might have overlooked one vital reason it is perhaps healthier to watch horror films than to not watch them:

Fantasy and speculation are no small part of what makes us able to evolve philosophically and strive for civilization. For speculative actions only bring about speculative consequences, and enable us to make better, more informed decisions on what to do or not do in the real world.

The cold fact is: Horror exists. The potential for violence and atrocity fills our history, threatens our present, and lurks in our genetic makeup. It would be foolhardy and bigoted to assume that any one of us is beyond the potential for becoming a monster, to not question the shadow's origins and motivations. For curiosity is yet another aspect of humanity that ensures our evolution. Without questioning the shadow's motivations, no understanding of it can be gained. The shadow wants more than simply to be fed; it wants to be understood and accepted. It's only when it's been starved for too long that it breaks free and demands nourishment, and then, more often than not, it's too late for reparations; it manifests itself as what we fear it to be: ravenous, unreasonable and uncontrollable.

Chapter One:
Shadows and Projections

What is a Movie?

Continual conscious realization of fantasies, together with an active participation in the fantastic events has...the effect firstly of extending the conscious horizon by the inclusion of numerous unconscious events; secondly of gradually diminishing the dominant influence of the unconscious; and thirdly of bringing about a change in personality.
—*The Collected Works of C.G. Jung, Vol.7*

To a filmmaker, a movie is a conscious projection of fantasies; to the filmgoer, it is like a dream. The filmmaker sees sets, costumes and actors when he watches movies, be they his own or those of others. He sees a succession of still frames depicting a fake world—stills that only *appear* to move when they are shown in rapid succession. The filmgoer, however, sees a living, breathing world entirely unto itself. And if it's good enough, it replaces the filmgoer's own world for the time that it's onscreen.

Suspension of disbelief, we call it. It's an ability that we have to fight to hold on to as we get older, because the adult world often demands that we remain rooted in reality. We forget how to play, and often we find the concept of *playing* as adults embarrassing. But there's a part of us that simply does not want to let go of that sense of whimsy and fancy, that refuses to grow up completely. We create forums for our adult selves that are acceptable to play within—role-playing games, as it were. The less inhibited among us play full-on, unabashed role-playing games like *Vampire: The Masquerade* or *Dungeons and Dragons*, or attend sci-fi conventions and Renaissance Fairs dressed up as whatever mythic figures best complement our alter egos.

Adults forget how to play (photo Library of Congress)

Most of us—even the most conservative among us—seek some sort of whimsy in our lives. And the act of engrossing ourselves in fiction, be it written or filmed, is rooted in the desire to *play*, to suspend disbelief as we did in childhood, and as the freaks and geeks in the adult world still seem to be able to do. Movies and books allow us easiest access to this world; society does not look as strangely upon a group of people gathering in one room to stare at two-dimensional images of other people pretending to do things, as it does upon people pretending to do things themselves.

Adults still crave the activity of playing, but require boundaries in which to do it—we have the need to prove to our peers that we're grown up: kids play cops and robbers; we play paintball. And as adults we like to know when the bounds of reality have become blurry; we like to maintain control, and there's an abundant element of control in the movie-going experience. The plot isn't a mystery, nor is the suspension of disbelief as intense as it is in dreams (sensory deprivation is limited to the dimming of the theatre lights, only submerging us so far in the fantasy). The outcome isn't ruled by chance, as it is in role-playing games (or real life, for that matter).

But we can still lie to ourselves enough to believe in what's happening onscreen. We still have the ability to escape into the world of movies. Therefore, we can rest assured that adulthood hasn't fully sunk its claws into us yet. By the same token, we can exit if we are unsatisfied with the movie we're watching, or if we have to go to the bathroom. Therefore, we can rest assured that we have control over our delusions. And, sitting in a special room with the lights off, gathered among a group of friends and strangers who are all watching two-dimensional people play make-believe, we can rest assured that we aren't weird. Or something.

What is a Nightmare?

The primitive mentality does not invent myths; it experiences them.
Myths are original revelations of the primitive psyche.
—*The Collected Works of C.G. Jung, Vol.18*

It is impossible for mankind to "outgrow" the need for myths—our capacity for inventing and entertaining myths is one of the traits that separate us from animals. (If somebody winds up proving that animals can not only speculate about their origins, but communicate their speculations to each other, I will humbly eat my words.) It is detrimental to human existence to reflexively equate the word "fanciful" with the word "immature" (he said, aware that he might merely be trying to subconsciously cover his fanciful ass). To suspend disbelief is simply to entertain speculation, and obviously our speculative abilities are an important part of our survival instinct; it would be wise for a driver to entertain the speculation of what might happen to him were he not to wear a seatbelt.

We observe our pets sleeping fitfully, and we (safely) surmise that animals can dream. It's not so far-fetched a notion to imagine *why* animals might dream: they are probably "practicing" certain relevant situations, like hunting and being hunted. It could be further (and still safely) speculated that with enough repetition, animals can learn from their dreams. But do we entertain the notion that animals understand

Dreamscape (1984), starring Dennis Quaid, uses psychics to enter people's dreams.

the *concept* of dreaming? And as for the notion of an animal having a neurotic dream about its dick falling off in front of its mother, well, I don't think any of us can suspend our disbelief that high.

So. Safely surmised, human dreams serve a myriad of purposes other than aiding in day-to-day survival. Our dreams are more than battle-plans for the next waking day; they are wishes, they are fears, they are examinations of what our minds cannot let go of, what our hearts desire, and what possibilities are available to us. Every time we go to sleep, we become simultaneous filmmakers and filmgoers; we fool ourselves and allow it to happen. Everyone talks to him- or herself once in a while. But how separate is this piece of us that we are *surprised* by what it tells us in dreams? We don't know what's going to happen next in normal, non-lucid dreaming, and we are usually unaware of our real, dreaming self. It's a disconnection so extreme we might associate it with schizophrenia if we weren't talking about our own sane selves.

Every night we occupy a new world made up of our own projections. And every day we wake up to a world that is the same as it was when we left it, and therefore "real." We think nothing of it, even though dreams are certainly real enough while they're happening. It's extremely difficult to address this subject from a Western standpoint without coming across as a stoner philosopher, but the idea of all things that we *experience* as real *being* real is fascinating. (Or is it only fascinating to those who have done their share of drugs?)

To the rational adult mind, the notion is perhaps more terrifying than it is fascinating. To dream is to venture across the line of control; it is to succumb to the unknown. It's much more palatable to a mind that has enough trouble coping with the waking world to assume that dreams are entirely fictional, and to dismiss them immediately upon awakening. The more fanciful among us keep ourselves up at night sometimes, in dread of not only what our subconscious has in store for us, but of how real it's going to seem, and how real our loss of control is in REM sleep. As Edgar Allan Poe wrote, "Dreams—those little slices of death. How I loathe them."

What is Paranoid Delusion?

Projection means the expulsion of a subjective context onto an object...the subject gets rid of painful, incompatible contents by projecting them... The general psychological reason for projection is always an activated unconscious that seeks expression.
—*The Collected Works of C.G. Jung, Vol.18*

Where are the lines drawn between dream, faith, art and schizophrenia? All these phenomena require a degree of suspension of disbelief, an aptitude for considering the intangible. In art, we play games with ourselves, immersing ourselves halfway into its illusions, but not enough to lose complete awareness of outside stimuli. If a figure were to jump into our peripheral vision, we would register it and likely snap out of our trance.

Dreams are much like the art-trance, but the immersion is deeper and the dreamer himself is both artist and patron. Still, the sleeping nervous system is on alert for any changes in the waking environment—temperature, sounds, and smells.

To have faith in something, be it in the loyalty of family or the existence of God, is to know in the back of one's mind that such things could be proven wrong. But yet we are moved to put emotional stock in the intangible, the *object* of faith. Faith is belief in what you can't prove.

With schizophrenia, we're in a darker, more vague area, but, I believe, a still relevant territory. At first glance, schizophrenia almost appears to be a combination of faith and dream. Schizophrenia encourages belief in things one cannot prove, because, due to some neurochemical misfire, one can sense things that are not there. One hears voices, sees demons, feels eyes watching one. I suppose a schizophrenic could hallucinate anything and dream. It is often souls such as these—souls that are incapable of differentiating between fantasy and reality—that are responsible for tragic manifestations of the shadow in the real world.

Nick Blinko managed to create this album.

On the more mild-mannered side, Nick Blinko—outsider artist, musician, and paranoid schizophrenic—has recalled moments spent in the grips of the illness, believing he was going to be crowned the next Pope, and planting his paintings in his garden to see if they would grow. And then of course, you've got folks like David Berkowitz, the "Son of Sam," who was "ordered" to kill by a demon that he believed lived in his neighbor's dog. For these people, the line is more than blurred, and it remains uncertain if that line can be established at all in such minds. Sometimes there's simply nothing we can do; sometimes a soul just seems born doomed.

It would be far too easy—as easy as it is to villify media violence—to blame bad parenting for real life shadow acts, like, for instance, the student shootings at Columbine High. There's garden-variety juvenile delinquency, and then there's the violence at an actual high school. If an explanation exists as to why those kids did what they did, it will not be arrived at easily. This certainty, to me, is even more frightening than the idea that "it could happen here." The idea that some human beings operate on a level beyond our comprehension, whether due to a chemical imbalance, unfortunate genetics, or something we're not even aware of yet. And that if the mental states of these people drive them to do something horrible, there might not be anything we can do to prevent it, or even see it coming.

What is Reflection?

> Reflection is the cultural instinct par excellence, and its strength is shown in the power of culture to maintain itself in the face of untamed nature.
>
> The shadow is merely somewhat inferior, primitive and awkward; not wholly bad. It contains even childish or primitive qualities that would in a way vitalize and embellish human existence, but—convention forbids!!!
> —*The Collected Works of C.G. Jung, Vol. 8*

In what modern-day witches call the "burning times," Inquisitors utilized, among many other things, a device known as a witch's cradle to extract confessions. The accused witch was first placed inside the cradle, which was nothing more than a sack made of heavy, thick fabric. Once the subject was placed inside the sack, the sack was subsequently tied off and suspended from a tree, rafter, or whatever was handy. It was then spun and rocked from outside, and the motion, combined with sensory deprivation, made for quite severe disorientation on behalf of the accused, encouraging hallucinations and delusions, often adding quite a bit of color to the ensuing confessions.

The witch's cradle was, in later times, adopted and utilized by witches themselves, allegedly as transportation to the *sabat* and definitely as a means of altering consciousness, sometimes inducing astral projection. Houston and Robert Masters modified the device in 1973 and renamed it ASCID (Altered State of Consciousness Inducing Device) before the inventors chose to settle, once again, for the decidedly more tasteful witch's cradle.

The adoption of the cradle by the people it was designed to persecute is a prime example of shadow play's alchemical attributes. Another example that springs to mind is the adoption of hateful slang by the minority groups the slang was meant to hurt. The fact that words like "nigger" and "fag" have become terms of affection by their targets simply, and beautifully, demonstrates the power of embracing the shadow (in these cases, the shadows of other people!) and transforming darkness into light.

The chemistry that makes BDSM work is more mysterious (people who like it are often hard pressed to explain precisely *why* they like it), but the results are no different. In the BDSM world, pain is quite literally transformed into pleasure, and non-consensual acts are transformed into consensual fantasies. Through this speculative confrontation and embrace of the shadow self, fear is removed from the picture, rendering the specters of rape and torture powerless, at least between the consenting parties, and if only for a little while.

Of course you see where this is leading. That's right: Horror films provide this very same alchemical transformation and release. We are taking everyday horrors, distilling them down to reflections, and deriving positive reactions from them, making them *fun*. To have fun while watching a horror film is to take away the power fear has over us the rest of the time.

It would seem that there is an inherent desire within the collective unconscious to turn negativity into positivity. To cite another example of this desire: Somewhere along the way to civilization, the human race invented black humor. The morbid joke is certainly the distant cousin of the horror story. They both provoke the same questions from the more puritanical among us: "Why would anyone want to?"

It's a valid question. Why *would* anyone want to relate a joke about defiling dead infants? Because, for many of us, putting horrible situations into humorous context is the only way we can begin to confront these situations at all. Indeed, joking about atrocity is not exploitation; rather, it's an attempt to de-fang the atrocity. If we couldn't (or weren't allowed to) do this, we might never mentally confront certain subjects, and denial and repression, according to our friend Jung, only serve to make our shadows bigger and denser.

We engage in a very similar sort of exorcism when we go to horror films. Certainly we don't go to punish ourselves; human beings seldom go out of their way to do things that they don't find entertaining. So yeah, we find horror films fun, or we wouldn't bother. It seems oxymoronic, sure, but no more so than the concept of morbid humor.

And when you get down to it, is there any humor that isn't at least a tad morbid? Obviously slapstick humor is damn violent most of the time—I remember being mortified by many of the antics I saw on *The Muppet Show* when I was too young to understand the concept of black humor. And, much like drama and horror, humor needs some sort of conflict at its core to work.

Drama and comedy are different perspectives on pretty much the same thing—conflict and exaggeration. If the victim of the conflict is likely to walk away permanently scathed, the mood of the piece will likely either be dramatic or horrific. But if the conflict is one that the characters could likely get over, then we have the potential for comedy (or light-hearted adventure).

Let's take the movie *Very Bad Things,* for example. You probably haven't seen this movie, and count yourself among the blessed for that. *Very Bad Things* billed itself as a black comedy: Bachelors accidentally kill a hooker and hilarity ensues. When the bachelors' botched attempts to cover up the incident lead to calculated murder, we are still receptive to the idea of *Very Bad Things* as a comedy, even though we haven't laughed yet.

But the film's last scene, in which the surviving bachelors and newlywed husband are left helplessly crippled, and the camera looms up into the air above newlywed wife Cameron Diaz, screaming and screaming, we have veered off into serious non-comedy territory. We are, in fact, left as uncomfortable as we would be at the end of a Neil LaBute film. The line of reparation has been irrevocably crossed, which places us in tragedy territory. Jason Biggs being caught humping a pie might be morbid and mortifying at the time, but it's his (and his dad's) ability to shrug it off that enables *us* to shrug it off and laugh, maybe even to entertain the notion that at that age, if I were horny enough...never mind.

There's an exaggeration present in horror that's not unlike the exaggeration in comedy. It really does want you to enjoy it on some level, just like the morbid joke wants you to laugh. The horror film wants you to react viscerally (and vocally) to a greatly exaggerated conflict. In this respect, laughing and screaming are much more closely related than we might have imagined.

It's taking the essence of human conflict and fear, blowing it as far out of proportion as suspension of disbelief will allow, containing it in a controlled environment, and looking at it more closely than we would be able to if it were *really* staring us in the face. This is the alchemy that lies at the core of shadow play. This is the witch's cradle we use to both explore our inner landscape, and take away the power of the witch-burner.

One Final Argument for Reflection

> If you imagine someone brave enough to withdraw all his projections, then you get an individual who is conscious of a pretty thick shadow. Such a man has saddled himself with new problems and conflicts. He has become a serious problem unto himself, for he can no longer say that they do this or that, they are wrong, and they must be fought against. He lives in the "House of the Gathering." Such a man knows that whatever is wrong with the world is in himself, and if he only learns to deal with his own shadow he has done something real for the world. He has succeeded in at least shouldering an infinitesimal part of the gigantic, unsolved social problems of the real world.
> —*C.G. Jung, Psychology and Religion, 1938*

Even now, it's the emotional reflex of those who survive a tragedy, such as the Columbine High murders, to want the instant solution, to want to link dark art to real life violence (ironically, it's most often these dark artists who address the lack of instant solutions in coping with loss). But any doubt about art's place in the world—as mirror or catalyst, chicken or egg—should be settled once he who is asking asks himself this question: When mankind first began to draw on cave walls, what did he depict?

Exactly. You got it. An artist can depict nothing *but* his/her environment. Our environments—personal, public, physical and spiritual—are our only frame of reference. It would be impossible *not* to reflect our environment in art, as it is impossible for me to use anything other than English characters to convey these thoughts to you; it's all I know.

Therefore, the violent act came before violent art, and it is only in this way—as a mirror—that we can truly link violent art with real violence. By their very definitions they couldn't be further apart. Violence is a destructive act; art, no matter how perverse, is creative and pacifist. Filmmakers cannot be held accountable for the effect they have on a public too stupid not to imitate the stunts they saw in *Jackass: The Movie*. It is in fact we, the people of this planet, who are responsible for the acts that inspire the art.

When I speak of the environment that art reflects, our physical environment—the landscape and the physical events that occur therein—is the most obvious subject. The collective unconscious of a culture, I think, is also a large factor in its environment and is almost always reflected in art. (Take a look at the Japanese for example, who in their cinema and anime, have been meditating on the destruction of major Japanese cities since the 1950s. Now why do you suppose they would do something like that?)

Art is simply a form of communication, like written, spoken and signed forms of language. And art is used, often unconsciously and unwittingly, to reflect *personal* environments. Our entire histories, from infancy to childhood, adolescence to adulthood, are stored in our bodies. And we are constantly communicating our histories—our personal environments—in every nuance of our body language, vocal inflections, handwriting quirks, habits and nervous tics. When we sit down to write, paint, sing or draw, all those tics and quirks contribute to our style.

So our environment cannot be limited only to physical surroundings, but includes the cultural hive mind, as well as our own contributions to that hive mind with our idiosyncrasies, urges and fears. The old phrase "Write what you know" seems kind of pointless—it's impossible for a writer to write anything but. Thus, I am trying to find philosophical meaning in horror films, and in our urges to watch them...but I write like a fanboy

Occult forms of divination—Tarot cards, Ouija boards, the *I Ching*, automatic writing and the like—are considered by their users ways in which to communicate directly with the subconscious. Since horror fiction deals with subject matter that we most often tend to repress or deny within ourselves, by its very nature it is the most subconsciously rooted of all forms of art. In fact, horror fiction deals with a very specific and select, if slowly evolving, group of archetypes. Unlike, say, science fiction, where new and creative ideas are the order of the day, horror writers spend their time finding new ways to interpret the old archetypes, and revealing more about themselves in the process. In other words: In horror, it's the singer, not the song.

If the film critics and fans of the world (me included) made a list of the scariest horror films ever, you'd notice quite a few redundancies. There are a handful of universally recognized classics in the genre, and I will not be writing about them here, unless I feel I can bring a different perspective to them. Volumes have already been written about *Halloween '78, Alien, Texas Chain Saw Massacre (1974), The Shining* and *The Exorcist*. To add any more text to the pile would be redundant, and redundancy is the last thing I want in these pages.

It's been decades since these films first graced the screen. The collective American psyche has been slowly changing as it grows up, and the horror film has changed along with it. Already ghosts and demons are becoming a thing of the past. Though we still feel their traces in our subconscious, and though they may not be through with us in films by a long shot, they are admittedly more rare than in the days before *Friday the 13th*.

Reading Stephen King's *Danse Macabre* today is interesting, and kind of alienating. King, being a child of the Cold War, and growing up under the shadow of Sputnik, focused much more of his analyses on those old-school, epic horrors: the nuclear mutant big bugs, the McCarthy paranoia flicks, xenophobic invasion movies *et al*. In fact, most of the contemporary (1970s) films he discussed have more in common with those movies made 20 or even 30 years before the writing of his book (*Prophecy, Phase IV, The Giant Spider Invasion*, etc.).

As I reflect on *my* childhood, *my* adolescence, and the collective unconscious of my generation, I realize that the gap between King and me is huge, and not just chronologically. Everything has changed, and of course, changing as well is the face of the American bogeyman.

Horror has grown more intimate and personal since the end of the Cold War. Small-scale, intimate stuff—groups of people dealing with man-sized monsters—have been the order of the day. This is the stuff that began with *Psycho* (1960), Mario Bava's *Twitch of the Death Nerve*, and of course, *Halloween*. The psycho slasher of the 1980s could arguably be seen to represent a modern mutation of the vampire or the werewolf.

And out in the modern world—a world leaving the '80s and '90s behind and settling into the post-9/11 mindset—our monsters have evolved yet again. They can perhaps be crudely compared to Frankenstein's monster: made by man, without regard to the consequence of its creation. Dr. Frankenstein is proud of his "son," as it were, but mainly so as a symbol of Dad's accomplishment. Perhaps some relevance can be drawn between this poor, misunderstood creature and the kids today that go strange and shoot up their schools. If Dr. Frankenstein were alive today, one could easily imagine him driving an SUV sporting a bumper sticker that reads "PROUD PARENT OF A JIGSAW OF BODY PARTS I ASSEMBLED AND RESURRECTED IN MY LABORATORY."

Modern movie monsters are largely recognizably human. There have been, of course, several wonderful supernatural exceptions (such as the Blair Witch and a dead little girl named Samara), but it was *Psycho* and subsequently *The Texas Chain Saw Massacre* that laid the foundation for the post-'60s American horror film. Given the source material for both these films, it could be said that Ed Gein was the founding father of American horror—our first backyard bogeyman.

From 1968 to 2001, American horror lived in the shadow of Gein, and it might even be said that Gein established the last *romantic* horror archetype of our age. The seemingly up and coming archetypes—the new faces of real life American fear—are colder, more high-tech, and, in many cases, younger. It is precisely this modern coldness that separates the new archetypes from the romantic (for want of a better word) trappings of the Gein mythos: creaky old houses, sharp-bladed weapons, direct contact between killer and victim, and intimate flesh fetishes (cannibalism, dressing in human skins, etc.).

Modern American monsters use handguns and live in suburban tract houses. They smuggle shoe-bombs onto airplanes and blow up buildings in the name of their gods. There's a lack of primal intimacy between monster and victim, a quality present in more traditional horrors of teeth, claws and chainsaws. While it could be argued that Tobe Hooper's introduction of the chainsaw into horror cinema ushered it into the modern age, I must counter that the chainsaw is still a *melee* weapon. The ever more popular handgun and pipe bomb just don't hold the same shudder factor as the more traditional implements.

As horror manages to leave Gein's shadow in the push-button, pull-trigger age, it will be interesting to see what direction it takes. Will we truly adopt these new archetypes—the gang-banger, the time-bomb family man, the trench coat Mafia, the terrorist—into our collective unconscious? After 9/11, are we making our way from the "intimate" horrors—not unlike Val Lewton's work of the 1940s—back into the epic horrors of the 1950s? Will the Devil continue to hold any cinematic power in a society that is quickly and efficiently killing God?

If there is, indeed, a new ugly head due to rear itself in horror, perhaps a few films from our past will help point the way to horror's future:

Assault on Precinct 13 (1976): The first film to give gun-toting gang-bangers the face of the Bogeyman;

The Stepfather (1987): A modern fairy tale in which Red Riding Hood's mother marries the wolf;

Hellraiser (1987): Helping horror evolve beyond the supernatural into the metaphysical, with an amoral, non-judgmental vibe that makes us question the reality of evil.

And, of course, the body-horror films of David Cronenberg: the guy's practically been our witch-doctor therapist as we transition into an ever more technological world. His films have addressed our fear of evolution more succinctly than perhaps any filmmaker's work before or since. Distinctly modern devices are meshed violently with human bodies in Cronenberg's world. Bodies become a symbol for the souls that inhabit them, hosting all manner of distinctly modern emotions and manifesting them physically. His characters are hurtled toward an evolution that, to the body, is simply "the new flesh," but to the civilized mind, ever clinging to familiar forms and systems, is death.

The drama continues: the projection of a sour soul's shadow onto its perceived enemies, and the delusions that drive it to commit horrendous acts in the real world.

The drama continues: the projection of a lucid soul's shadows onto the movie screens of the world, and the atrocities that drive it to commit horrendous acts of violent illusion.

Preface to Chapter Two

This is the autobiographical chapter. I've kept it short, and I add this preface only to warn you ahead of time, and allow you to skip ahead if you are anxious to get to the movies themselves. I include this chapter only because I think it's nice to have the perspective of someone who grew up on horror and didn't wind up shooting up his or her high school. It keeps balance in the universe.

Chapter Two: Me and My Shadow

> We know that the wildest and most moving dramas are played out not in the theatre, but in the hearts of ordinary men and women who pass by without exciting attention, and who betray to the world nothing of the conflicts that rage within them, except possibly by a nervous breakdown.
> —C.G. Jung, *New Paths in Psychology*, 1938

I was maybe five years old when I discovered the concept of taboo, and my introduction to it was profanity. My parents cursed all the time, and I had begun hearing these words long before I knew how to speak, let alone what they meant. As any parent of a small child will tell you, kids are ruthlessly curious—particularly about rules.

I figured out pretty quickly the difference between societal rules and physical laws. Laws made cruel sense that I didn't question: The balloon floats away if you let it go, the ground hurts when met with high velocity, that kind of thing.

Rules, on the other hand, made sense half the time at best. Rarely could I figure out why they were there—not that adults were much help. "Because I said so" was more common an explanation than I could stand. The very idea of profanity made no sense to me whatsoever. These words were "bad," I was told, but nothing ever happened to me when I said them: I was never struck by lightning; my tongue never fell out; I never broke out in hives; in fact, the only thing that ever happened was that grown-ups got pissed off. Besides, Mom and Dad used these words all the time, so how bad could they really be? This was a fucking stupid rule, I decided. My subsequent obsession got me into loads of trouble over the years, which of course only made the obsession grow, and I'm still obsessed to this day.

I remember very vividly a first grade assembly in which I was first exposed to what I suppose we could call *Grand Guignol*. My classmates and I sat watching a magician whose act, for the most part, was quite mystifying and hilarious to my six-year-old ass. At the halfway point of his act, he took a volunteer from the audience—a very pretty girl not much older than me. He reached under his table and withdrew a device that looked like a large cigar-cutter. He set the device on the table, and asked the girl to put her hand through the wrist-sized hole.

It was a sort of low budget "saw the lady in half" trick, and it was the first time I'd ever seen anything like it. He used the arm-guillotine to slice a carrot in half to demonstrate the potential of the device, and when he asked, the girl stuck her hand into the hole much more readily than I would have. My heart was pounding for this girl.

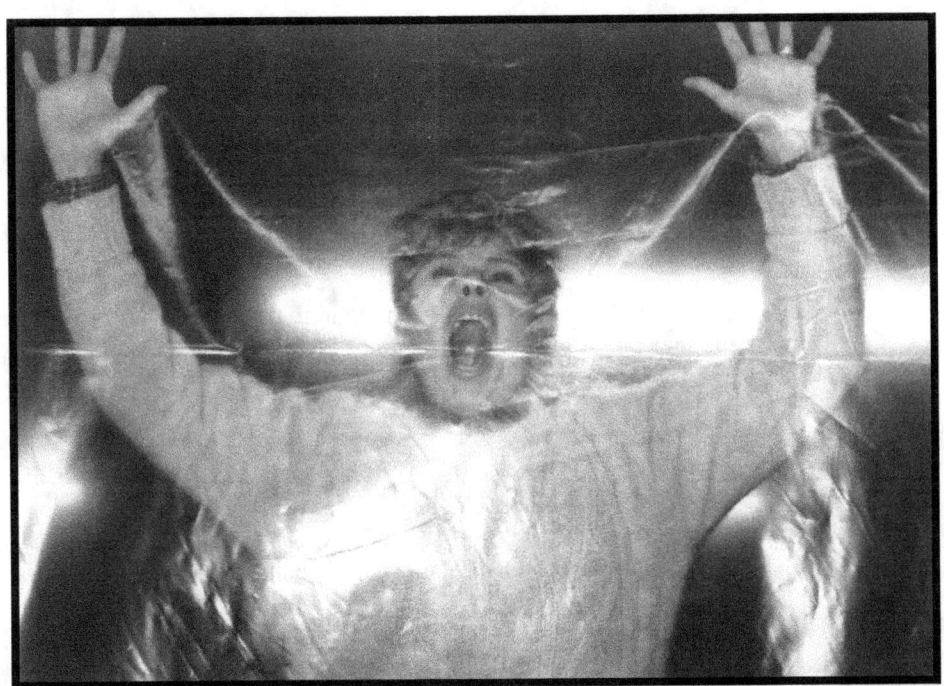

***Friday the 13th* on TV brought splatter movies into the home.**

Of course I knew that it was a trick, but I couldn't figure it out, and the magician wasn't letting on. He false-started three or four times before he finally brought the blade down. After the girl removed her hand, he had her hold it tightly at the wrist, and told her, "Hold it together like that and don't drink any liquids for the next few hours."

My interest in horror movies began when I heard a radio ad for a movie called *Dogs*. I was maybe six or seven, old enough to know that movies and TV were somehow, miraculously, not real (a year or two before, I had seen *Star Wars* and had to be told why I couldn't go back behind the screen afterwards to say hi to Han Solo). The scariness of the ad touched me in a weird way, but what really got me was the spoken statement "Rated R: Under 17 not admitted without parent." Here was yet another thing deemed too mature for the likes of me. I scoffed at this absurd notion, but try as I might, I could not convince my folks to take me to see *Dogs*.

The first time I successfully sought out R-rated horror, I was maybe 10. My teenage friends David and Sandra were babysitting me, and we discovered that on cable was none other than *Friday the 13th* (1980). We decided to go for it.

It was amazing.

I knew that something was happening to me while I watched this movie. At the time, I could not articulate that I was experiencing something both indulgent and therapeutic, but every time we screamed or "ewwed" at a murder scene, I felt a tiny euphoria counterbalance the shock. I was seeing something taboo and coming away unscathed. And, just as it was for every other youngster in the 1980s, the "chair jumper" at the end was a landmark experience. We talked about it for half an hour after the movie had ended.

Every time I hung out with David and Sandra after that, we frantically searched cable for splatter movies. We would scan the cable guide, eschewing movies listed as simply containing "violence" in favor of those which contained "graphic violence." David and Sandra would later give me my first hardcore horror drive-in experience: a double feature of *Humanoids from the Deep* (1980) and *Piranha* (1978).

I now had a secret, something that belonged to me; and *older* kids, no less, had made it all possible. For the first time in my life, I felt kinda...cool.

> I watched the whole procedure. She thought it terrible, but the slaughtering and the dead man were simply matters of interest to me.
> —*Memories, Dreams, Reflections*, C.G. Jung

One night I managed to talk my Mom into watching *Friday the 13th* on cable with me, and it wasn't long into it before she began fuming. She stormed off into the kitchen, muttering, "I don't know why in God's name you want to watch *innocent people* getting killed." I guess I somehow convinced her that I knew it was just a movie and didn't take it seriously, because we wound up finishing it.

Mom was pleasantly surprised when Betsy Palmer showed up, and giggled in spite of herself when she turned murderous. I seem to recall she even squealed with amusement when Betsy got decapitated. But either I'm romanticizing the past, or the camaraderie with Mom was short-lived. Later that same year, *An American Werewolf in London* was released theatrically, and I demanded my Mom take my friend Greg (who was a year younger than me) and me to see it. Halfway though the movie, Greg ran out of the theatre to the bathroom, on the verge of throwing up, and Mom remained furious at me for weeks. When Ike, a grownup friend of Mom's, offered to take me to see my movies from then on, she gratefully accepted.

Thus began an entirely new kind of childhood enchantment at the movies for me. I was now allowed into the *theatre* to see the damn things—a world forbidden to most kids my age. It was the highest form of cool to me, and really the only form of cool I had access to. I was above having to be a kid at horror films, which I craved much more than I craved being accepted by my peers.

It also got me into loads of trouble. Teachers would write notes in my report cards saying "Willy is more interested in monsters than in his homework. I'm very concerned." But bless their hearts, Mom and Dad grudgingly allowed me my obsession.

So now I offer up myself as an example in the ongoing debate over youth and fantasized violence. Has movie violence desensitized me? Yes—to movie violence. I now consider myself a gourmet of gore, but only in relation to film. Real violence still makes me physically ill. Nightly news and reality shows often slide horrific images of real violence—sometimes fatal—into their programming, and when I see them I feel as though I have been hit in the stomach with a hammer.

I will also state for the record that I spent most of my school years not unlike the kids who called themselves the trench coat Mafia: very few friends, stuck in the lowest social caste, angry and depressed. As a maladjusted youngster, I certainly had

An American Werewolf in London

my share of aggressive feelings roiling away inside. No doubt there was a shadow-self in the making since the first day of kindergarten, eager for revenge on my peers in school. Revenge for all the teasing, for the rejections I got from girls, for everyone else's seeming ease at adapting and moving gracefully through the system while I stood on the sidelines with my fists clenched, convinced that there were better things to do with my time.

For smashing up my KISS lunchbox.

KISS, yeah, there was an indication of my aesthetic right there, I suppose. Gene was my favorite—the "monster" of the band. The guy that breathed fire, spat blood, and sang about being the "God of Thunder." It didn't get any cooler than that for me. Probably Alice Cooper came slightly before KISS in my life, courtesy of my parents. Mom and Dad were huge Alice fans, and I remember being entranced by his album *Welcome To My Nightmare* at five years old. I remember being glued to the stereo speaker, like Ralphie listening to "Little Orphan Annie" in *A Christmas Story*. I remember the narration by Vincent Price, the creepy voices in the background during the "Steven" trilogy on side two, the pre-John Carpenter instrumental drones, all sending chills down my spine. I remember being severely creeped out, and not being able to stop listening. I would reckon that this is why Mom and Dad never forbade me my interest in macabre theatre—it was probably their fault to begin with.

But we were talking about a lunchbox, weren't we? One day after recess, I returned to the little sanctioned-off lunch box area to discover that my prized possession had been kicked to smithereens. This is going to sound silly, but...that day, something died inside me. I accepted the possibility that everything that I put out in the open, be it material or emotional, might be trod upon in this self-contained universe known as the school system. I knew that I would have to be ridiculously protective of my self-esteem; I knew that there was something wrong in the way others saw me, not in the way that I was. And I will testify that one element that kept me from going down the path of the trench coat Mafia—aside from the fact that I knew the difference between fantasy and reality and didn't worship monsters like Hitler as heroes—was that I had an outlet in horror.

Horror would come to be my escape from the shackles of youth, and my reassurance that there was indeed an adult world waiting for me, if I could find the strength to wait for it. It was also, of course, my glimpse into the shadows of my own heart, a chance to indulge my primal urges, as well as a forum in which to analyze them and decide that most of them belonged in my head, and would stay there

I used art—creating my own and experiencing others'—to vent. To this day, I have never hit another human being, and I have explored my fascination with both shadow work and shadow play to an extent that has catalyzed major self-discoveries, with hopefully many more to come.

And, as I write this, I find that I am settling back into my memories of escaping into horror with a warm, fuzzy content. These were among the only happy memories I have from my school years. You may consider that sick or sad, but hey, to each his own.

I also experience a poignant sadness when I read Joe R. Lansdale's or Joe Bob Briggs' writings on the lost Texas drive-in culture, or *Psychotronic*'s Michael Weldon waxing poetic about the old 42nd Street grindhouse theatre of Times Square. The fact that I couldn't be a part of those eras fills me with a longing I suppose Goths and Ren Fair geeks feel for more ancient eras. Home video has pretty much killed off the drive-in and grindhouse markets, but I suppose that the access to every movie under the sun that video provides compensates a little.

The question might remain in the minds of certain readers: Watching such violent films at such a young age, did I merely indulge in my prurient impulses and figure out ways to rationalize it all as I grew older? Did I truly know what I was doing long before I could articulate it to myself, much less to the public? Since I've arrived at a civilized, non-violent adulthood after a childhood and adolescence soaked in red food coloring and Karo-syrup, does it matter whether I had the answers then or figured them out later?

I believe the only thing that truly matters is that, whether or not my conscious mind was aware of shadow play's therapeutic properties at age 10, I knew that movies weren't real. It's that awareness—the awareness of the line between fantasy and reality—that needs to be instilled in humans as soon as possible. Children without awareness of this dividing line are capable of hurting themselves and others whether or not they listen to Marilyn Manson. In my childhood, kids into Superman were jumping off of roofs and out in front of cars. They were hitting each other in the head with frying pans because they saw Jerry do it to Tom. Many kids learn about physical laws the hard way, and these were the worst-case scenarios, many of which could've been avoided if the kids in question had been made aware of negative consequence.

Or, to put it another way: enlightened by making the darkness conscious.

Fans of Jerry Bruckheimer–style action flicks and first-person shooter games, I believe, entertain more fantasies of full-blown aggression than fans of horror films, because that stuff tends to establish audience identification with killers, good guys though they might be. And even though the first reel of John Carpenter's *Halloween* is seen through the eyes of little Michael as he stalks and murders his sister, it never encourages us to identify with the killer, as Siskel and Ebert fretted in their anti-splatter campaign of the 1980s.

These are *horror* films, after all, and it is their whole reason for being to establish the murders as horrifying and horrific. Never in any of these films is murder presented as cool. In most action films, of course, the opposite is true. In fact, *The Matrix* takes that idea to its extreme, positing that the world is merely an illusion, and that we can don our black latex combat outfits, blow the crap out of everything, and not worry

about killing real people. Life, literally, becomes a videogame, and it's this sort of thinking that I imagine went through the heads of the trench coat Mafia; a sort of sociopathic narcissism: *All these figments are here for my amusement, and they are all disposable.*

A child who is allowed to watch *The Matrix* might begin to view the world a bit differently than one watching *Halloween* or other R-rated horror fare. The *Matrix*-watching kid is not only identifying with killers, he is unaware of the concept of consequence. If children are not told, they don't know that every action in the real world carries consequence with it. Consequence, however, is the subject of practically all horror cinema. Horror identifies itself with those who are afraid of death: those who have to pick up the pieces and cope with the aftermath, and with those who are in danger of *becoming* the aftermath.

Even in campier, midnight-movie situations where audiences cheer for a particularly grisly effect (as Harlan Ellison referred to with revulsion in his essay *The Thick Red Moment*), or "root for the killer," they are merely looking death in the face and reacting viscerally. It has precious little to do with audiences identifying with Jason Voorhees (for who among us possibly could?). Rather, the audience is reassuring itself that it's ready to look the next horror in the face and cope with it. Death in horror films, even when played for a laugh, is always ugly. There has to be that element of ugliness, or it simply would not *be* a horror film.

Rather than establish audience identification with monsters or serial killers, the horror film derives its true power by encouraging identification with victims and survivors. Makes sense, then, that many horror fans are what we like to call wimps and geeks (myself certainly included)—people who would *naturally* identify with victims and survivors. (This notion is expanded upon greatly by Carol J. Clover in her book *Men, Women And Chain Saws: Gender in the Modern Horror Film*. In it, she posits that the young male demographic of these movies is not only identifying with victims and survivors, but with women, specifically and always.)

We, the horror geek culture, process and react to our childhood traumas in varying degrees. The *hardcore* horror geek seeks out the most intense, grueling, disturbing fare out there, proving that he "can take all that and more, what else ya got?" These guys tend to drink copious amounts of beer, wear T-shirts that depict serial killers (usually post-execution) and listen to whatever form of metal music is most brutal this week.

Then there are the more Goth and conventioneer-type fans, who create fantasy worlds around themselves in which only their own kind exist. They play role-playing games and often dress as post-apocalyptic vampire Cenobites, or some combination thereof, when going out for coffee in the morning. Red wine is their beverage of choice and they listen to music featuring chorusy, flangey guitars and drum machines programmed with power drill samples.

And then there's *my* sub-cluster: the DVD geeks. We think that the fact that we can quote every Romero movie line-by-line makes us cooler than you. If we were offered the ability to travel time, we'd use it to catch the original *Toolbox Murders* (1977) at some flea-ridden grindhouse in pre-Giuliani Times Square. We tend to wear the same *Evil Dead 2* T-shirt every day until laundry day, at which point we will go shirtless. We drink Jolt cola and eat Mac n' Cheese religiously, and our CD collections consist only of Ennio Morricone, John Carpenter, Tangerine Dream and Goblin. Still, inexplicably, we seem to possess a preternatural ability to talk good-looking women into posing for perverse photos to promote our fanzines/blog pages/bootleg T-shirt companies.

Many people from all horror geek subgroups share interests in tattoos, body piercing, BDSM and roller coasters. Aesthetics may divide us, but the fundamentals of shadow play are universal. Exposed in some way to fear in childhood, we spend our adulthoods chasing our fears down. And we do it on our own terms, of course, which gives us more control over said fears than we had in childhood.

And it's safe to say that virtually every childhood is traumatic in some form or another—the process of birth

Phantasm II

is in and of itself a trauma. No one gets to adulthood without going through some form of fire, though individual degrees of fire certainly vary. But if we had no negative experiences to react to and struggle against as we grew up, if we did not form a shadow-self, we literally would not be half the person we are today. To live the human experience is to be affected by it, to experience some form of scathing. Without it we would be less than human. It's all part of the process, part of the alchemy.

The physical law mirrors a psychological and spiritual truth: Casting a shadow is proof of substance.

When I was 19, I got all my acid at the Hippie House, in Fresno's Tower District. A few of my bandmates lived there, and a girl I was seeing lived under the stairwell. Tenants came and went, and you could count on at least one person to be tripping at any time.

One night, I went to a party at the Hippie House, bought five hits from some guy in the bathroom, and dropped one of them. A half-hour later, as it began to kick in, I wandered into the living room and said hi to one of the tenants, who was watching TV on the couch. "Dude," I said, "you're watching *Phantasm 2* on *acid?*" He shrugged and said "Yeah," as though it were the most natural thing in the world. "Hm," I said, sat down and watched with him.

It was like being thrown into Archetypeland. The zombie with the sewn-up mouth had become a symbol for all the things we fear about death: the silence it brings, the indignities of the embalming table, the attempts at beautification that cannot fully hide the rotting reality. The lovely blonde heroine became, of course, the damsel-in-distress…one of my favorite archetypes, by the way. Strapped to a gurney, being wheeled by the evil henchman to the crematorium, she, Uberdamsel, had my strictest attention, my empathy, my libido, and my love. (She winds up saving herself, so now the feminist readers have only me to be pissed at.)

Listening to Reggie the ice cream man and the hitchhiker girl fuck while Mike and Uberdamsel overheard in the next room made me embarrassed and giggly, the way one might feel listening to their parents do it. And when the Tall Man got embalmed alive with hydrochloric acid, I watched with a mild shudder of revulsion and a childlike sense of wonder. When it was over, I realized that I had been transported back to that magic place in my childhood, when horror was more taboo. I felt like a bad little boy the rest of the night, and I loved it.

The first time I ever confronted a personal horror vicariously through film, I was 22. The experience, compared to most of the fucked-up stuff I've seen in movies, was relatively benign, but still incredibly unsettling.

Mandy, a very close friend of mine, was trying desperately to kick heroin and relapsing repeatedly. She had come close to death several times. I slowly began to withdraw emotionally from her and our circle, terrified that I was going to lose her forever, and, I guess, deciding that I would lose her on my own terms if I had to.

The Basketball Diaries was not a horror film, but I watched the withdrawal scenes the way a resident of 1960s Nagasaki might watch a *Godzilla* movie. I felt as though I were staring horror—my friend's and my own—square in the face. It turned a cold knife in my belly, and the blade never got warm inside me. This was what I was unable to face. I was a coward, and I knew it.

And at the time, I could do nothing about it. I pushed myself further away, and when I did communicate with Mandy, only hostility would come out. Eventually, Joe, a better friend than me, would take Mandy under his wing, locking her in the backroom of his office, taking care of her as she languished through that nightmare week. When Mandy came out of that backroom, she walked away from junk permanently and is now a professional pilot, sober and happy. I am beyond grateful to Joe for being able to provide what I could not.

So, watching that movie, I stared my demon in the face...and blinked. Today, those events are 10 years behind me. I wonder, quite often, if I would have the strength to do things differently today. To be honest, I hope so, but I don't really have any idea. But I know one thing: I will find out again someday. Life has a way of putting your ass on trial, doesn't it?

And after being exposed to a fair amount of horror in my life, and my share of violent death, horror films have lost none of their appeal to me. I am as obsessed as ever—perhaps more so, now that I'm a grownup and can watch them whenever I want (you never get over certain perks that come with being an adult—sometimes I eat birthday cake for breakfast). And if I'm at least thinking about the real life shadow acts that inspire artists to create horror fiction, maybe I stand a chance against the monsters. Maybe I stand a chance against *becoming* a monster.

In fact, I feel pretty good about the odds. But let's not get cocky.

Chapter Three:
Defending a Mountain of Crap

No work of art is invalid, no matter how seemingly immature or awkward it might be. To make art is to be fully human, striving to do more than simply survive and procreate, striving to touch the intangible.

Using this perspective, no horror film is less than a work of art. Even the most crass and exploitive B-movie can be a catalyst for the viewer asking him/herself very important questions; even questions as simple as, "Why did I want to watch Udo Kier fuck the Bride of Frankenstein in the gall bladder?" The question has been asked, the viewer will hopefully find an answer someday, and director Paul Morrissey has just helped humanity evolve one tiny—but welcome—fraction.

66 Days In The Gutter

I've seen upwards of 1,000 horror films in my career thus far as a horror junkie. That amounts to over two months of onscreen mayhem, not counting repeat viewings (I'm sure *that's* a ridiculous total…good God). Take into account that maybe 300 of these—or 18 days' worth—were really very good, and I'm a prime example of someone whose brain would've rotted away to a nub if it were going to.

I can usually find pleasure in even the crappiest of horror films. The most familiar feeling I experience is this fuzzy nostalgic warmth, reminding me of staying up past my bedtime to watch my movies on cable, breaking taboos.

Flashpoints of memory linger in my head, flashes of images that blew me away as a kid:

The teenage protagonist's head ballooning up twice its normal size, his skin splitting open to reveal *The Beast Within*;

The climactic pig head chainsaw battle in *Motel Hell (1980)*;

The tail of the *Alien* rip-off monster skewering a girl through her vagina and out her back in *Forbidden World*;

The same girl (earlier in the film, of course) and her equally naked lady-friend taking some kind of "laser shower" in *Forbidden World*;

The Alien rip-off monster puking to death in *Forbidden World* (a memorable movie, this was);

The girl getting eaten by pigs while taking a shower in *Evilspeak;*

The fisherman's ripped-off head tumbling down the waterfall, smashing against the rocks below in a shower of blood and brain in *The Incredible Melting Man;*

The woman giving birth, *Alien*-style, to the offspring of one of the *Humanoids from the Deep*;

The dead woman popping out of the dryer, after obviously having been through the High cycle a couple of times in *My Bloody Valentine* (1981);

The dead woman getting up off the slab in the morgue and slow-motion-ambushing the camera in *Blacula* (this scared the living shit out of me as a kid);

The girl getting raped by a giant worm in *Galaxy of Terror*;

And, of course, the big scene in *Scanners,* we mustn't forget that.

Lotta Corman stuff in there, huh? Yeah, good old Roger was there for me as a kid, just as he would be during my adolescence. (I shan't soon forget *The Big Doll House* or *Barbarian Queen*...Lana Clarkson, God rest your soul; Phil Spector, may you rot in hell.)

There were more eye-popping moments throughout my movie-watching life, to be sure. But these were the first ones; the ones that lured me down the path of damnation, the path to the irrevocable "creepy nerd" label. There was plenty of just plain crappy cinema, too—stuff that, for some ungodly reason, I still remember. Like *The Boogens*, for example, or *Funeral Home*, or *Jaws of Satan*, in which Fritz Weaver battles the Devil in the form of a cobra; if memory serves, he kills it by showing it a crucifix. Woo-hoo.

There were movies with a message, like *Humungous*. (The message: Babies conceived by drunk rapists who are subsequently killed by wild dogs in front of the victim's eyes, and, once born, left to fend for themselves on an island, will grow up to be monsters that like to eat teenagers.)

And, God help me, one of my favorite filmic experiences of all time was getting to see *Friday the 13th Part 3* in 3-D as a kid. Arrows, red-hot fireplace pokers and eyeballs shooting off the screen at me; God it was bliss.

Go ahead; cast the first stone, I dare you.

There are those of us who love the stuff. Crap-ass horror, the worse, the better. As Joe R. Lansdale so rightly put it: "You develop a taste for it, sort of like learning to like sauerkraut."

Lordy it's true. I know I could be spending that valuable time out of my life hiking through rainforests or listening to Bach or learning Italian, but this is what my soul thirsts for. Give me the lawnmower-zombie-bloodbath in *Dead-Alive*, the woman giving birth to a full grown half-alien man in *Xtro*, the fat kung-fu guy strangling his opponent with his own intestines in *The Story of Ricky*.

There are several reasons why I occupy my precious time with this stuff, I guess. For one, it's a coffee break from being civilized, a chance to be base and primal for an hour-and-a-half. Other times, it's a chance to laugh at some truly incompetent filmmaking and feel superior and smarmy. And sometimes I actually discover some overlooked gems—both well-intentioned works of cockeyed passion and the occasional through-and-through quality film: the pony in the mountain of crap.

What lands a movie in this chapter is not necessarily its crap value alone. These "ponies" I mention are often films that were released though the exploitation markets—drive-ins, grindhouses and direct-to-video—because the distributors didn't know what else to do with them. This will be the main distinction drawn between *art* and *crap* in this book. Everyone by now acknowledges *Night of the Living Dead* (1968) as an art film, but it was released through exploitation markets and found its niche slowly by word of mouth, rising from the shit-pile as though hefted aloft by some Arthurian Lady of the Septic Tank.

Many films that we'll discuss in the Crap section are certainly works of art, but they had to be sought out as such in the drive-ins and grindhouses of yesteryear. They needed to be discovered, and they still smell a bit like the grindhouse, even after all these years and all this praise. They're proud of their heritage, and proud of that stink they'll never quite wash off. It's the money from backers normally used to producing straight sleaze that forever taints these films with the exploitation tag, and the movies don't mind at all.

And sometimes, the simply crappy films have at least some unintentional value. Sauerkraut films, like the man said, but most of these do manage in some way to entertain.

From my perspective, it takes a special kind of ineptitude to make a film without even the barest kitsch value. The adaptation of Stephen King's *Thinner* came close, but watching the lead actor in a fat suit, trying to act fat, was fucking hilarious.

One flick that struck true mediocrity pay dirt also had King's name attached to it—in a big way. *Maximum Overdrive* looked like it had not only been directed, but also acted, photographed and edited by people who had never tried it before. King himself called it "the cinematic equivalent of a Big Mac and fries." He's flattering himself. Trying to laugh at this movie is like laughing at a guy with no arms or legs.

Slasher Films and The Goddess Complex

The fear that Siskel and Ebert had about the damaging effect of "splatter movies" was that viewers might eventually become desensitized to real violence. Another common argument in the anti-splatter campaign of the 1980s was that slasher films might tend to teach adolescent boys (their target audience) to view women as helpless objects, often portrayed in these films as either virgins or whores.

Aside from embodying the last vestiges of the child archetype, virgins in horror films also contain equal aspects of the mother archetype. The Catholic underpinnings of the "virgin mother" are obvious, and as kids, we simply can't conceive of the mother and the father being sexual. (Later in life, when we do find out, boy do we wish we hadn't.) Ed Gein worshipped his mother in such a way, and after she died, he boarded

Jamie Lee Curtis as Laurie in *Halloween*

off the rooms of the house that she most often occupied, preserving them as a kind of shrine to her.

Thus, the virgin, archetypally speaking, is on a pedestal, removed in similar ways from primal humanity. We don't think of her "in that way," and this is often descriptive of the virgin in slasher flicks (even if she's beautiful, she's usually dressed and made up too frumpily for us to notice). She is also, of course, usually an adept babysitter (made evident by Laurie Strode in Carpenter's *Halloween*), and this reminds us even more of the mother archetype (although it could be argued that her affinity with children is linked to a lingering identification with them, not yet having undergone the sexual rite of passage that would make her a maid, no longer a maiden).

And the virgin in these movies, of course, always seems to have the strength, intelligence, repressed anger, sexual frustration or grace of God (take your pick) to defeat the killer in the last reel. These films—nearly every one of them—are about the journey of the virgin out of childhood and into womanhood. In the Tarot, she is the Fool, beginning her journey into the real world. In confronting and defeating the killer, she is in essence taking back womanhood from the (usually) male monster who has been stealing it from the other girls; she becomes a maiden by avenging those who went before her.

The slut in these films, however, is only looked upon as such on the surface, in the superficial minds of men and women. In Archetypeland—in the subconscious—she is the maiden: a sexualized, playful female creature. In the subconscious, there is no such thing as a slut, for fucking is a celebration of life.

Yet another aspect of Jung's "Triple Goddess," the maiden is the woman that we, alpha male, love and strive to protect, but we love her in different ways—ways that aren't suitable for the virgin mother. And maidens, as we all know, usually meet disturbingly sexualized deaths in slasher films. The argument that protesters of these films once used was that the sight of women being sliced and diced might "turn on" impressionable young minds. Adolescent males who have a bit more of a tough-guy attitude built into them by their environment might express ideas like that outwardly in order to impress their peers. And if one's mind were weak enough, one might convince himself he believes it. I, however, am not a weak mind, nor am I a tough guy. So, I'll share with you the prurient appeal these flicks might've had for me as an adolescent.

If seeing a woman get carved up in a movie has any effect on the baser, primal side of my brain, it certainly isn't misogynistic. That side of my brain, I suppose, *does* view women as beautiful creatures, archetypes of life: nurturing, mothering, if not delicate, then worthy of protection. And at the core of these films—the knife-kill flicks, where the victims are often female and the weapons always phallic—is the woman as an archetype rather than a stereotype. Really.

Years before puberty came into my life, I thought my mother was a goddess. And I remember very vividly a dream I had in which my mother and I were out on the front lawn of our house. Just five houses down the block was Cedar Avenue, an extremely busy cross street. That street claimed a lot of neighborhood cats. "I'm gonna go down to the store, hon," my Mom said, "I'll be right back." And then she smiled and walked down the block, and began to cross Cedar Avenue. I never saw her get run over, but the traffic suddenly thickened a great deal. My mother was engulfed in a sea of metal, and I could no longer see any glimpse of her. I waited for her to resurface on the other side, and when she didn't, I began screaming. I had never known true helplessness until that moment, in that dream, standing on my front lawn, screaming for my mother.

The conscious mind of a misogynist filmmaker (or filmgoer) might think of female victims as helpless, but I believe the conscious mind has to be *trained* over many years to see women in this way—and by influences much more potent than media. The subconscious, however, sees only archetypes everywhere it looks. In the sleaziest of these films takes place the desecration of the maiden—an aspect of the Goddess. At the core of my alpha male dog-brain, I experience horror at these images. It's blatant manipulation, sure, and it's popular, because it *works*.

These films appeal much more to the alpha male protector in us, I think, than to the sleazo woman-hater. When the beautiful young maiden onscreen falls prey to the guy in the mask, the alpha male feels helpless to defend the woman he loves (and Mr. Alpha Male loves *every* maiden, I think). When the final surviving girl (often a virgin, and often embodying traits identifiable with both mother and child) remains to do battle with the killer by herself, all he can do is watch (and Mr. Alpha Male loves the virgin as well, albeit in a different way). Thus he experiences the closest approximation of horror in movies as crappy as these often turn out to be.

I am speaking for myself here, being honest with my inner caveman and offering up his thoughts as an example. It feels like good work for me to give you a real opinion from someone interested in the subject, rather than spouting out a bunch of statistics at you. At the end of the day, all I can tell you is that I love horror films, many of which happen to include scantily clad women in peril, and there is nothing in my mind that entertains any notion of a weaker sex.

I hope that helps.

Okay, enough with the psychobabble. Let's talk about some movies.

PROPHECY (1979)
Dir. John Frankenheimer

I remember seeing *Prophecy* in a theatre when I was a kid (it had a PG rating). It was one of those experiences, like Philip Kaufman's (also PG) 1978 remake of *Invasion of the Body Snatchers*, where I felt like I had been accidentally shown more than I was supposed to see. Kaufman's film had Brooke Adams doing full frontal nudity and Donald Sutherland smashing in the face of his slimy doppelganger with a shovel. And *Prophecy* had some gnarly, twisted mutant puppets, a guy getting his head bitten off, and a kid getting mangled by an inside-out grizzly bear.

Prophecy is, as I think most horror geeks would agree, a fairly entertaining turd. It boasts a ridiculous lead performance by Robert Foxworth, ineptly directed horror set pieces (helmed, to our amazement, by John Frankenheimer), a forest campground set that's less realistic than anything you ever saw on *Gilligan's Island* or *Land of the Lost*, and a truly retarded giant mutant bear creature. It's a throwback to the great and terrible monster flicks of the '50s—as has been stated with extreme reverence by King in *Danse Macabre*—and it is indeed terrible in the greatest ways. It's actually kind of heartbreaking upon first viewing, because the opening credit sequence—involving the slaughter of a rescue team, ominously lit with nothing but their headlamps—is quite creepy and effective. After this promising opening the film pretty much completely turns to shit.

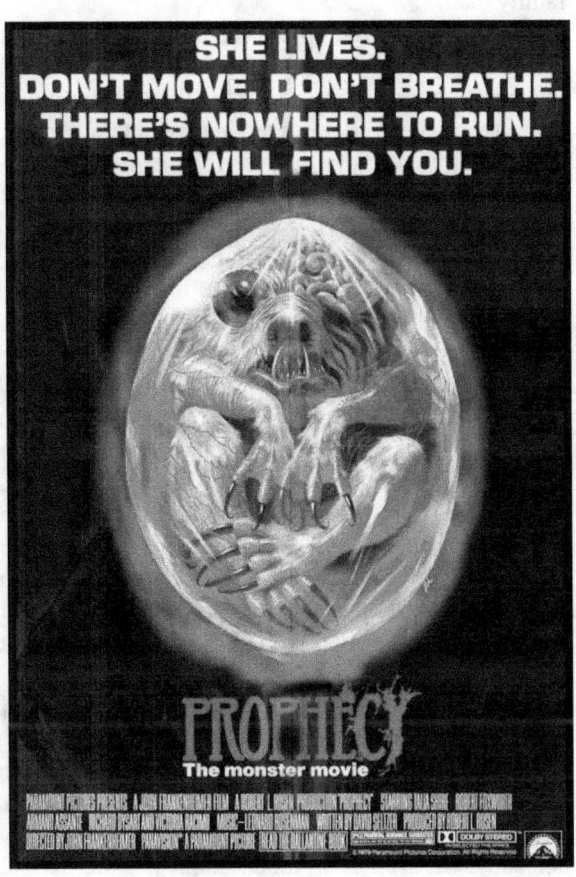

However, some respect needs to be paid to David Seltzer's screenplay, which is actually brimming with subtext. The story deals with a doctor, Robert Verne (the aforementioned Foxworth, in a performance that's somehow simultaneously over-the-top and wooden), struggling to better the lives of minorities whose basic rights and needs are being stepped on by big

Prophecy

business. He is married to a classical musician named Maggie (played by Talia Shire), who is keeping from him the fact that she is pregnant. He says he doesn't want to bring children into a world so polluted and corrupt, but it's also pretty clear that he is obsessed with his career and doesn't want to put his crusades aside in order to be a family man.

He drags his wife up to a section of wilderness in northern Maine, where the heads of the local paper mill are at war with the local Indian reservation. His job is to try to uncover corruption on the part of the mill in the form of pollution. Both he and his wife are dragged into a secret that will literally mark them forever: The mill has been dumping mercury into the water, contaminating the lake and the local fauna. Robert happens upon giant salmon and tadpoles, as well as an Indian chief who doesn't feel pain after burning himself with cigarettes. Unwittingly, the good doctor feeds his wife some of the mutant salmon, contaminating the new life growing inside her.

There's some interesting stuff to chew on here, before the inside-out bear shows up and begins chewing on the cast. There are a multitude of examples of how the left side of the brain goes to war with (and seemingly always defeats) the right side: masculine/feminine; science/art; industry/spirituality; foreigner/native. In every case here, the masculine (evil) side wins out. Maggie puts her cello aside to accompany Robert on his medical/political quest; the mercury contaminates her child; the paper mill wins its Supreme Court case against the Indians, destroying their heritage as well as their DNA. In the film's climax, the mutant bear chows down on the evil head honcho of the paper mill (after he sees the error of his ways, no less), but then she goes ahead and eats everyone else, so it's obvious she's not on anyone's side but her own (and, of course, her mutant cub's). She's the embodiment of pure primal nature, cruel and unforgiving, which is the element in nature that remains unchangeable after the thoughtless humans tamper in God's domain.

The film ends with the couple flying off in a prop plane. On board the plane, a pregnant Maggie wonders what she's going to give birth to (and maybe even reconsiders her stance on abortion), just as, down below, a new mutant pops up to replace the bear killed by Robert in *Prophecy*'s ridiculous climax.

It would make sense if Maggie's character were considering getting rid of her baby; the film is as much about her arc as it is about Robert's. Maggie grows to experience Robert's cynical world-perspective firsthand, as the corruption of the human race infiltrates her own DNA. And Robert has to revert to "native ways" to kill the monster; when firing a rifle from a distance doesn't stop it, he must fight it face-to-face, killing it with an arrow—a *native* weapon—clutched in his bare hands.

But the script is where *Prophecy*'s intelligence ends. It's not a film like *The Howling*—a B movie that's almost too smart for its own good. This is a film so stiffly, wrong-headedly executed, one must sometimes simply stare at it in wonder and disbelief. *Prophecy* was made for 12 million 1979 dollars, and it looks about as good as something American International Pictures might've put out in the same time period. Where the hell did all the money go? Not to the forest sets or the monster suit, that's for flippin' sure. I really don't know if I can do the inside-out bear suit justice with words; I feel more strongly motivated to simply urge you go to your local liquor store, buy a fifth of something dark brown, and check out (or revisit) *Prophecy* for yourself. It's pretty surreal, and great fun, to watch every unbelievably hokey puppet (most of the time, only the monsters' mouths are articulated, and the final monster head can be seen, for a glorious split second, to be nothing more than a head and shoulders, as it pops up too far in the frame), every fake-ass set, every visible wire, every misfiring scare scene, and think to oneself, *John fucking Frankenheimer made this*.

THE BEYOND (1981)
Dir. Lucio Fulci

It is commonly recognized that Lucio Fulci was more than a tad influenced by Dario Argento, on more than one occasion. There are some who posit that the influence went both ways. Oh, fucking *please*, people. The gore in Fulci's films, don't get me wrong, is magnificent, and I count myself among his fans, but good fucking lord, for someone who slagged so hard on Argento in the press…

Well, I suppose there are *seven* damned buildings as opposed to three, and the boiling wax actually *is* applied to a human face this time, and a guy gets eaten alive by *tarantulas* as opposed to rats. To some, I suppose that's enough of a departure from the source material. But as much as *The Beyond* is practically a remake of Argento's *Inferno* (borrowing a fair share from *Suspiria* as well), I admit it outdoes *Inferno* in gore, as well as in plot cohesion, which still, really, isn't saying much.

Certain movies (most of them Italian) are still unsurpassed in the gross-out department, even after 30-plus years. Among them are *City of the Living Dead, Buio Omega, Cannibal Holocaust* and *The Beyond*. I'm especially fond of Fulci's eyeball fetish; in *The Beyond*, eyes get gouged out, impaled upon nails, and eaten by spiders. It's amazing stuff. Combined with the subplot of the blind woman on the run from the afterlife, and the final image of the last survivors ending up in hell, their eyes gone white and blind as well, the eyeball mutilations drive home the not-so-subtle symbolic link between death and loss of sight.

In the scene where Zombie Joe kills Marta, impaling her head upon a nail, which then bursts out through her eye-socket, taking the eye with it, there is also a vague sexual parallel. Eyes in horror films are often stand-ins for female genitalia, and their desecration is often symbolic of sexual violence, in films dating as far back as Dali and Bunuel's *Un Chien Andalou*. Argento would later exploit this theme further in his own *Opera*—the first instance I know of in which Fulci possibly influenced Argento.

In its pacing and narrative, *Inferno* starts off amazing, but the second half of it completely falls to pieces. Whereas *The Beyond*'s story and momentum are *okay* from beginning to end, and therefore it feels like an all-around more competent film to gore buffs who aren't paying a whole lot of attention.

But Fulci just didn't have that focus, that manic vision that Dario had in his golden age. *Inferno* is at least half-brilliant, and in his whole life Fulci never came close to realizing anything on the scale of *Inferno*'s underwater ballroom scene; he never had it in him. But I don't fault him for that. I praise him for the outrageousness of his own *mise-en-scene*, and wish he hadn't felt the need to berate (and then visually quote so liberally from) someone he so obviously idolized.

As I said, there is more plot cohesion in *The Beyond*, but only to a certain point. I mean, what exactly are we to make of a scene in which a man is struck by lightning, lies paralyzed on the floor, and is slowly eaten alive by spiders...all in the *reading room of a library?*

Besides *Suspiria* and *Inferno*, Fulci also quotes ideas and images from *The Sentinel* (1976)*, Carnival of Souls* and *Les Diaboliques*. And there are some famously hilarious gaffes, like the sign over the hospital door reading "DO NOT ENTRY," and the line, "You have carte blanche, but not a blank check." There's also a rather non-sequitur monologue from a librarian (played by Fulci himself) about bold labor unions fighting for the right to a longer lunch break.

But despite its flaws (which are really only flaws to someone who takes this stuff a little too seriously...and what are *you* looking at?), *The Beyond* is deliriously entertaining. And what makes it shine like a little bastard are the visual set-pieces: the spider-scene, the blind woman plagued by zombies, the zombie ambush in the hospital (including the now-archetypal image of the little zombie girl getting the top of her head blown off), and the ending tableaux, in which the two leads wind up in a dusty, corpse-strewn vision of hell. This last scene is both beautiful and nihilistic, and certainly the most original visual conceit Fulci gave to *The Beyond*. In fact, I wouldn't be surprised if it made Argento a tiny bit jealous.

GINGER SNAPS (2000)
Dir. John Fawcett

Too rare is the teen horror film that gives a damn. Personally, I can only think of three or four, and *Ginger Snaps* is one of them. It gives a damn on all fronts—it bristles with great ideas, great dialogue, believable characters with believable motivations, great direction and great gore. No one of these elements is more or less important than the other; the whole film can fall apart if one element doesn't convince. For example:

Show of hands, please: How many of you saw *An American Werewolf in Paris?* Okay, 13 of you. Now, how many of you actually *finished* it? Ah-ha; nobody, just as I thought. And was not the reason for everyone's passionate lack of interest in that film—I mean besides the inept screenplay, acting and direction—the remarkably, mind-blowingly unconvincing CG werewolf?

Those involved in the production of *Ginger Snaps*, I believe, knew that a mechanical monster, while maybe not entirely convincing, is still loads more convincing than fucking CGI. Even if a man-made creature doesn't move as fluidly as a real animal, it still looks like it's actually *there*, taking up the space the characters have left for it. It belongs there. Ninety-nine percent of computer animation looks like precisely that—animation. This removes the creature from the reality of the movie and ruins any suspension of disbelief the viewer might've had going in. Fortunately, the makers of *Snaps* chose the romantic, organic route, which not only makes the film's fake world easier to slip into, but it also gives *Snaps* a rather unique look compared to its filmic contemporaries.

The story is slightly familiar; lycanthropy as metaphor for adolescence was admittedly used in *Teen Wolf*, but any inspirations *Snaps* might take from earlier films are turned on their ear quite nicely here. The first two reels of the film make referential nods to *Harold and Maude*, *Heathers*, and *An American Werewolf in London*. We have the size and shape of the small town laid out for us, as well as the dynamics of the characters. Once the bite happens, though, the movie veers off on its own wonderful trajectory.

Ginger and Brigitte are two "creepy" (read: gothic and hot) sisters living in suburbia, whose lives change drastically when Ginger, the older and more dominant sis, gets her first period: The scent of her menstrual blood attracts a marauding werewolf. Ginger survives the attack; the werewolf does not.

As Ginger begins to manifest *the change*, references are of course made to puberty and adolescence—

Ginger Snaps **is the most thoughtful teen horror film since** *Carrie*.

specifically, to female adolescence. Ginger's moods become dark and unpredictable, and her body seems to be rebelling against her. She begins acting in ways that alienate her from her family. The spin given to the lycanthropy mythos here is that Ginger doesn't change with the full moon and return to normal after the moon wanes (a bit too obvious a metaphor for menstruation, perhaps?). Rather, her transformation is gradual and permanent. She is evolving into something mysterious and alien to both herself and Brigitte.

This metamorphosis is experienced not through Ginger's eyes but through those of her weaker sister. Brigitte views her sister's transformation into a sexual animal as a change into a *literal* animal; Ginger's first period attracts an animal that contaminates her. Hence, lycanthropy is portrayed in the film almost as a venereal disease, in addition to its symbolizing puberty. Is it, in the process, comparing puberty to a venereal disease? In Brigitte's eyes, it could very well be seen that way.

Snaps also presents lycanthropy, of course, as female empowerment. From the get-go in this movie, all the males are pretty much ineffectual, from Ginger and Brigitte's wimpoid father to the jocks at their school. The most damage they can inflict is by labeling girls amongst themselves. Ginger realizes this after practically date-raping her new boyfriend. Even though she took the initiative, to the point of making him bleed (and of course infecting him), she realizes that "I'm just a lay to him. He's the hero and I'm the lay." She tells Brigitte that, in a man's eyes, a girl can only be "a slut, a bitch, a tease or the virgin next door."

All the girls seem to know this, and thus the ones that take on the title of "bitch" get to wield the power. By embracing the lycanthropy that is taking her over, Ginger decides to become a bitch. Ginger's embrace drives a wedge between her and Brigitte, and Brigitte must find the strength within herself to force her own evolution—not into a monster, nor a bitch or slut or virgin next door, but into a fully human woman, capable of the love, strength, and compassion it will take to either save or kill her sister.

The protective instinct is quite strong in this family, at least among the women. Brigitte is all for the idea of covering up Ginger's messes and helping her split town. And once Mom catches on to Ginger's murderous impulses, she tells Brigitte that she's going to take her girls, burn the house down, escape town and start fresh somewhere else. "Dad'll blame me," she says, "everyone will." Even Mom knows the petty power that men wield by calling names. And she doesn't seem that concerned with losing Dad. Only the creatures capable of having periods, linked to the earth and moon, familiar with the agonies of bearing children, are able to exhibit this kind of altruistic love.

Indeed, all the guys in *Ginger* are pawns, a concept not only entirely calculated on behalf of the screenwriter, but absolutely necessary to the plot. Drug dealer and bad boy Sam has a bit of real service to offer in creating the werewolf antidote, but other than that, he's prey in the girls' power struggle. This is a world where women rule either subliminally or overtly, and where one woman must decide to stop another woman who has taken her power too far. Initially, the head bitch of the story is Trina Sinclair, but she has to be taken out to make room for the up-and-coming Ginger. Ginger, of course, winds up being worse than Trina had ever dreamed of being, and Brigitte is the next in line to challenge the queen's authority.

Before their final confrontation, only a mortally wounded (and infected) Sam stands between the two sisters. He hovers between life and death, between humanity and monstrosity, and on either side of him are human (but infected, and slowly changing) Brigitte and fully monstrous Ginger. When Brigitte tries, and fails, to drink Sam's blood, she makes her choice to remain human—to stop trying to be like Ginger. And now Sam, the film's damsel-in-distress, doesn't have a prayer. Ginger kills him in a heartbeat, and the final battle is on.

Brigitte, cornered by Ginger, retains her humanity in the face of primal animal conflict. With the antidote in one hand and a knife in the other, she offers Ginger a choice between living as a human (accepting the antidote) or dying as an animal (forcing Brigitte to fight her off and destroy her). "I'm not dying with you," she screams before Ginger makes her choice; she leaps at Brigitte, and practically onto the knife itself (the pounce almost seems suicidal, actually). We are left with Brigitte lying over the corpse of her sister, and we are never quite sure if she administers the antidote to herself. We assume she does, but the film leaves her with a choice to make—to accept or reject this primal power.

Ginger Snaps is going down in my book as the best, most thoughtful, most important teen horror film since *Carrie* (1976). And given how long ago that was, I'm a little disturbed. Has it really been that long? If I think of a worthy predecessor to *Ginger,* I'll come back to this page, but I'm actually hard pressed to think of another teen horror film besides *Teeth* or *Carrie* that isn't pandering or patronizing. Sad, really.

CREEPSHOW (1981)
Dir. George A. Romero

William M. Gaines' EC Comics captured the imaginations of many a male youth in the 1950s, and turned many a parent into a potential lynch mob member. Gaines was put on trial for distributing harmful matter to minors and driven bankrupt in the process. His comics (including *Tales from the Crypt*, *Vault of Horror*, and *The Haunt of Fear*) were shut down, and he had nothing left but *Mad* Magazine, which he, of course, parlayed into quite a success. *Creepshow* is Stephen King and George Romero's open love letter to Gaines' gory glory days, and it's one of those films where the viewer can feel its makers' love for its subject matter oozing off the screen.

Creepshow opens with a little boy being viciously scolded by his conservative father for having an issue of the comic. This could be seen not only as representative of what many kids went through in the 1950s if they were caught with a dreaded EC comic, but if you squint real hard, you can also almost see it as representing Bill Gaines on trial against closed-minded, conservative Establishment types; the kid's name is even Billy! The father throws the comic away, much as said Establishment ran EC out of business.

Gaines didn't necessarily obtain revenge by way of a voodoo doll in real life, but he did exact revenge by getting richer off *Mad* Magazine than he had been during EC's heyday. And, of course, his old *Tales from the Crypt*s eventually rose from their moldy graves via reprints to infect the minds of every consecutive generation since. I'm positive that, in his own moldy grave, Gaines is laughing his ass off.

Father's Day

The story here is about as classic EC as it gets: murdered person comes back from the grave to exact revenge on those who killed him. But screenwriter Stephen King does manage to inject a little complexity into the story here. The murder victim in this case, Nathan Grantham, was indeed a sick, vicious bastard who deserved to die. He controlled the lives of his family with his money, and he was maniacally possessive of his daughter Bedelia, going so far as to arrange to have her suitor murdered, in order to keep her close to him. If any gnarly old bastard deserved a marble ashtray in the skull, it was this guy. In fact, you could almost end the story with the patricide and it would still be pretty classic EC.

But there are other factors here. All of our "protagonists" make choices to stay close to the family, under its cloud of insanity, in order to be closer to Nathan and his money. And, justified though she might have been in killing her father, Aunt Bedelia returns to his gravesite every Father's Day because she's "overwhelmed with guilt." This is a universal truth: Engaging in murder—the ultimate shadow-act—is never without its consequences, no matter what the justification. Certainly a movie like *Creepshow* isn't interested in preaching philosophies about the consequences of violence. But sometimes, even when we're just trying to have fun writing stupid little horror stories, our subconscious betrays a bit of truth, does it not? As previously mentioned, the consequence of violence is certainly more often a factor in horror films (and comics) than it is in your standard action films.

So then, what exactly is it that brings Nathan back from the grave? Is it Bedelia's guilt? The Grantham family's greed? Nathan's own maniacal need for control, even

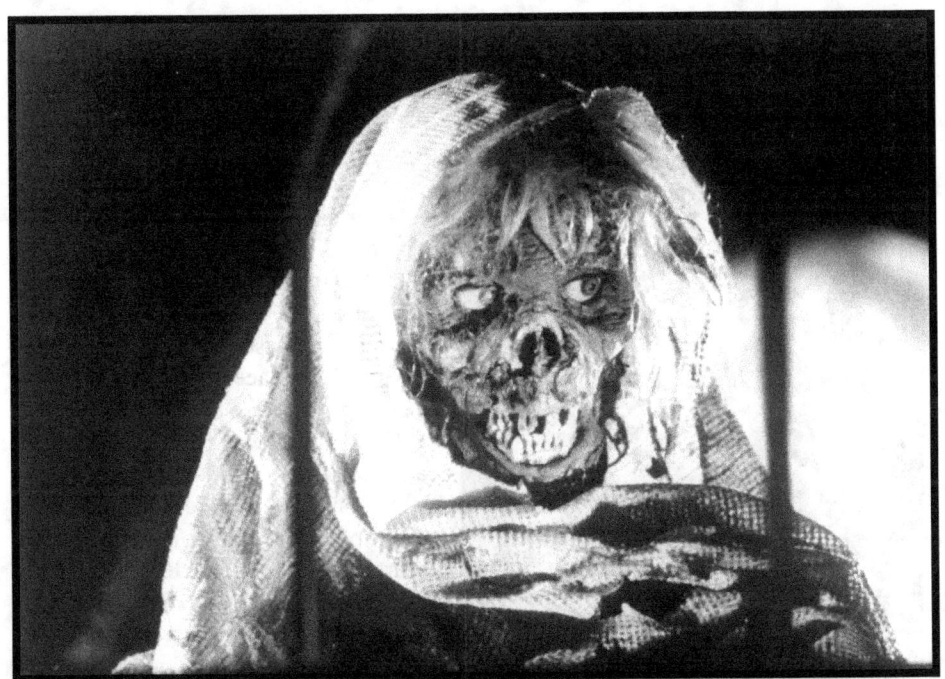

Creepshow is a love letter to E.C. Comics glory days.

in death? That certain absurd magic that only seems to happen in EC comics? All of the above, probably. It could in fact have been one of the reasons the adults of the 1950s were so outraged by *Tales from the Crypt* et al.: they inspired kids to believe in justice and karma—notions almost more absurd than those of the Easter Bunny or Santa Claus.

The Lonesome Death of Jordy Verril

At the risk of sounding rude, this is the role Stephen King was born to play. Am I saying King is a hillbilly? No—King himself is; he did, after all, write the screenplay. This is the only story that King as an actor could've carried as the one-man-show it practically is. And yes, there's subtext going on here too:

Jordy Verril is killed not by the growing fungus from the meteorite that crashes on his front lawn, but by his own hillbilly ignorance. He doesn't know any better not to pour cold water on an unfathomably hot meteorite; he doesn't think that the local university's "Department of Meteors" will accept a broken specimen, much less pay for one; he doesn't know that going to see a doctor about his "growing" fingers will not result in an unanaesthitized meat-cleaver *fingerectomy*. He may or may not have had a fighting chance against this fungus from space, but the absurdity with which he expedites his own demise makes this episode of *Creepshow* play like an airtight argument for natural selection.

Something to Tide You Over

This one is pure, basic, EC corpse-revenge stuff: bad guy kills good guy in a particularly nasty way; good guy rises from the grave and subjects bad guy to the same fate. Not much else to say about this one except: Man, that's one nasty way to go, and King knows this, and makes it the centerpiece of the story.

The Crate

In terms of subtext, characterization, and gore, this is the most rewarding story in the lexicon. The two protagonists in question, Dexter and Henry, are university professors, and most of this chapter takes place in Amberson Hall, the university where they teach.

Dexter and Henry are both stuffy academic types, so it's easy to see the school as symbolic of the academic brain. In the upper level of the "brain" are the research rooms, libraries, databases, and—except for right now—students and teachers. But in the basement we find the Laboratory (definitely more id-like down here: we perform experiments, and only if they succeed—if they please the ego and superego, maybe?—are they allowed into the sunshine of academia) and the dark recesses under the stairs.

Mike the janitor and Charlie Gereson—the only student around during Summer break—are hanging out in the basement, and of course, also hanging out in the basement, carefully hidden and locked away in a crate, is *something else*. Mike stumbles across the crate, and alerts Dexter to its presence. Dexter, who seems to have a thing for his younger female students, probably spends his fair share of time "in the basement" as it were and is immediately curious about this crate locked away in the shadows.

Together, Dex and Mike make a great deal of effort (and a great deal of noise) unearthing the crate and prying it open. What they discover inside is an animal in the most basic sense of the word—an id with teeth. The shadow-self that lurks in the substrata of the civilized mind.

Both of our professor-protagonists come within feet of the monster during the course of this segment, but they are never truly menaced by it, implying that they have some kind of control over it, maybe. That maybe it *belongs* to them. Mike and Charlie, curious and naïve, fall prey to the id-monster, and Dexter, a witness to both these deaths, is shaken to his core. Once confident, arrogant and suave with the ladies, he is now a babbling wreck—the very personification of fear.

With nowhere left to go, Dex runs to his colleague Henry, a mousy little man endlessly henpecked by his obnoxious wife Wilma. "Two people are dead," Dex says, "and I could be blamed." The guilt he feels stems from his subconscious knowledge that the monster is his responsibility; he let it out. He, if not lured, *allowed* Charlie to go down into the basement and meet his fate. And now, Dexter's fear of his shadow renders him unable to control it. As Dex tells his story, a change begins to occur within Henry. A cool confidence overcomes him, a level-headedness and willingness to take charge of the situation. When Henry subsequently drives to Amberson Hall to clean up the blood, waiting for his wife to read his note and meet him there, he accepts and embraces the monster/shadow, thus making it do his bidding.

Though everyone in the audience wants Wilma to get eaten as badly as Henry does, the comic-book morality, as well as the universal truth about the shadow, insists that there be consequences for letting our monsters loose in the real world. At the segment's conclusion, Henry and Dex try to lay new bricks of civilization over the dark places in their subconscious, rationalizing their actions to each other ("I haven't done anything to anybody!" "Neither have I!") and playing chess—that most civilized of games (and perhaps the beginning of a perpetual power play between Henry and Dex, now that their roles have been reversed). Meanwhile, at the bottom of the quarry where Henry dumped the crate, walls are being broken down from the inside. The shadow is coming home, whether the professors like it or not.

They're Creeping Up On You

Upson Pratt "grew up in Hell's Kitchen." And, given the man he is now, we can assume he did whatever he had to do to escape it, to put as much space between the ghetto and him as possible.

The end result: Upson Pratt is a heartless bastard, and a damn rich one to boot. He lives in a hospital-sterile penthouse apartment that he apparently never has to leave. He's just engaged in a hostile business takeover that has driven a man to commit suicide.

And now…he's got bugs: crawling memories of his childhood, of the hell that he fled at a cost that now includes at least one human life (it is not coincidental, in my opinion, that the bug infestation occurs at the same time as the suicide). Pratt, living in a completely sterilized environment, has greatly reduced the strength of his immune system—his *strength* in general. Shades of Poe's Prince Prospero as the Red Death overtakes the castle that he built to keep it out.

Roaches—creatures that thrive in shit, rot and waste—are the toughest species on earth. The sonsofbitches will outlive every species currently extant on the planet. The people Pratt left behind in the ghetto, the ones who stuck it out, who struggled to live under adversity Pratt would soon forget, developed strength that Pratt would never know in his most noble dreams. Creatures with hard lives become survivors. And the roach is perhaps the greatest example of a survivor species: One that eats shit and builds muscle tone.

Pratt lives in the Tarot archetype of the Tower, a card that signifies eminent and drastic change. Not a happy card.

The uprising against the Establishment (Pratt) is led by the lowliest of inner-city life. And the army is *huge*.

ALIENS (1986)
Dir. James Cameron

I wanted James Cameron to burn in hell long before he foisted *Titanic* upon us. Why? Because I am an *Alien* geek. In my humble opinion, not only one of the most frightening films of all time, *Alien* is, after nearly 30 years and numerous technological advances, still one of the most visually stunning films in history. Ridley Scott's visual

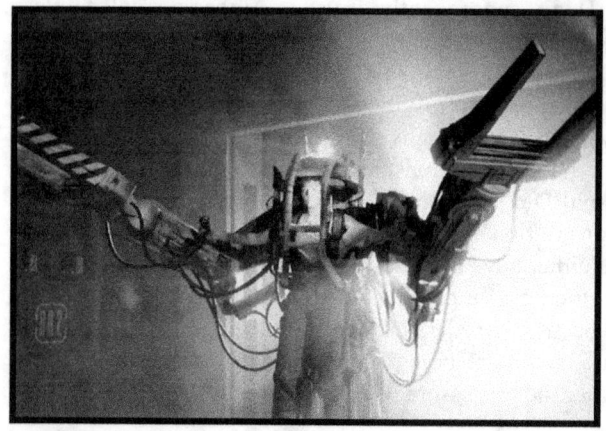

aesthetic is so strong that he's one of the few contemporary directors worthy of being called an *auteur*. And let us not forget the dark magnificence invested in the title creature by H.R. Giger. Hell, so strong was the design that forgetting is not an option.

Enter James Cameron and his *Aliens*, which attempts to de-fang the greatest movie monster of the last 50 years. Cameron once likened *Alien* to a haunted-house ride, and his own *Aliens* to a rollercoaster. This analogy needs slight amending:

Alien is, as Stephen King so rightly put it, Lovecraft in outer space. The look given to the creature by Giger is nothing short of otherworldly, nothing short of Lovecraftian. When Kane, Dallas and Lambert step out of their craft onto the barren planetoid and venture into the derelict spacecraft, we are plunged into a world we've never dreamed of. It simultaneously blows us away aesthetically and brings out the xenophobe in us.

Aliens, on the other hand, is *Rambo* in outer space. Let us not forget that Cameron had a hand in the screenplay of *Rambo: First Blood Part Two*, and apparently his imagination wouldn't stretch too far beyond this world when writing *Aliens*: "Let's throw some Marines in there or something." *Aliens* is saturated with Cameron's obsessions: soldiers, robots, a potential love story (which is nearly consummated while Hicks shows Ripley how to shoot a gun—Freud would have had a field day with that one), and body-building tomboy women grunting stoically. At one point in the film, Ripley is lugging a wounded Michael Biehn to safety, barking orders and words of encouragement like a drill sergeant, exactly as Linda Hamilton did (again, to a soldier played by Michael Biehn) in *The Terminator*. What the hell is up with this? The repetition here is positively fetishistic. I can't help but wonder: Is Biehn some sort of stand-in for Cameron? Is Cameron directing these scenes, lurking off-camera, clucking to himself, "Michael, you lucky bastard"? If it were more exaggerated, like the films of Russ Meyer, it might be kind of perversely enjoyable, but, like Tarantino's foot fetishism, once the viewer notices this repetition, he or she realizes they're learning more than they ever wanted to about the director. Other Cameron-isms present in *Aliens* include the standard gun fetishism and dialogue like, "Now you're ready to rock and roll." It works in *Rambo*, but here it's sorely out of place.

On its own, without the original to compare it to, *Aliens is* a great popcorn movie, a great actioner. But compared to the baroque, stately *Alien*, it's a case of Mozart vs. Salieri, Hitchcock vs. DePalma. There's a reason why fans and critics still rank *Alien* among the 10 scariest movies ever made: Scott and Giger worked very hard to invest in the title creature a dark mystique, a cryptic history, and invincibility worthy of one of Lovecraft's Elder Gods, the bogeyman, or the Devil himself. In *Aliens*, Cameron reduces this magnificent enigma to a videogame zombie; a drooling target that pops up in a PlayStation first-person shooter. There are lots more of them this time around, but they are apparently stupider in numbers. They pull off one strategic trick—ambushing the troops via the ceiling—and that's about it. The rest of the time, they are mere drones, mindless pursuers.

Speaking of drones, let us not forget the other plot contrivance Cameron threw into the *Alien* mythology. Hardcore fans of Scott's film know the original life cycle given the creature by Giger: The alien cocoons its victims, turning them into eggs. Yet another enigma Cameron decided to piss on in favor of his own uninspired, adolescent conceits. Why change the mythos? Why introduce a queen alien? So Ripley can have something to fistfight at the end, of course. You can't end a shoot-em-up (or a video game) without the hero engaging in a fistfight with the head goon, now can you?

Well, actually, yes you can, but Cameron isn't one to mess with a formula. It doesn't matter that the film he's building off of succeeded because of its uniqueness. Cameron gives us formulas we've seen in every action movie before it, and in its quest to be a great action thriller, it often forgets to be a horror movie. All its characters, save for Ripley, are painted as broadly as we would paint the side of a barn: we've got the lion-hearted lieutenant, the chicken-shit infantryman, the gruff, cigar-chomping sergeant, the corporate weasel, the cute kid (gag) and the bodybuilding *Chicana* bull dyke. Thus, as two-dimensionally as these characters are rendered, we don't ever really feel a sense of loss when they bite it.

No new tricks are brought to the table when it comes time to generate real suspense. Stylistically, Cameron brings us the same flashing lights, hissing steam, sirens and female voices counting down self-destruct sequences that Scott gave us in the original. As if the aping of stylistic motifs were not enough, Cameron goes so far as to "borrow" the climax from Scott's film wholesale: Ripley has to journey into the bowels of the structure that the alien has taken over, racing against the self-destruct clock, in order to retrieve a cute, mewling accessory (Jones the cat in the original, Newt in *Aliens*). In both cases, Ripley and her little friend make it onto the escape ship in the nick of time, and so does the alien. Ripley dons a special suit to confront the monster, flushes it out into deep space, and then drifts off to sleep. So basically, we're left with more or less the same film, with more monsters, more explosions, cheesier characters and a sexualized military fixation.

So much cinematic piss had Cameron left on the *Alien* landscape, in fact, that director David Fincher felt he had to scrub it all off in the first five minutes of *his* sequel, killing Hicks and Newt before the opening credits had finished. Kind of a jarring transition, but Fincher knew that it had to be done. Perhaps he overcompensated a bit by killing Ripley at the end, trying to exhibit some cinematic altruism and ensure that no one could risk screwing things up with another sequel.

His efforts, of course, proved fruitless, and another sequel was indeed made. This is, after all, a world where James Cameron wins Oscars.

53

SILENT HILL (2006)
Dir. Cristophe Gans

It's a backhanded compliment calling *Silent Hill* the best movie ever made from a video game, but there you go. It's got some of the creepiest, most disturbing and beautiful imagery I've seen in a long time, but so does the game. It's got some of the silliest dialogue I've ever heard, but then, so does the game. It changes the plot of the game considerably, but it stands up easily on its own.

Before I proceed, I must reiterate how clunky the dialogue is. It's downright horrible, in fact, and one might be shocked to find Roger Avary credited as the sole screenwriter for the film. Many of the performances are horrendous as well. But the dialogue and the performances aren't the point of the movie. *Silent Hill*'s real story is told visually and sub-textually, and in those departments it's simply amazing. The contrast between the film's graceful qualities and its ineptitude make it truly idiot savant cinema.

In the video game, *Silent Hill*'s protagonist is a man searching for his daughter in a literal ghost town. In the film, however, we follow a woman named Rose, who is quickly growing estranged from her husband, through the ash-covered landscape of Silent Hill in search of her child. The policewoman, Officer Cybill Bennett, is portrayed as slightly more, shall we say, *butch* than she is in the game, and your humble author must admit that his deviant mind concocted several decidedly *unfrightening* scenarios when Officer Cybill handcuffed our plucky heroine and led her around the deserted streets like her own personal lipstick lesbian slave-girl. But I digress.

I don't believe that the lesbian underpinnings of the relationship between Rose and Officer Bennett are accidental. *Silent Hill* is most certainly a film about women—about the varying ways in which femininity is oppressed by patriarchal religion, and the inevitable backlash that it creates.

Rose takes her daughter Sharon to the town of Silent Hill to try to cure her dangerous bouts of sleepwalking. Sharon has called out the name of the town several times in her sleep, and Rose believes there may be something there that will help solve the dilemma. Rose's husband wants to seek more conventional treatment (hospitalization), but Rose opts to use intuition rather than logic in order to help her daughter.

Various issues that are frowned upon by Catholicism and Fundamentalism are touched upon in *Silent Hill*: divorce, pre-marital sex, witchcraft, childbirth out of wedlock, and same-sex relationships. In fact, when Rose and Cybill finally team up to find Sharon, the film can be seen as commenting on same-sex couples trying to adopt. It's a stretch, sure, but stick with me, okay?

Once Rose makes the choice to take Sharon to Silent Hill, she literally cuts herself and her daughter off from the men in their lives. Her husband and the male police officers are stuck in the real world, futilely searching for the females, while Rose, Sharon and Cybill are trapped in what seems to be a parallel universe full of horrifying creatures.

Rose slowly unravels the clues, which lead her to a fanatical religious sect led by a woman named Isabella. She and her congregation are, of course, warped out of their gourds and believe that the only way to stay pure is to burn all evildoers. The only men in Silent Hill are either monsters or henchmen (and the most threatening monster—

known in geek circles to be named Red Pyramid—lugs around with him twin butcher knives that are as big as he is…you don't have to be Freud to figure that one out, do you?).

The religious loonies burn Cybill to death, snarling and overacting as though they're in a high school production of *The Crucible*, before justice is finally served in a wonderfully bloody finale involving the shadow half of Rose's daughter and miles of razor wire. In fact, Isabella's death scene is rivaled only by the most twisted of Japanese *Anime*.

Silent Hill is, in many ways, about as imperfect as movies get, and yet I find myself compelled to defend it, even though I agree with virtually every condemnation that has been leveled against it. The

dialogue isn't the screenplay's only shortcoming; there are flaws in the script's very structure that just make you want to cry. For example:

The child, Sharon, suffers from nightmares and somnambulism, and she draws pictures with images she doesn't remember putting in. It would seem only appropriate to anyone with an interest in screenwriting that the initial clue—the name of the town—be given in one of these drawings. The child draws a landscape she's never seen before, with a sign that says "Silent Hill" or some such thing. Right? But no: For whatever reason, Avary chooses to have Sharon yell out "Silent Hill! Silent Hill!" in her sleep. It's unmotivated and terribly awkward.

And when Rose finally breaches the core of the mystery and makes her way to the room in which Sharon's dark half resides, the girl explains every last missing element of the plot to Rose, in far more detail than any James Bond villain would ever bother, in a six-minute-long scene. She even goes so far as to spell out that she is the child's dark half. Are videogame players really this dense?

I *know* this movie is a problem child, but I believe it has merits that warrant it a second opinion. The dialogue is awful, but the dialogue is superfluous; it is not there to advance the plot. The visuals tell the story, and they are absolutely sumptuous from start to finish. The ending of *Silent Hill*, in which Rose and her husband experience a sort of metaphysical divorce, occupying the same house but never to come in contact with each other again, is the most haunting part of the movie, and not a line of dialogue is spoken.

And I suppose, being who I am, I simply have to love any movie in which a Fundamentalist loony gets raped and split in half by razor wire, while a little girl dances in the rainstorm of the loony's blood. There, I said it; I feel better.

VERSUS (2000)
Dir. Ryuhei Kitamura

A band of Japanese mobsters, a couple of prisoners they have just boosted prematurely, a girl they're ordered to hold hostage, and a couple of cops in pursuit of the prisoners set foot in an enchanted forest. All hell subsequently breaks loose. That's pretty much all you need to know.

Versus is two hours of hyper-stylized gunplay a la Tsui Hark, anti-gravity kung fu a la Yuen Woo-Ping, firehouses of zombie gore a la old school Peter Jackson, steely-eyed standoffs a la Sergio Leone, and even a little dry-witted zombie existentialism a la Michele Soavi's *Dellamorte Dellamore*. All of these influences are chewed together and regurgitated in that typically Japanese psychedelic collage style that has practically become its own language—a language of pure aesthetics.

As the plot progresses and the body count rises (and doubles, as this is the Forest of Resurrection and everybody has to be killed twice), we're let in on some enigmatic mumbo-jumbo about a mythical trio of Hero, Villain and Damsel who are locked in a seemingly eternal struggle for power. And it seems that whoever is currently the dominant one takes mystical power unto him or herself, and subsequently takes on the qualities of Villain. But the plot is secondary to the visual Bacchanalia taking place before our ever-popping eyes.

Versus exists in its own world in terms of both narrative and aesthetic. The film's hero and damsel have no memory of who they were before they entered the forest, and they worry that if they try to leave, they'll die. And as firmly as its characters are confined to the boundaries of the forest, the film is bound to its own aesthetics. So many of the Yakuza men are concerned with looking cool that their obsession with visual aesthetics defines their characters. And the movie itself is similarly obsessed. An amazing amount of care has gone into *Versus'* photography, choreography and editing.

Versus is so much fun it should be illegal. It contains everything that makes exploitation movies great—with the exception of rampant Japanese female flesh—and throws everything else out the window. Its hero oozes with cartoony testosterone, *and* he's a feminist (we know this because he tells us). Perhaps he has sway over the overall tone of the film, because no breasts are bared but gallons of blood are shed. Heads, hands, intestines and movie cameras fly willy-nilly. Blood-soaked Yakuza men gaze stoically through the gaping, spurting holes in their victims' bodies and heads. Hearts are punched out and eaten. *Versus* is fucking ridiculous. *Versus* is maddeningly giddy. *Versus* is sheer poetry.

Ryuhei Kitamura's film *Versus* is so much fun it should be illegal.

Like Alex Cox' *Straight To Hell*, Peter Jackson's *Bad Taste*, Sergio Leone's

Westerns, and the underrated Chris Elliott classic *Cabin Boy, Versus* creates a world with its own logic and plays by its own set of rules, with love and virtuosity.

In terms of the artfulness and technical skill with which *Versus'* vision is executed, it's pure, perfect cinema. It does what it sets out to do with fevered focus and loopy grace. And because *Versus* is practically nothing but style, style becomes its substance, media its message, and eye-candy becomes a three-course meal.

HOUSE OF 1000 CORPSES (2003)
Dir. Rob Zombie

Nothing screams "American laziness" like the cinematic disease known as *homage* (except, maybe, the remake glut that shows no signs of stopping, but more on that later). And it seems we've been getting an awful lot of *homage* to specific horror subgenres lately: We had *Scream*, of course, which paid tribute to the slasher movie craze of the 1980s; we had *Dead Hate the Living*, which bowed down at the altar of the late Italian shlockmeister Lucio Fulci; countless variants on Romero's zombie films; and Rob Zombie's long-delayed *House of 1000 Corpses*, which is all gaga over those old school psycho family classics like *The Texas Chain Saw Massacre* (1974), *Mother's Day, Spider Baby* and *The Hills Have Eyes* (1977). The biggest influence on *Corpses* is actually *The Texas Chainsaw Massacre 2* (1986), with its over-the-top cruelty, corpse-strewn underground labyrinth, and the casting of Bill Mosely as the psycho with the most dialogue.

The trouble with homage, obviously, is that it's all too easy to recreate what you love and bring nothing new to the table, and most of these movies are guilty of this. *Dead Hate the Living*, a tribute to one of cinema's mavericks, is as cutesy and cloyingly referential as *Scream*. Some might argue that the bizarre last reel of *Corpses* brings something new to the table, but is it enough, really? Is it enough to justify the film's existence? Does it say anything new about the sub-genre it's paying homage to or update the formula in any way?

Corpses is trying really, really hard to get into the hardcore club; you can feel Zombie's desperation to impress horror writer Chas Balun. He's already in a precarious position as a B-movie schlock-rocker. In this day and age of Norwegian black metal and autopsy-photo-lovin' grindcore, Zombie's theatrical horror rock is more than obsolete. Danzig? Danzig who?

Zombie's career seems nothing more than a catalog of references. His song *Living Dead Girl*, itself an homage to the Jean Rollin film of the same name, has an accompanying video that is pretty much an exact recreation of the German Expressionist classic *The Cabinet of Dr. Caligari*. So, having won the prize for "most obscure," Zombie tried to go after some "brutal" cred with *Corpses* and prove that he's not a poser.

Horror freaks and metal-heads love to try to out-brutal each other. It's fascinating to observe how metal album covers have evolved from Black Sabbath to Brujeria. By the same token, it's interesting to see where the indie horror film has gone since the original *Texas Chain Saw*. Filmmakers around the world have worked hard to raise the bar for gore and grimness, from Jorg Buttgereit's *Nekromantik* to Joe D'Amato's *Beyond the Darkness*, to Jim Van Bebber's sicko serial killer stuff, to Nacho Cerda's *Aftermath* (a short film which Chas Balun thought went too far!).

So now Mr. Zombie turns out *Corpses*, a tribute to the downbeat grindhouse flicks of the 1970s. References to most of Tobe Hooper's early stuff: *Chain Saw 1* and *2*, *Eaten Alive* and *The Funhouse*—as well as *Motel Hell* (1980), *Halloween*, and oddly enough, a few Marx Brothers films—abound. *Corpses* certainly matches *Chainsaw 2* in the nastiness department—it's a very mean-spirited affair—but the theatrical cut (the only one I've seen thus far) is a bit lighter on the gore than I was hoping for. It certainly wasn't "hard-gore porn" as one local newspaper touted it. (I know, that's a very promising phrase, isn't it?)

The Firefly family in *Corpses* isn't as fleshed out as those of the *Chainsaw* films or *Hills Have Eyes*, either. The most we know about them is that they're psycho-ass hillbillies who worship Satan and celebrate Halloween. All Bill Mosely and Karen Black really get to do is jump around and yell in half-baked Southern accents. There's no father figure in the household, and this might provide some insight as to why Mosely's Otis dresses up as "The Father" for Halloween—in the skin of one of his tormented guest's murdered father, no less. It's definitely the most disturbing scene in the movie. Maybe it's supposed to be symbolic of the disintegration of the nuclear family? Hell, I don't know. Probably Zombie doesn't either. But it's moments such as these that make *Corpses* more depressing than scary.

There are, of course, some nice visual touches in the movie. This is where Zombie always shines, as his animated mushroom sequence from the *Beavis and Butthead* movie will attest to. Captain Spaulding's museum and "murder ride" are great, as is the image of a coffin being lowered into an underground chasm, its living occupants screaming away inside, and the reveal of the stupidly named (but effectively realized) Dr. Satan.

Chain Saw '74 had a strong, clear aesthetic vision and a frighteningly precise grasp of the mindset of its villains; you feel, at the end of the film, like you genuinely *know* the Sawyer family, which is almost more uncomfortable than watching the dinner party Marilyn Burns endures at the film's climax. But Zombie's vision is unfocused and twitchy, like a kid with ADHD. The narrative often cuts away to nonsensical, unrelated bits of bargain-basement psychedelia and weird digressions that are supposed to represent—I guess—what's going on in the minds of the Firefly clan. But even these don't fit into the narrative. Nevertheless, Zombie tries to hammer them in, like a kid with a jigsaw puzzle and no patience. Watching *House of 1000 Corpses* is like watching your metal-head high school classmate drawing pentagrams on his Pee-Chee folders during Spanish class, hoping someone will notice.

THE DEVIL'S REJECTS (2004)
Dir. Rob Zombie

Almost immediately after the release of *House of 1000 Corpses,* Rob Zombie all but apologized for it, saying (and I'm of course paraphrasing here), "Aw, dude, that really wasn't the movie I wanted to make, it's too cartoony, studio interference, blah blah blah. The next one's gonna be fuckin' *hardcore!*"

So he pretended Dr. Satan never happened, had Captain Spaulding take off his clown makeup, and tried to get down to some reality with *The Devil's Rejects.* This installment finds the Firefly clan in trouble with the law. Sheriff Wydell (William Forsythe) is out to avenge the death of his brother (played by Tom Towels in *Corpses*) and leads a blazing police raid on the Firefly house, killing Rufus and capturing Mama. Otis and Baby escape, round up daddy Captain Spaulding, and hit the road for adventures in mayhem, rape and ritual slaughter. Wydell goes increasingly insane in his search for the marauding clan members.

In case we didn't catch that Zombie is paying homage to the horror films of the 1970s last time around, he *really* lays it on here, with gratuitous freeze-frames, zoom shots, handheld camera, bleached-out colors, and grainy film stock (I found myself wondering if the scratches on the print I saw in the theatre weren't CGI, added by Zombie in post-production). The look of the film is so self-consciously 1970s, in fact, that it plays more like a Beck video than a drive-in flick from horror's golden age. The attempts at grit and grimness come off as even more pretentious than they did in *Corpses.*

As if the film's visuals were not enough, Zombie jam-packs *Rejects* with cult stars from the 1970s: Steve Railsback, Ken Foree (who is fantastic, as always), P.J. Soles, Geoffrey Lewis, Priscilla Barnes, Michael Berryman, Ginger Lynn Allen, and more. And there's a ton of '70s tunes straight off of K-TEL on the soundtrack. And, perhaps most sadistically of all, Zombie subjects us to "Freebird" in its entirety during the film's climactic shootout. Fuck this goddam song, man. How obvious can you get? Redneck killers in the '70s. "Freebird." How goddam cute.

In spite of the sledgehammer stylistics, *Rejects* is definitely a better film than *Corpses.* It's almost even a *good* movie. As one-dimensional as the lead characters are, as monotonous as the film's dynamic is, and as juvenile as the attempts at shock are, this film actually appears to be saying something. We spend the first half of the film watching the Fireflys torture and kill innocent people. Since the victims are far more believable than the villains, we identify with them fairly easily. When Otis and Baby hijack two couples in their

motel room and torment them sexually for what seems like a half-hour of screen time, it's pretty grueling, indeed.

The second half of *Rejects* focuses more on Sheriff Wydell's slide into psychosis as he ramps up his quest for revenge. And damned if we as an audience don't want him to catch up to these guys and make them suffer as horribly as possible. So, weirdly enough, we as an audience undergo more of a character arc than any of the characters in the film; we go from being voyeuristic masochists in the first half of the film to being voyeuristic sadists in the last half. This also happens in various rape/revenge films from the 1970s—most obviously *I Spit on Your Grave*—but it works here too. It does, genuinely, make the viewer question why s/he's watching.

So, maybe by his fourth or fifth film, Zombie will finally become a filmmaker to watch. Here's just hoping that one day he'll be able to focus more on the craft of filmmaking rather than focus his quest for street cred.

GHOST SHIP (2002)
Dir. Steve Beck

It feels like taking the easy road, bagging on all the bigger-budget Hollywood flicks, as I am wont to do in these pages. But I, and you, must keep in mind that I am rating *The Ring* and John Carpenter's *The Thing* as all-time classics herein. Hollywood has, indeed, produced some of the best stuff in the genre, but as I mentioned before, *The Shining*, *The Exorcist* and *Alien* have all been written about to death; it feels like wind in sails at this point to write anything else on them.

That having been said, *Ghost Ship* is a piece of crap. Not a complete waste of time like the remake of *The Haunting*, or *Thirteen Ghosts*, but more like the remake of *Black Christmas*—more of a "fun if you are loaded enough to not care that precious time is ticking off your life" type of film. Even better if you don't have to actually pay much, or any, money to see it—you know, catch it on cable or Netflix it or something. And while you're at it, maybe you're better off just watching the opening sequence and then turning it off.

Like *Blade* before it, *Ghost Ship* has a doozy of a bloodbath opening. In a wonderfully edited and executed (by the new kings of splatter, KNB FX) set piece, a group of ballroom dancers on the deck of a luxury liner are simultaneously sliced in half by a wired-up booby trap. Everybody pauses for a very long time, then, just like in the *Lone Wolf and Cub* films, their upper halves all slowly slide off of their lower halves. It's the goriest thing I've seen in a while in a mainstream film, and yes, I loved it to pieces. It's truly inspired.

The rest of the film, however…

Okay, do any of these images or set pieces sound familiar to you?

An empty ballroom that comes to life with the spirits of formally dressed ladies and gentlemen, with old music playing in the background;

A sexy, naked temptress turning into a shriveled ghoul;

A ghost offering a recovering alcoholic a drink.

So we've got *The Shining* on an ocean liner here, populated by the hokey, horrible-dialogue-spouting salty sea crew from *The Perfect Storm*. There are a couple of tacky CGI pans over the span of the Really Big Ship a la *Titanic*, and Gabriel Byrne even gets a monologue in which he gets to pretend he's Quint from *Jaws*.

It's hokey as all hell; it's riddled with logic holes (twice in the movie, people get thrown overboard and swim away easily from sinking ships, as if there were no such thing as suction), and it's more than a little predictable. But if you realize you're supposed to laugh *at* this movie and not *with* it, you will enjoy truly some lowest-common-denominator schlock.

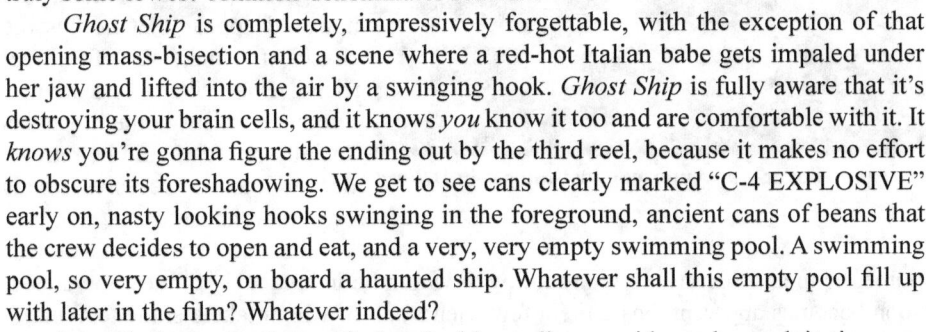

Ghost Ship is completely, impressively forgettable, with the exception of that opening mass-bisection and a scene where a red-hot Italian babe gets impaled under her jaw and lifted into the air by a swinging hook. *Ghost Ship* is fully aware that it's destroying your brain cells, and it knows *you* know it too and are comfortable with it. It *knows* you're gonna figure the ending out by the third reel, because it makes no effort to obscure its foreshadowing. We get to see cans clearly marked "C-4 EXPLOSIVE" early on, nasty looking hooks swinging in the foreground, ancient cans of beans that the crew decides to open and eat, and a very, very empty swimming pool. A swimming pool, so very empty, on board a haunted ship. Whatever shall this empty pool fill up with later in the film? Whatever indeed?

So yeah, in the pantheon of what the big studios consider to be exploitation, you could do worse with something like *Thirteen Ghosts*, but you could do better with *Deep Blue Sea*.

WILLARD (2003)
Dir. Glen Morgan

Anybody who has the slightest iota of taste in cinema will attest to one fundamental, unshakable truth:

Crispin Glover is the shit.

He simply is one of the greatest living presences we've got in cinema, and every second we have of him captured on film belongs in the Smithsonian. Remaking *Willard* with Glover in the lead was one of the most divinely inspired acts in recent cinema history, and I bow my knee and tip my hat to both those studio executives who pitched, and those who green-lighted, this project.

Crispin Glover—an American instituion—in *Willard*

In the remake of *Willard*, the lead character's house is the symbol of his psyche. Bars line its windows; the inner rooms reek of must and ennui. Willard's house is a decaying shrine to his dying mother. His mother is the only friend he has in the world, and she's slightly batty and more than a little frail.

Outside of home, Willard is bullied and brutalized by his boss, who seems to be waiting for Willard's mother to die so he can lay claim to Willard's house. His boss goes so far as to try to replace Willard at his job with Cat, a sweet, pretty lady played by Laura Elena Harring. Cat immediately takes pity on, and grows to like, Willard, and it would appear that he has the chance to make his first real friend. But Willard is a hermit, smothered by his home life and is socially retarded, and he retreats deeper into the recesses of his own mind/house.

In the basement of his home, he meets Socrates, a white rat, with whom he immediately bonds. Socrates, it soon becomes apparent, has quite a few friends, all of whom take a shine to Willard. He spends more and more time in his basement, befriending and training his new subterranean friends. Socrates is his favorite and the only rat he allows into the upstairs of the house. Envious of Willard and Socrates' relationship is Ben, a rat named by Willard because of his size; "Big Ben" is the first thing out of Willard's mouth when he spies him. Ben is large, sinister-looking, and not as cuddly as Socrates by a long shot. Socrates is what Willard would like to be: smart, charming, capable and cute. Ben is, of course, a manifestation of Willard's shadow: he embodies all the things Willard loathes about himself: he's unattractive and awkward, the kind of rat that scares girls. Willard recognizes these shadow aspects of himself in Ben and, accordingly, shuns him. He won't let him upstairs, won't say encouraging things to him, belittles him in front of his peers—in short, Willard treats Ben precisely the same way Willard is treated by his boss.

When Willard's mother finally dies, the rats bubble up from the basement, taking over the house, as Willard's rage bubbles up from the depths of his subconscious. His mind is pretty much gone by this point, and this is further symbolized by the arrival of representatives of the State, attempting to foreclose on Willard's house, which his parents were not financially adept enough to keep in their name. Willard is now a hopeless case. He goes rifling through his deceased father's belongings, coming across a rusty old pocketknife. He makes a feeble attempt to cut his wrists with it and is saved by squeaky pleadings from his furry friend Socrates. When Cat stops by his house, offering her sympathies to Willard in the form of her pet housecat, Willard accepts her offering. She offers it for warmth and company; he accepts it as blood sacrifice to the ravenous id swarming freely in his house.

When Willard's boss fires him, tries to convince Willard to sell him his house, and winds up killing Socrates (who had been lurking in the storeroom with Ben), Willard completely loses it. He allows his madness to roam free. Under Willard's command, the rats swarm into the office and devour his boss alive.

And now, in the film's third act, the center of Willard's world falls to pieces. The whole of the outside world is now pounding on Willard's door: Cat, because she's worried about him; the State representatives, because they want his house; the police, because they suspect him in his boss' death. And inside the skull of Willard's house, a war is taking place. Willard is in a desperate battle to kill the rats. But the one rat he can't kill, of course, is the one he wants the worst.

Ben is leading the revolt against Willard. Ben is waiting for Willard as he tries to climb above the swarming masses on the floor of the house. Ben gnaws at Willard's face and fingers, sending him back down into the revolt of tooth and claw. Willard's crashing to the floor happens to bring his father's pocketknife down with him. Once the implement of Willard's literal suicide attempt, it now becomes the implement in his figurative suicide, his murder of shadow-self Ben. Fade to black.

We cut to a scarred but relatively intact Willard, sitting in a small room in a mental hospital. He is talking to himself in voice-over and quietly petting a new white mouse. The parallel in both imagery and dialogue ("We've got to be quiet as a mouse") obviously suggests *Psycho* ("Why, she wouldn't hurt a fly!") more than a tiny bit, and I suppose that's only appropriate. Only Crispin could get away with such an over-handed homage to the late, great Tony Perkins. Just as only he could get away with trying to kick David Letterman in the face and still be invited back on his show.

Crispin Glover, folks. An American institution. Worship him, would ya?

DARKNESS FALLS (2003)
Dir. Jonathan Liebesman

The only truly unforgivably bad movies are the mediocre ones. Movies that provoke no reaction—not even laughter—are the only ones that truly disappoint. These movies are few, but they exist. John Carpenter's *Ghosts of Mars* and Dario Argento's remake of *Phantom of the Opera* are such films, doubly disappointing in the fact that they were made by masters of the genre…miserable failures, unfinishably mediocre, unforgettably forgettable.

But some films are so bad they are beyond funny—they are downright fascinating. And such a movie is *Darkness Falls*. Dear God, where to begin? It's difficult to merely pick out the film's most important faults—there are just so damn many. Should we start with the plot? For the back-story isn't hideous: It attempts to recreate the Tooth

Fairy in the guise of a vengeful ghost. Not a horrible idea. According to the film's lore, before the old hag was wrongfully executed, she placed a curse on the town of Darkness Falls. (Yeah, I know, perhaps the fact that the town is named Darkness Falls should be the starting point in the *great fault* list...but we'll let that slide.) As a ghost, she begins visiting and murdering the town's children on the night they lose their last baby tooth. But as soon as she makes her first cinematic appearance, she kills the protagonist's *mother*, so I guess the curse isn't really that strict (and no, we won't even start here, with the fuzzy logic of the curse!). The boy is, natch, accused of the killing and grows up to be a mental case. This makes him a convenient murder suspect once bodies start piling up.

The Tooth Fairy herself resembles a female Freddy Kruger wearing a *Phantom of the Opera* mask and a *Scream* cloak purchased for $7.99 at Walgreen's. That's where we'll start, I guess. We'll call the derivative hodgepodge of the Tooth Fairy's look Important Flaw Number One. Okay: onward.

2: When a movie doesn't know how to set up its back-story with its screenplay, it often resorts to opening title cards that explain it to the viewer. *Darkness Falls* sets up its back-story with no less than *five minutes of illustrated narration!!!* The narrator's voice does not belong to any character in the movie. So, this makes it the equivalent of one of Criswell's opening monologues for Ed Wood's films. It's five minutes of a guy with a *scaaaary voice* saying, "This is what the mooooovie's about, mua ha ha…" This is what your creative writing teachers mean by "Show, don't tell."

3: Twice in the film a scene occurs where characters turn their back on the darkness in front of them to face the person behind them, the camera frames them with plenty of room on either side, and the character says, "Everything's okay." Everyone who has ever seen a horror film knows what's going to happen next. Come to think of it, so does everyone who hasn't.

4: Apparently this whole Tooth Fairy Curse is the stuff of legend in the town, so why do any of the kids bother to put their teeth under their pillow?

5: *Darkness* telegraphs its ending not 30 minutes in when the heroine is flipping through some book about ghosts and finds a page on which a female specter is killed by a giant lens refracting light at her. Oh yeah, and the town has a prominently featured lighthouse. Too obvious to be legitimate foreshadowing, this is simply, and terribly, telegraphing.

6: The protagonist says the line, "Stay in the light" over 50 times throughout the film. Maybe this is supposed to represent some obsessive neurosis on his behalf. Instead, it just annoys the fuck out of you.

7: The Tooth Fairy is repelled by light, but it is apparently not bothered by the 600 or so flashes of lightning that pepper the last 30 minutes of the movie.

8: Every line of dialogue in the movie is not only wooden and inane, but sounds like it was looped—overdubbed by the actors in a recording studio during post-production. Many foreign movies are shot this way—without live sound—to save money. Subsequently, even the original language prints sound like they were dubbed. The words have that lack of ambience and that lack of emotional immediacy that removes the dialogue from the world of the movie *just enough* for us to notice. Every line in *Darkness Falls* sounds like this. Every. Line. Was it shot without live sound? I don't know, and I'm not gonna access the special features on the DVD to find out.

9: Do we count regular dumbshit movie things? Like guys crashing their cars into trees, going headfirst through the windshield, and picking themselves up like nothing happened? We don't count it if it's *Evil Dead 2*. If the movie's trying to take itself even a little bit more seriously, it counts.

10: The Tooth Fairy can short out the power to the *whole town* but can't disable the emergency lights in the hospital?

11: In the climax, the surviving characters—none of whom have ever had any experience running the lighthouse, and one of whom hasn't even set foot in the town since childhood—can get the lighthouse up and running in less than five minutes.

A textbook film, this. There are more examples of how not to make a movie in *Darkness Falls* than in anything I've seen since *Sgt. Pepper's Lonely Hearts Club Band*. Film students would be wise to take note of its treasure trove of glorious faults. But as unbelievably wrongheaded as it is, *Darkness Falls* does not commit the crime that *Ghosts of Mars* or Argento's *Phantom of the Opera* commits: It is not un-amusing.

CHRISTMAS EVIL (1980)
Dir. Lewis Jackson
MARTIN (1977)
Dir. George A. Romero

In the movies, they call it suspension of disbelief. In organized religion, they call it faith. In abnormal psychology, they call it paranoid schizophrenia. The subject places himself in the hands of the intangible, and lets it lead him where it will. In the case of both *Christmas Evil* and *Martin*, the childhood faith in mythic figures is taken to somatic extremes in adulthood.

Strange how our parents, who we are supposed to trust to play fair with our growing minds, encourage us to develop that sense of fancy that borders on delusion. We are encouraged to believe that Santa will reward us for being good by breaking into our homes and giving us things rather than stealing them. However, were we to suffer from a nightmare or two about Dracula after having seen one of the movies or read part of the book, our parents soothe us by telling us that Dracula doesn't really exist, that there are no such things as vampires. Well, *jeez!* Is the notion of Santa Claus any more preposterous than that of Dracula?

No two films embody the multiplicity of "suspension of disbelief" more than *Martin* and *Christmas Evil*. Children are encouraged to suspend disbelief by their parents in order to install that sense of wonder that is supposed to make childhood magical and great. Adults who eagerly practice suspension of disbelief, however, are looked upon as kind of batty. Indeed, many of them *are* batty, but perhaps only in retaliation for society ordering them to "put away childish things." Sometimes insanity is the last option for a grown mind that wants to cling to the idea of playing.

Christmas Evil opens on Christmas Eve in 1963, with little Harry, his mother and his brother Philip hiding on the stairs, hoping to spy Santa at work in their living room. They do, of course, and Harry is absolutely stunned. Later, in their room, Philip tells Harry that it wasn't Santa at all, but their father in disguise. Harry refuses to believe this and rushes back to the stairs for a second look. He catches "Santa" about to go down on Mom, and his world shatters.

We cut ahead to the present day (or 1980…perhaps it was a pun on writer/director Lewis Jackson's part to call it the "present" day in the film's title cards?), and Harry has grown into a quiet, troubled man-child. He has just been promoted off the assembly line at the toy factory, where he works at an administrative desk job. He is not happy; he misses making toys, and he cannot motivate his coworkers to share his passion for it. He is exposed to the corrupt thinking in the factory's top brass. This promotion should be Harry's final shove into adulthood, i.e., giving up on childish concepts like hope, wonder and common decency. Instead it pushes him backward into the childlike dreamland he has built for himself.

"I can play the tune now" is a phrase Harry says over and over to the adults in his life. It's his cryptic way of saying he's learned how to exist in the grownup world. The grownup world is telling him that there is no Santa Claus. And according to his own fuzzy logic, if Santa does not exist, it will be necessary to invent him.

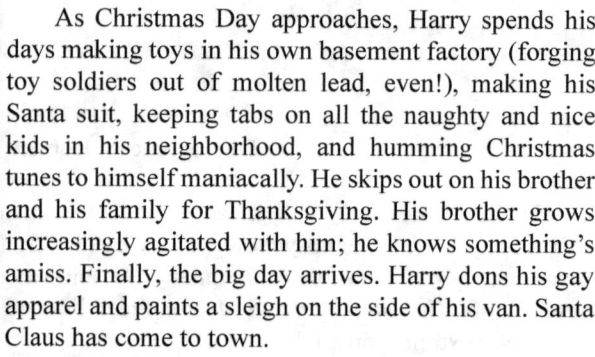

As Christmas Day approaches, Harry spends his days making toys in his own basement factory (forging toy soldiers out of molten lead, even!), making his Santa suit, keeping tabs on all the naughty and nice kids in his neighborhood, and humming Christmas tunes to himself maniacally. He skips out on his brother and his family for Thanksgiving. His brother grows increasingly agitated with him; he knows something's amiss. Finally, the big day arrives. Harry dons his gay apparel and paints a sleigh on the side of his van. Santa Claus has come to town.

Christmas Evil received typical exploitation distribution, and at the time, the grindhouse audiences didn't know what to make of it. The actual carnage in the film is extremely minimal—Harry only kills three adults—and most of his interactions with children and adults in the film are actually quite funny. *Christmas Evil* and *Martin* both technically reside in the Art chapter according to the logic of this book—they're too sophomoric for the Jarmusch crowd but too dry for the splatter set. But they both have that grindhouse taint on them that lands them in the Crap section. Both splatter fans and "real" movie critics overlooked *Christmas Evil* then and now; it was silly to the snobs and pompous to the geeks. It treads that magic ground that *Dellamorte Dellamore*, *Santa Sangre* and many others would later tread—that shaky middle ground between art and trash. *Christmas Evil*'s camera hangs out alone with Harry for slow stretches of time as he hums to himself, breaks into the toy factory at night, and gets stuck trying to climb down a chimney. These moments have a creepily voyeuristic feel, and are ever more revealing of Harry's mindset. They're simply great.

When action does happen in the movie, it's all quietly absurd. Harry robs his workplace of its toys and distributes them to the children at the local hospital. Immediately after this, he dispatches a couple of non-believing adults on the steps of a church. He is "kidnapped" by an office Christmas party where everyone's a little too drunk. Things here could easily turn ugly, but the presence of children saves the mood—and possibly the lives of the adults in the room. Harry's interaction with these kids inspires warmth all around, and soon he is dancing with the kids, as well as a few of the ladies. He leaves the partiers and their offspring with the words, "If you're bad boys and girls...I'll bring you something...horrible," and is off yet again.

Soon word of his crimes gets out, and the grownups are on the hunt for him. The police round up a gaggle of Santas and subject them to a lineup. Harry is pursued by an angry mob, complete with torches. Beautiful! Anyone who had complaints about these little touches needs to buy, borrow, or steal a sense of humor quick, before their hearts explode.

Harry makes it back to little brother Philip's place for one final confrontation (Philip is the ultimate grownup, having been the first to take a potshot at Harry's belief in Santa) before he is again running from the angry mob. He swerves his sleigh/van off of a bridge, and *Christmas Evil* delivers its final *coup de grace*: Harry's van goes soaring off into the night sky, sleigh bells jingling in the background, to his exclamation of "Merry Christmas to all, and to all a good night." The house lights come up and the credits roll. Every yahoo in the audience who was expecting a Santa slasher film a la *Silent Night Deadly Night* pries their ass out of the puddle of congealed PBR that's soaked into their seat and begins screaming for a refund. No one cares until years later, when film geeks rent it and are as pleasantly surprised as when they rented Carpenter's *The Thing* years after it bombed in theatres.

As far as I'm concerned, this is one of the three greatest endings in a horror film ever (the other two being *Dellamorte Dellamore* and *Alone in the Dark*, 1982). It pushes the movie over into Spielberg territory—the idea that "if you just believe in something completely, magic happens, garsh golly." *Christmas Evil* tells us, "Yes, Virginia, *now* there is a Santa Claus. And he's coming back next year, so you'd fucking well better behave."

Humankind has needed mythology in its life since its very beginning. To believe in and sustain mythology is to not only fill in some narrative gaps in history and nature, but also to believe in magic. Definitely in Harry's case, and probably in Martin's, a fervent belief in their respective myths compensates for innocence that was taken prematurely.

Martin gives us a protagonist who has rejected the idea of magic, but who has somaticized a mythological icon into his own psyche regardless. Martin believes he is a vampire, 84 years old, but according to him, it's merely a sickness. "There is no

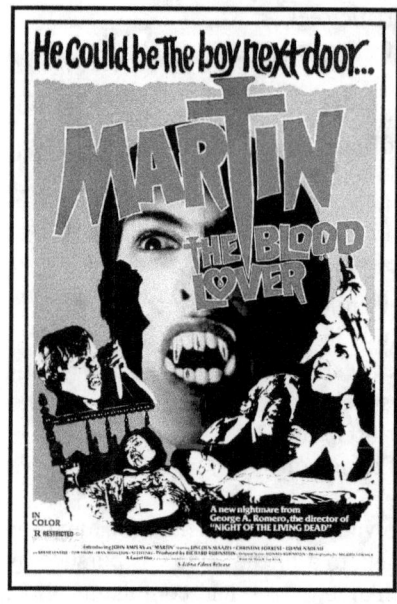

magic," he says, referring to the superstitious trappings of the Catholic Church. He uses syringes and razors to take his victims, rather than fangs. Cousin Cuda has taken Martin under his wing, and believes, just as fervently, that the lad is a vampire. Being two generations removed from Martin, he *does* entertain the wackier superstitions of the church. He tries to keep Martin under control with garlic, crosses and exorcisms, to precious little avail.

The women to whom Martin delivers groceries in the neighborhood all seem to like him a lot. They're drawn to his gentleness, his strange androgyny. He is the quiet, oddly handsome young halfwit they might fantasize about initiating in the ways of carnal love. In other words, he is the exact opposite of each of their husbands. One such woman is Mrs. Santini, a depressed, cuckolded housewife with sad and lovely eyes. She recruits Martin to do odd jobs around her house, offers to put some booze in his lemonade, and tries to get a tad fresh with him. Martin ain't havin' it, and he high-tails it out of there (for now).

The cynicism of Martin's generation has permeated the world of the film and infiltrated the new guard of the Church; the new generation of priests smoke, drink, go to see horror films and preach from makeshift altars made from TV sets. (Romero has stated that *Martin* was his revenge on the Catholic priests of his childhood; wonderful, then, that Romero plays the young priest, overturning all the traits we associate with clergy.) The sacrament of marriage is trod completely under; there is no marriage in the film that is happy, much less faithful. Infidelity begins to complicate Martin's life more and more; not only making his stalkings more difficult, but also possibly making him question his sexuality. You see, for all his rebellion against the old guard, he is still a bit developmentally disabled, at least sexually. He has trouble getting it on with conscious women. He has to "use the needles" to do it. In the film's harrowing opening murder, Martin rolls his drugged victim on top of him before he cuts her, letting her blood spurt onto his chest in a decidedly ejaculatory fashion.

This vague allusion to homosexuality was no accident, in my opinion. When Cuda addresses "the family shame" that Martin has inherited, he believes it is a curse, and that Martin is demonic. Martin, on the other hand, believes that what he has is "just a sickness." The Church has not left his soul unscathed, try as he might to resist its guilt.

Later in the film, when Martin accidentally catches an intended victim in bed with her extramarital lover, the ante is upped considerably. Not only does Martin now have two people to sedate against their will (the man requiring much more sedative than Martin had anticipated), he now has to wrestle internally over whom he wants to kill. He drags the guy out back, into the woods, yelling at him over and over, "You weren't supposed to be there," and it sounds more like Martin is more pissed at the guy for *tempting* him than for screwing things up with the lady back at the house. But Martin gives in to his impulse. He skewers the man's neck with a stick (Freudian imagery a given here, yes?), ripping his shirt off and drinking deep of the man's fluids. Back at the house, Martin fools around with the girl a little, but does not kill her; he does not take out his latent rage on her, having already spent it back in the woods.

Immediately after this incident, Martin tells a radio talk show host that he would one day like to try "the sexy stuff, but without the blood, with a woman who's awake." The host has no real idea what the hell Martin's talking about, but it's a pretty big step for Martin, just the same. He's now ready to try to explore sexuality with a conscious woman, having just completed his little dirty ritual with a man.

This new phase of Martin's life, the script's third act, begins with Martin succumbing to Mrs. Santini's advances. It marks the first time he has sex with anyone consensually. And it's also the cruel reminder that Martin will never be able to escape who he is—what the family and Church have made him. His romance with the melancholy Santini is as doomed as she is, and this actually might be what attracted Martin to her in the first place. His train murder at the beginning of the film was very carefully set up to look like a suicide; is it possible that he subconsciously sees Mrs. Santini as an easy target? Or, more dramatically, perhaps he *identifies* with her as someone who cannot get along in the world, who doesn't see much point to it, who feels more pain than pleasure.

The hope Martin might have had for salvation is shattered when he comes over one day to find that she has killed herself. He discovers her corpse in the bathtub, her eye peering sightlessly out of the bloody water (one of the most truly remarkable shots in the film, along with the earlier shot of the garage door closing, each slit in the wood allowing us a glimpse of Martin's snakelike eyes as it passes down). He looks genuinely sad observing Mrs. Santini's corpse but not entirely surprised.

He now tells the talk show host that he's through with people, and that he's ready to kill again. He had his chance to become human, and now that it has all crashed down around him, he has written the human race off. He is, again and finally, a monster. And he does not attempt to clean up the mess that Mrs. Santini left behind. It doesn't seem to occur to him that it might get traced back to him.

In the film's giddily surreal penultimate scene, Martin stumbles across a parade on his way home, and just kind of slips into it, ambling around as though in a dream. He is in the world, but no longer of it. These creatures are

Martin (John Amplas) believes he is a vampire.

merely interesting diversions for him now, and somehow he is in the parade with all of them, but he just cannot relate to it. After a while, he wanders off home, to accept who he is and meet his fate.

Both Harry and Martin live completely in their own heads, and communicate in strange, obsessive dialects: Harry prattles on and on about being able to "play the tune," and Martin repeats most of the lines he utters in the film at least once, and goes on and on about "the sexy stuff" on the talk show.

And both characters actually *become* the mythic figures they believe themselves to be. Harry completely absorbs the Santa mythos unto himself, even inheriting magic powers in the process (although you could see it as a wish-fulfillment fantasy on Harry's part before his van crashes…but I prefer not to). And if he wasn't before, Martin is *made* a true vampire at the film's end, when Cousin Cuda stakes him in his bed. The other clichés about sunlight and garlic may not have applied, but the wooden stake sure seems to do the trick.

In both films as well, the lead characters are, at some point, pursued by a mob of angry townsfolk with torches. It's a subtle parallel, but an important one, considering the mythic proportions of the character arcs in these films. Both films are relatively quiet character studies, depicting the inner lives of mentally fragile man-children, following them as they make real their obsessions with mythology.

Christmas Evil and *Martin* are dependent, to say the least, on their lead actors Brandon Maggart and John Amplas—every bit as dependent as *Taxi Driver* was on DeNiro. And the two leads carry these movies to never-before-seen places, which is the most exalted task film asks of filmmakers. You will not see movies quite like these anywhere else. Maggart and Amplas pull off the trick of making mentally ill, murderous characters believable and likable. Perhaps Martin is a bit less likable than Harry, for all his dark perversions—he would certainly have made Harry's "naughty" list. But still, we never lose identification with Martin as a protagonist. We never really want him to get caught, and his death is every bit as jarring as Ben's was in *Night of the Living Dead*.

BLUE SUNSHINE (1976)
Dir. Jeff Leiberman

Jeff Leiberman is a criminally underrated horror film director. Exploitation cinema is far the richer for the three films he gave us in the 1970s and 1980s: *Squirm, Blue Sunshine* and *Just Before Dawn*. Proudly prancing shit-ponies are lurking here in this little trilogy, waiting for lonely, bottle-bottom-bespectacled film archeologists to discover and take a ride on them.

Sunshine, at first glance, seems to almost take a moral stance: *You deserve what you get when you put street drugs under your tongue*. The cautionary interpretation is not without merit—in this day and age, street acid is even more ominous than it was in the '90s. Lord knows I'd never do it again; my body's simply too old for strychnine, let alone whatever else acid is cut with nowadays. But I believe *Sunshine* is saying something more than, "Just say no." It starts off interestingly enough, revealing a seemingly random set of characters and watching them freak out, lose their hair and go homicidal, killing their lovers, friends and families. A guy named Zipkin, who witnessed the first rampage (and is of course the prime suspect), is driven

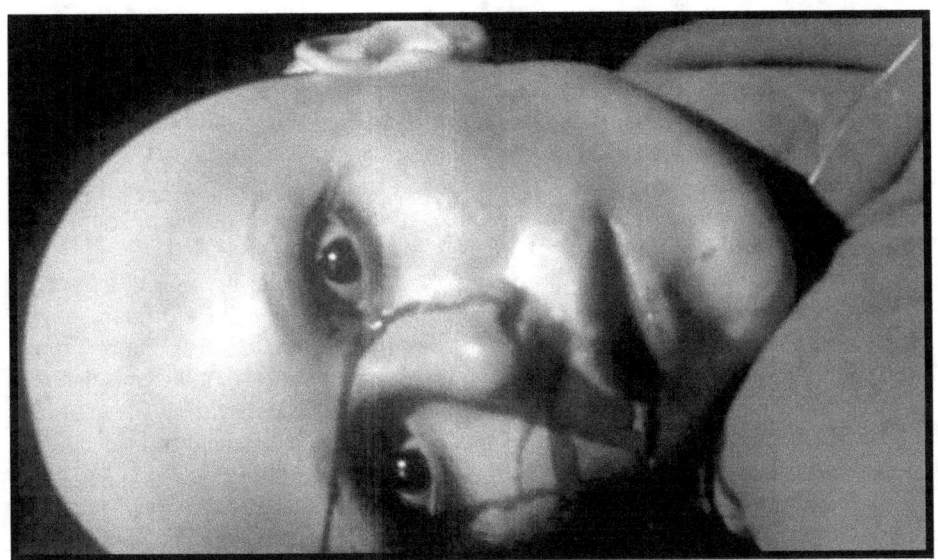

*Blue Sunshin*e can seem a cautionary tale to the hippie generation.

to investigate. He discovers that all the bald perpetrators graduated from Stanford University 10 years before, and he begins looking for a deeper connection.

He soon finds his connection in Ed Fleming, a charismatic fella running for City Council. As it turns out, Fleming, once upon a time, was also a charismatic *acid dealer*, and he dealt a little batch called Blue Sunshine to many of his classmates. Ten years later, the recipients are having some nasty flashbacks. They are roasting their girlfriends alive in fireplaces, attacking the children they babysit with butcher knives, killing their entire families, and ripping discotheques to pieces.

The idea of the slackers/stoners of yesterday's generation becoming today's parents, doctors, bodyguards and political leaders is a bit creepy, I admit, and it's a reactionary fear that *Sunshine* toys with—the Hippie Generation, who wouldn't take responsibility for their own bodies as teenagers, are now responsible for the welfare of both their own children and the elder generation—but there is something else at work in the subtext. You *can* look at *Sunshine* in this reactionary way if, in fact, you *are* terrified that the generation you don't seem to even be on a linguistic parallel with will be taking care of you when you grow old.

But the film can also be (and wants to be, I think) seen as a cautionary tale to the Hippie/Boomer generation itself. The characters in this movie—even the ones who aren't tainted by Blue Sunshine—are all seriously stressed about something in their inner lives. They once were a generation of hope for the future, and now they've pretty much all sold out, taking jobs in the Establishment. The guys who still have Sunshine lingering in their DNA, maybe still tripping after all these years, are looking at this new, modern, cold world and freaking out in a big way. The babysitter loses it when the children begin repetitively screaming for Dr Pepper and numerous other corporate products. Wayne, Ed Fleming's bodyguard, agrees to meet a girl in a disco, and the lights and music make him crazy. When he loses it and rips the place apart, her only hope is to isolate herself in the DJ booth and *crank that disco up*! He begins stomping and grunting like Frankenstein's monster and leaves immediately, probably looking for some orange juice and a nice Allman Brothers record.

It is not inappropriate to mention that this discotheque is housed in a shopping mall—and that Ed Fleming is also holding a campaign rally at this very same mall. Perhaps *Sunshine* would make a nice double bill with *Dawn of the Dead,* eh? Yes indeed, and *Sunshine's* climax is littered through and though with racks and racks of consumer goods. At one point Wayne stumbles past rows of televisions, all portraying Ed Fleming's smiling visage.

Being in every wrong place at every wrong time, Zipkin becomes a suspect in all of the murders, and he has to go underground…shades of Abbie Hoffman, maybe. (He even asks his girlfriend if she was followed to their rendezvous point one time.) And, ever the true hippie (note the rhyme with his nickname, even), the conscientious objector, Zippy cannot kill his enemies. He has to bring Wayne down with a tranquilizer dart. In exchange for the proof of drug-induced rage in the dormant form of Wayne, Zippy can now come out of hiding and turn himself in.

Littered throughout the film's interiors and exteriors are campaign flyers that read: "Ed Fleming—Here is the Future." And for the poor slobs in this movie, Fleming most certainly is. He has become a modern product, like Dr Pepper…or Blue Sunshine. And he is certainly no less hazardous to the health of the consumer.

HORRORS OF THE BLACK MUSEUM (1959)
Dir. Arthur Crabtree

Jekyll and Hyde are mentioned late in the movie, so it's no stretch to apply most of what goes on in *Horrors of the Black Museum* to the concept of civilized man vs. primal man, ego vs. id.

A killer is picking off beautiful young women in ghastly ways. The first one we see is a doozy of an opening for the movie. A woman looks through a pair of binoculars (that were a gift from someone mysterious), adjusts the field of focus, and collapses to the ground, screaming in agony. You see, a pair of spring-loaded spikes has just penetrated her orbs and shot though to her brain. (Eyeball mutilation is one of my real squirm-inducers, so this proved to be particularly effective for me.)

After this murder we are introduced to Edmund Bancroft, played by Michael Gough, who was better known as a villain in British movies like *Horror Hospital* before he became Bruce Wayne's butler in the 1990s. Bancroft is a true-crime writer, and his column addresses the murders that are currently plaguing the young women of London—the most recent of which was the binocular case.

Bancroft shows up to talk with police about the killings (and to subtly taunt them for their inability to catch the killer), and during their discussion much talk is made of Scotland Yard's Black Museum, in which grotesque evidence from past cases, solved by the Yard, are stored and catalogued.

If, in symbolic terms, a house can be seen as a projected body for the people who inhabit it, than a museum can be seen as a projected body for the collective unconscious of a culture. No less, a "black museum," such as the one in this film, is a projection of the collective shadow of a culture. It's a physical representation of the pit of the human mind—the kind of mind that would *create* devices intended to *destroy.*

But this morbid chamber is given a slightly more positive perspective once we get a look inside Mr. Bancroft's house. For he has been building his own Black Museum, and if we thought the police version was morbid, we now stand corrected. It is no more morbid than the museum that is the ruins of Dachau; a reminder of a reality that we would like to evolve beyond. Bancroft's museum is dedicated especially to the killers who eluded capture by the Yard in the past, and who currently remain at large. His collected weaponry includes medieval, modern and futuristic implements, and his secret dream is rooted in the present, and in the future as well.

Bancroft buys his artifacts at the antique shop of an old lady named Aggie. Aggie and Bancroft banter dryly about each other's sex lives and chatter about the murders during his visits. She mentions that the new string of murders makes chills run down her spine. He responds with, "Until the killer runs out of young women, you're quite safe." He buys a long dagger from her and departs, only to return to his private museum. It is here that we meet Bancroft's protégé Rick, a young, directionless fellow who is a little too easily trusting and eager to learn from Bancroft. Rick obeys every order Bancroft gives him, and soon enough we find out what those orders are.

We follow Bancroft to the flat of June, a woman whom he is, more or less, keeping. He pays her rent and buys her food and doesn't like her to leave, or to be seen in public with him. When he arrives, she hits him up for money; when he refuses, she dumps him cruelly. She makes fun of his age, his looks, and his disability (he walks with a cane, which she immediately snatches from him so she can play with him some more). Standing facing into a mirror on the wall, June looks at him while grooming herself, and she scolds him for his conceitedness. A nice image here: she, a reflection in a mirror, is the face of vanity. Ego berating ego.

Bancroft leaves the flat in shame (and simmering rage), and the girl goes out to a pub to have fun (i.e., get drunk and dance). At the pub she tells the bartender that she is now an independent woman and she will no longer be kept by men. She goes home to her flat, and of course, she has a surprise waiting for her. Rick, whose face has transformed into something low-budgetedly monstrous, dispatches the lady with a portable guillotine. He scoops both his device and her head into a bag and runs off into the night, plowing through all the concerned neighbors in the hallway.

Bancroft shows up at Aggie's antique shop again, and she tries to interest him in a grisly-looking pair of ice tongs, telling him that they will cost him 1200 pounds. She's onto him, and now she wants money. Being the misogynistic and greedy cuss that he is, Bancroft dispatches Aggie with the very same tongs. So far in the movie, she is the first victim to die directly by Bancroft's hand. She is neither young nor beautiful, and therefore *approachable* to him.

Rick (Graham Curnow) and Bancroft (Michael Gough) take viewers on an enjoyable tour of the *Horrors of the Black Museum*.

    Distinctions are now being made in the movie. Lines are being drawn. The Jekyll/Hyde metaphor, which Bancroft so liberally applies to Rick, can be drawn elsewhere in the film now. The Yard's Museum is a grim museum of the id. In fact, we can go so far as to see it as metaphorical for horror cinema. It's a collection of frozen moments, on display to educate, inspired by humanity's dark past and present, and hopefully to prevent similar events in the future. (Those who do not remember the past are condemned to repeat it.) Bancroft's museum, however, is not actually a museum at all, but an *arsenal*. No outsiders must even know the room exists, but Bancroft and Rick can take the weapons off the walls and use them in the way their makers intended. It's a playroom for Bancroft's cavorting id.

    Two outsiders *do* wind up inside the museum, of course; you can't have *Bluebeard* without someone going into the secret room, now can you? The first is a nosy doctor, who almost immediately pays the price. The second is Rick's new girlfriend Angela.

    If Rick is a twin for Bancroft, a twin with the barest smidgen of humanity, than Rick's girlfriend Angela is a twin for June—a woman who thirsts for independence, who is a bit eager to manipulate her man, but for less malevolent reasons than June. Angela's power is such over Rick that she soon finds herself necking with Rick in the museum…and gets caught by Bancroft. He asks the girl to leave them for a bit, lectures Rick on the evils of women, injects him with what is apparently the Jekyll/

Hyde drug, and sends them off on their date to a carnival. Once there, she attempts to placate Rick by asking him to ride with her in the tunnel of love.

Here is the film's most fascinating scene. The lovers drift along in their little boat, submerged mostly in darkness, the occasional red or blue light passing over them. We don't see much of anything, and we don't hear anything said between them. Rick and Angela kiss once before the light passes by. The dialogue we do hear is eavesdropped from lovers in the other boats, as lights briefly illuminate Rick and Angela, and then strand them in darkness.

A girl slaps her groping boyfriend, calling him an "octopus." The boyfriend responds, "No one can see anything in here."

Angela is now on her own side of the boat, her face in comic shock at what she can hear. Rick is not smiling.

"Jerry, kiss me again, I like it"—"Aw, leave me alone, will ya, sit over on yer own side and leave me alone! You always wanna neck!" Two pairs of opposites: positive male/negative female, negative male/positive female. Angela is amused by the voyeurism; Rick is scowling. No one's getting laid tonight.

The boat emerges from the tunnel. Angela has a pleasant expression on her face. Rick turns to her, and his face is that of the monster we saw earlier, in June's bedroom. Angela screams and Rick plunges a dagger (the one Bancroft purchased from Aggie) into her. He barrels off through a hall of mirrors, wigs out when he sees his own reflection, and runs from the bobbies by climbing to the hub of the Ferris wheel.

The police show up, with Bancroft in tow like a vulture. When Rick spies Bancroft, he pleads with him to save him, yelling, "I did what you told me!" Bancroft orders the cops to shoot, and, realizing the betrayal, Rick leaps from the Ferris wheel, dagger outstretched in his arm. Both Rick and dagger land squarely on Bancroft, and the circle neatly closes. Hyde kills Jekyll and, subsequently, self. Well, I suppose Bancroft was never at any time fully Jekyll, but rather more like Hyde with table manners. Conversely, Rick had Jekyll's humanity, but no self-control. He uses his last bit of humanity to destroy the monsters lurking within both himself and his mentor.

All this might read better on paper than it plays onscreen, but *Black Museum* is a thoroughly enjoyable ride. A little more gore couldn't have hurt, but those binoculars are certainly suggestive enough.

HOUSE BY THE CEMETERY (1981)
Dir. Lucio Fulci

My introduction into the Fulci oeuvre has been slow going, and this is the most impressive I've seen from him thus far. It's nowhere near as derivative as *Zombie* (which is mainly derivative in Italy, where it was plugged as a sequel to Romero/Argento's *Dawn of the Dead*) or *The Beyond*, though there are large hints of *The Shining* in this one's plot. *House by the Cemetery* is about a guy who moves his wife and son to a spooky old building so he can quietly get some research done. The boy has premonitions of terrible things that will happen in the house, and he eventually communicates with a dead little girl. Seems some horrible murders took place in the house many years ago, and the spirits of the killer and victims still walk its grounds. But any similarities to *The Shining* end there; the rest of *Cemetery* seems inspired

mostly by the bonehead stalk-n-slash flicks of the American 1980s, with the obligatory Italian blood-sprays, body parts, and maggots.

There is a veritable plethora of stupid behavior on behalf of every last character in the movie. You could base a drinking game on how many times someone wanders through the titular house with nothing but a flashlight, incessantly calling out the name of a missing character. And it's funny how none of the victims in Fulci films ever raise a hand in their own defense when being skewered or having their throat ripped out. Their hands are always at their sides, and they never even bother to so much as scrunch up their shoulders to try to protect their necks. Not that I'm complaining. We do not watch Fulci films for believable character motivations. We really don't watch for plot of any kind. We watch Fulci the way we watch porno: fast-forwarding through the dialogue, in search of the money shots.

The porno metaphor perhaps applies more succinctly to Fulci than any other splatter director. No other filmmaker lingers as long or lovingly on the arterial geysers, and no other director gets as pornographic a reaction from the viewer; the uninitiated squeal in disgust, and the fans make decidedly different primal noises. And in Fulci's films, more than any other horror directors', the porno reaction is the name of the game.

The murder of the lady real estate agent in *Cemetery* is the prime example of this. A long black spear penetrates her three separate times. The first one happens in the stomach, and the camera zooms in as the phallus twists inside her, blood pulsing out to soak the shaft. The spear then withdraws and hovers over her breasts as she writhes and moans, the tip dripping blood onto her white blouse. It rams her again in the chest, and finally the throat, where we zoom in and out, in and out, on the spurts of blood that spatter her face. And as sensualized as many of the female victims' deaths might be in Argento's films—even the heart stabbing in *Suspiria*—they are just that compared to Fulci—*sensualized*. They're all seductive lighting and pulsing, throbbing soundtrack. They're Cinemax soft-core porn compared to this blatantly *sexualized* murder scene in *Cemetery*.

As previously mentioned, *Cemetery* takes much stylistic influence from the American slasher films of the '80s; you have to love a movie in which a woman accompanies her boyfriend to an abandoned, dilapidated house on the outskirts of a graveyard to *fuck*. You might be inclined to argue whether or not you *have* to love a movie like that. You would be wrong. You also have to love a movie with a line like, "This ain't New York. Most of the old houses in the area have tombs in them."

There are several almost-artsy touches, like the boy's connection to a ghost-girl he sees in a picture of the house. He sees her first through the pane of glass that separates him from the picture, and later through a car window. To the adults she only appears as a doll, I guess. The ghost girl is later seen looking through a plate glass window at a female mannequin that looks a bit more realistic than your average showroom dummy. To the ghost-girl's shock, the mannequin's head falls off in a welter of blood. This mannequin later shows up in human form as the boy's babysitter. Panes of glass doubling as veils that separate the living from the dead; sure, I'll buy it.

The creepiest element of *Cemetery* is the sound design. Whenever the undead Dr. Freudstein is on the loose, shambling about in his cellar or above ground, we hear the crying and whimpering of children. Late in the film, we realize these sounds are supposed to be emanating from him. A final title card quoting Henry James rams this idea home: "No one will ever know whether children are monsters or monsters are children." And in *Cemetery*, Fulci certainly seems to leave us with the latter being a reasonable summation. As for the former, though, the kid in this movie isn't exactly cruel by any means. He might be warped into being a monster by the film's end, but he certainly didn't begin that way. So what the hell is Fulci trying to say with that quote? I'm not exactly sure, but I do give Signor Lucio points for making a half-assed stab at artsy-fartsy enigma.

THE PROWLER (1981)
Dir. Joseph Zito

The Prowler's reputation as drive-in sleaze precedes it. But the film is surprisingly well done, thoughtfully acted, executed, photographed and costumed. We open up in the 1940s, at a graduation dance coinciding with the return of several young soldiers from their WWII tour of duty. We know, via a narrated Dear John letter, that a young lady named Rosemary abandoned her lover while he was still oversees in combat; her reasoning being that she has to live her life now, and doesn't know when, or if, he's coming back. Rose attends the graduation dance with another beau. They twirl among the white, red and blue streamers (but white holds dominance over all other decorative colors herein), go outside to make out under a gazebo, and are summarily dispatched by a man in an Army uniform.

We'll call him the Unknown Soldier for our purposes in this essay, for that, to me, is what he most represents—the face of many men who came home after fighting for our country and felt abandoned by those they were fighting for.

As the narrative jumps ahead to the 1980s, this metaphor becomes even more appropriate after the Vietnam War. It could be said that many, many soldiers coming home from Vietnam received an equivalent of that opening letter. A graduation dance hasn't been held since that fateful night so many decades ago, and the spunky youth of the '80s have decided to take back their right to party. And, of course, a certain someone in combat fatigues has been waiting for just such a night. He's got his bayonet and pitchfork at the ready, and he, too, is ready to party. *The Prowler* rather cutely plays by the rules that *Halloween* helped set up for the slasher film. We are soon enough introduced to the requisite slut, pothead, and virgin that our tale will revolve around. We have our list of suspects quickly introduced and take very little time in figuring out who the killer really is.

The differences between the new grad party and the old one are certainly noticeable: not only has the soundtrack changed from Benny Goodman to cheesy white-boy butt-rock, but the décor has changed from virginal white to vaginal pink. The interior of the ballroom is decidedly womb-like. This is not a romantic, patriotic

ceremony like it was back in the day. This is an event where the kids sneak off into the basement to fuck.

While dishing out punch at the dance, the Virgin (wearing white, of course) has the red liquid spilled all down the front of her dress. This symbolizes to me that she has lost her innocence (especially since said spillage was caused by the hunky deputy, who seems to like her but can't keep his hands off other women). Call it a loss of innocence at betrayal by the deputy, call it symbolic of her getting her period and becoming a woman, but she is now a target of the Unknown Soldier. She has to go back to the house, disrobe, and change into a dress much less, er, white. The Soldier spies her and chases her out of the house, and once she escapes, she has part of her dress ripped away by a pervy old Army Major in a wheelchair. Losing more innocence by the second.

Later, the Soldier has his murderous way with a nubile who is taking a dip in the pool. During this scene I could imagine myself in a Times Square grindhouse, sitting in a crowd full of paint-sniffing yahoos, all of them hooting and hollering. I imagined how easy it would be to get caught up in the moment and start yelling myself. It was a warm, fuzzy feeling. This particular effect is remarkably jarring, even though we can figure out pretty easily how it's done. But watching that bayonet saw back-and-forth through the unfortunate lady's pretty throat is certainly eye-popping while it's onscreen.

Anyway, the climax takes place in the pervy Army Major's mansion, where all the furniture is draped with white sheets. It's great imagery; almost a return to the virginal whites of the films beginning, but the sheets look like shrouds, so we have sort of emerged from the womb of the dance to the tomb of the mansion. It is here that the killer is unmasked and has his head blown off in an effect that surpasses Savini's head explosion in *Dawn of the Dead*.

The Prowler is in the interesting position of being an exploitation film, but the film also demonstrates some quality. You can tell that director Joseph Zito actually gives a damn about filmmaking and telling a story. But he also knows what sells films like these, and Zito makes no apologies for diving into the seedier aspects of the slasher film with true gusto. The same is true of his *Friday the 13th: The Final Chapter*—you can't argue with how well made it is, no matter how badly you might want to, and I think critics of the day had a tougher time with *The Prowler* and *F13:TFC* than other films of the era for precisely that reason; they weren't quite as easy to write off.

THE TEXAS CHAINSAW MASSACRE (2003)
Dir. Marcus Nispel
DAWN OF THE DEAD (2004)
Dir. Zack Snyder

If the '00s have distinguished themselves at all in horror cinema history, it is for the outrageous glut of remakes Hollywood is pumping out. While the horror geeks of the world might be scratching their heads at the notion of remaking some silly William Castle flicks and remaking *Willard* with Crispin Glover in the lead (which might easily be the most inspired notion in the remake glut yet), the two films that best symbolize the modern American remake are *The Texas Chainsaw Massacre* and *Dawn of the Dead*.

Both films attempt not only to fix what isn't broken, but also to make classic stories palatable to a generation of viewers who apparently can't be bothered to delve into low-budget 1970s fare. But in terms of what they accomplish, *Dawn* and *Saw* are different animals indeed.

Dawn of the Dead is cynical and gratuitous, retaining none of the original's wit, compassion or social commentary, and this actually serves to make *Dawn* 2004 as reflective of its culture as the original was of *its* culture. The new one starts off grim enough and only gets worse. Where the original implied that humanity had an iota of hope against the zombie epidemic, the remake allows us no such luxury. Once our protagonists reach the mall, our darkest suspicions are confirmed. We meet up with a young girl whose father has been bitten, as well as a young man whose pregnant wife has also been bitten. So, in symbolic terms, the young adult (the demographic audience of the film) is stuck between its corrupted parent and its corrupted unborn child, waiting to be either devoured or corrupted itself. You can either join forces with the bad guys or die, *but you cannot remain human* in this movie's encroaching future.

It is this perspective, I believe, that makes *DOTD* 2004 the first official post—9/11 American horror film. True, it does borrow an uncomfortably heavy amount from *28 Days Later*, which began production just prior to 9/11, but *28 Days Later* was positively bursting with humanity and hope in comparison with *Dawn*. All its characters and

Horror remake *Dawn of the Dead*

The remake of *Texas Chainsaw Massacre* brings nothing new to the screen.

their motivations are pretty much unbelievable, and this seems to be part of the movie's point. *Don't get too attached, DOTD* 2004 seems to tell us, *these people are all fucked. Sit back and enjoy the violence, because it's all you're gonna get for the next hour-and-a-half.*

And enjoy it we do. The gore in *Dawn* is thick, relentless, and very entertaining. There's a chainsaw death that might be the high point of the movie, as well as the cornucopia of bullets to the head and zombie carnage one would expect from a remake of *Dawn of the Dead*. And, at the end of the day, the unborn baby is born a zombie, and not even islands are safe from the undead infestation; nobody survives. If the mutant big bugs of the 1950s were symbolic of the Red Menace, or a similar horror too big for us to have visualized at the time, than *DOTD* 2004 presents us with a nemesis that isn't alien or greatly exaggerated; it is a distorted reflection of ourselves, and deadlier than any "foreign" menace could possibly be. The fall of civilization comes quickly and mercilessly. And for the handful of survivors we take up with the duration of the movie, this *Dawn* is much darker than the night before.

The remake of *Texas Chainsaw* features the same cinematographer from the original, and John Larroquette narrates once again. It also manages to achieve that queasy, knotted feeling the first one is famous for. But really, it brings nothing new to the table. It can't be considered an update because it's set in 1973 as well. The *Dawn* remake calls itself a "re-imagining," and this is decidedly appropriate, but the *TCM* remake is more or less a mere "re-shooting."

The characters (except for Leatherface) have been changed, but the situation and mood are pretty much the same. The look is a strange combination of washed-out film stock, grainy color, and MTV editing and Ridley-Scott–style shafts of light. It's as though producer Michael Bay spent millions of dollars trying to make this movie look like a hundred grand.

This "grimy-yet-fashionable" motif is present in the costume design as well; everyone's clothing is filthy, soaked with sweat, and decidedly un-1970s. I don't recall jiggling nubile Jessica Biel's low-rise jeans being in vogue in 1973. But I'm not complaining, and the camera complains even less. It leers at her nonstop, focused intently on her glistening tank top, which is pasted so tightly to her implants it becomes clear that the only reason she isn't naked through the whole of the movie is that it wouldn't make any logical sense, and the critics would get pissed off.

The remake also seems to play the hick stereotype card far more heavily than the original. *TCM* 1973 seemed like a ride into another world, a nightmare fairyland. It's been called a modern fairytale many times, and this description is quite apt. But *TCM* 2003 lets us know that we are in its particular vision of Texas, where the law is corrupt, everyone is inbred and brain-damaged (David Dorfman's Billy-Bob teeth are particularly hilarious), and flies swarm over all the slowly rotting meat in the general store.

The fact that the head of Leatherface's family is (or was) a cop can be considered a comment on the relationship between the police and youth counterculture of the time. By the same token, the debate between the guys and girls on whether or not to dump the body of the hitchhiker can be seen as symbolic of the battle of the sexes. But that's about the extent of the remake's depth. The rest of the time, the going is pretty dumb. It's the kind of movie where one of the kids is searching the spook-house for his missing friend, while another kid distracts the owner outside. There's a serious shortage of time here, and the house is full of shreds of hanging, drying meat, but the doofus kid inside takes his time, dipping his fingers into bowls of red liquid and looking in the refrigerator.

All in all, it's not a horrible movie, not disrespectful of the original, and not without its share of intensity. But it's completely unnecessary. It doesn't provide any insight or visceral experience the original does not. And for its vastly increased budget and sick/slick visuals, I found it kinda funny that they could impressively sever Leatherface's arm but they couldn't sufficiently hide his real arm under his costume, while he rolled around on the floor screaming. We can clearly see it tucked under his clothes, and we have the urge to heckle the movie as though it were, well, cheap.

ALONE IN THE DARK (1982)
Dir. Jack Sholder

Were William Peter Blatty's *The Ninth Configuration* a bona fide horror film, I would likely be doing a double-essay. Both films' centerpieces are rather esoteric insane asylums, where doctors prescribe the most eccentric treatment. Both films also raise questions as to behind what side of the wall the asylum really lies.

We are introduced to *Alone*'s asylum along with newcomer Dr. Daniel Potter, a replacement for the recently transplanted Dr. Martin. He first introduces himself to the "receptionist," who tells Potter he cannot see the head, Dr. Bain, because he is invisible. Soon enough, Potter meets Bain (portrayed wonderfully by Donald Pleasance) and is introduced to his rather odd techniques. In Bain's work, patients are never called psychotics. Rather, they are referred to as "voyagers." When he is asked about some of the more violent behavior of his high-security patients—those that reside on the infamous third floor—he replies, "Well, all right! They're insane! Isn't everybody?"

In their defense, he says, "A man's violence is a cry of pain, but nobody hears it."

It would seem his methodology, though a bit cracked, does work. One of his patients complains to him that her intestines slither out at night and try to strangle

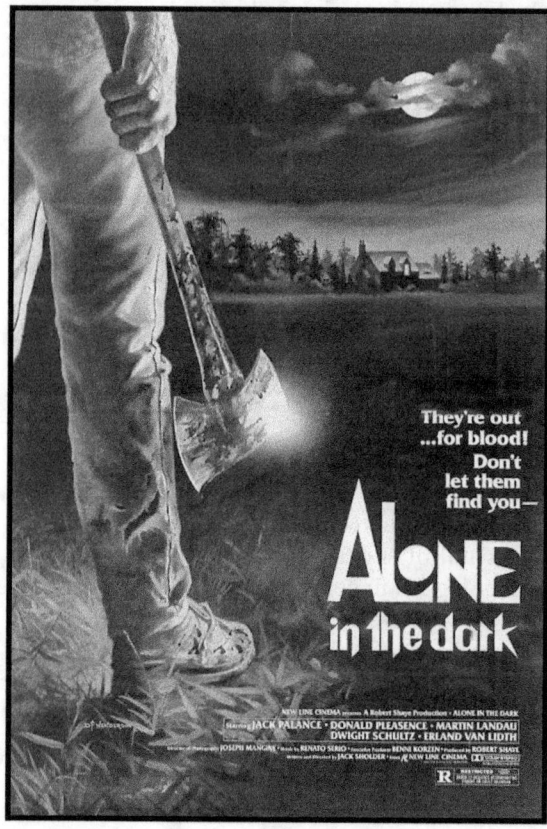

her. He gives her a simple little ritual to repeat and promises that if she performs it, it won't happen again. She seems satisfied with this treatment.

Before long, we meet up with the denizens of the third floor—the ones who have to be reined in by electricity (motion-sensitive alarm systems and whatnot). There's Hawks, the war veteran and seeming leader of the group (who has got it into his head that the newbie Dr. Potter killed Dr. Martin and wants to kill the third floor posse next), Byron, the religious fanatic, whose "trip" is burning down churches (preferably while there are people inside), Elster, whose trip is raping little girls, and Skank, who hates for his face to be seen and suffers from nosebleeds under stress. An intern named Ray is the "floor monitor" for this wily bunch, and he confesses to Dr. Potter that he is afraid of them. "The only thing between me and them," he says, "is electricity," referring to the electric security door to his room.

A little insanity pops into Potter's home life as well, when his sister-in-law shows up for the weekend. She has apparently just suffered a nervous breakdown, and is recovering quiet flamboyantly, thank you very much, embracing punk rock and anti-nuclear activism. Both of these activities she immediately introduces to the Potter family. First, she takes them out to see a band called the Sic Fucks. Dr. Potter doesn't know what to make of it, all the freaky behavior and violent, ritualistic dancing and lyrics encouraging the crowd to "Chop Up Yer Mother."

And then, the power goes out.

The Bacchanalian frenzy that was the concert, just seconds ago, dwindles down into nothing. Everybody politely vacates the premises and goes back to their homes (cells?) to wait for things to get better. But on the opposite end of the spectrum, somewhere else in the city are a whole gaggle of "regular" people whose shadow-selves were being held at bay, rather than achieving catharsis, by electricity. And now that the power is out, these normally docile people head straight out to the local strip mall and begin rioting and looting. And, of course, the denizens of the third floor waltz right out of the asylum and into the chaos. They fit right in with the looters. Skank dons a hockey mask and kills a bystander. They gather up a few weapons and head straight for Dr. Potter's place.

As the Potters drive home, the radio broadcaster attributes the blackout to either "an act of sabotage or an act of God."

The next day, Mrs. Potter accompanies her sister to an anti-nuclear power rally, and both are arrested. This leaves the youngest of the Potter family, Lila, at home alone and in the clutches of Elster. He repeatedly asks her to join him upstairs for "fun with scissors," and eventually he talks her into it.

Between the time that the girls make bail and Dr. Potter gets home, Lila's emergency babysitter and her boyfriend are murdered, but we find that Elster has not laid a hand on Lila. We discover that Dr. Bain's methods are not entirely unsuccessful. But as night falls, the trio finally lay siege to Dr. Potter and his family as they sit trapped in their home. Lives are lost, battles are fought, twists in the plot occur and precious mental ground is lost by the recovering sister before Elster, Skank, and Byron are finally (and viciously) dispatched by the Potter family.

The final confrontation occurs between a crossbow-wielding Hawks and the Potters. "So," Hawks says, "it's not just the crazy ones who kill, is it, Doctor? We all kill when we have to, and we all die when it's time."

And then (almost as if it were an act of God), the power comes back on.

And, coincidence of coincidences, whose smiling visage should appear on the TV screen? Why, Dr. Martin, of course, alive and well! He is being interviewed about the escape of his ex-patients. When asked by TV reporters of the homicides his former charges committed, he calmly replies, "Well, they were probably quite confused at the time," and continues to reinforce the possibility of their rehabilitation. Upon having seen that, Hawks, with apparent embarrassment and confusion, leaves the house.

His travels take him to—where else?—a Sic Fucks concert! A drugged-out girl at the gig immediately takes a shine to him, telling him that the music they're listening to is very "pink." When he pulls a gun on her, she grows even more aroused, lifting the barrel up under her chin and telling him all the while, "You're really there!" Here, with this girl, Hawks smiles to himself, realizing he's right back in the asylum where he belongs, and that we're all voyagers.

FRIDAY THE 13TH PART 3 (1982)
Dir. Steve Miner

In terms of traditional cinematic "quality," it is widely (and safely) surmised that *Freddy Vs. Jason* (2003) is the best *Friday the 13th* film yet made. But I feel compelled to defend another chapter in the series. While I readily admit that this defense is rooted in personal bias, I still have faith that I can rationalize it. Maybe.

Sometimes it's enough to ask of a film: Does it accomplish what it set out to do, and how well, exactly, does it accomplish it? Using this standard of analysis, I believe that *Friday the 13th Part 3* is pure, perfect cinema. Sure, by this standard of measurement I suppose it could also be said that not only much exploitation horror (including the first two *Fridays*), but also most porn, is pure, perfect cinema. Well, all right, why the hell not? (One begins to wonder, using this track of thought, *what exactly would constitute a bad porno*? I assume it would have to be either an unconvincing female lead or a poorly lit cum-shot.)

F13 3-D is trying to be two things at once: a slasher film and a 3-D movie, which gives it extra points compared to the other *F13s*. Neither one of these genres, of

This scene from *Friday the 13th Part 2* was used as a recap in *Friday the 13th Part 3*, which was shown in all its 3-D gory.

course, is famous for nuances of acting or screenplay. Hence, the barest minimum of attention is paid to both of these factors: "*How little time can we spend on dialogue and direction and still convey, in the most vague sense, that these 'actors' are playing 'characters?'*"

No, the paradigms of the subgenres in which this film resides demand two things: That at least 10 people get killed in ultra-violent and creative ways, and that an object comes flying out at the audience at least every two minutes. Not only does *F13 3-D* accomplish this, it often kills two birds with one stone. Case in point: Jason squeezes a guy's head so hard that his eyeball pops out at the audience.

As a 3-D film, *F13 3-D* tries pretty hard. Not only do projectiles pop off the screen on a nonsensically regular basis, but there is also some surprisingly nice screen composition using 3-D's depth as well—a factor that only Hitchcocks' *Dial M For Murder* seemed to care about up until this point. Shots showing long clotheslines with billowing sheets receding into the background are actually quite arresting, as well as shots in the climax that feature the final girl running in the foreground and Jason pursuing in the background. These shots are actually quite moody and effective.

There are eight kids staying at the cabin on Crystal Lake this time around, and they all stay alive until the last two reels of the movie. So, to fill in time and keep the audience interested, the filmmakers throw some extra adult characters into the mix as machete fodder—a bickering husband and wife, who own a grocery store, and a trio of bikers. In the last 20 minutes, however, Jason dispatches teenagers at the seeming rate of one every three minutes, and the effect is well worth the wait. The pace is pretty breakneck.

Likely the main reason I find myself compelled to write about *F13 3-D* is because I caught it again just yesterday, at a 3-D festival here in Portland. It had been over 20 years since I had last seen it on a big screen, and at that time I was 11 years old. As I've mentioned before, that experience was one of the most powerful I've ever had in a movie theatre. It was far more visceral and genuinely involving of the audience than any screening of *Rocky Horror* I've ever attended. Nobody in the audience harbored any illusions about what to expect from the film, and none of us were the slightest bit disappointed.

The second time seeing *F13 3-D*, as God intended it to be seen, was amusingly different in comparison to the first. The festival I attended was part of a 3-D convention being held in town. The audience comprised primarily 45-to-65-year-old men, most of whom were wearing Hawaiian shirts and had stereoscopic cameras slung about their necks, and all of them looked decidedly unlike anybody who would ever have seen an *F13* movie of their own volition.

Before and after the movie, an emcee all but apologized for the subject matter of the movie. "This movie," he said, "is basically one of a long string of successors and imitators of *The Texas Chain Saw Massacre*. It's a slasher film." I found it unbelievable that anyone could live in America for the past 30 years and not know that the *Friday the 13th* series were slasher films. But perhaps that just defines the difference between this crowd and myself. I was the only horror geek in a room full of 3-D nerds, which made the proceedings only more amusing.

After the film, the emcee announced, "Our next feature, *The Little Magician,* is the first-ever G-rated 3-D feature film. It's kind of strange that this is the first 3-D feature film that actually tries to *please* the viewer. So many 3-D films that were released in the 1980s revival featured beheadings and dismemberments, that it's refreshing to see some pleasant imagery."

If the emcee was truly representative of the audience in attendance, this meant that I was the only one present who found cinematic beheadings and dismemberments "pleasant."

F13 3-D's purity and perfection stem not only from its delivering precisely, neither more nor less, what it promises as a 3-D theatrical experience, but also from its ability to involve the audience, unite them as a hivemind in a way that most films do not. Here is where even porn fails; even if you go to see a porno movie in a theatre, and even though you may be united with the audience in what you're doing with your hands while you're watching, viewers generally not only watch porn alone, but as anonymously as possible. (Porn audiences don't usually cheer the screen after they cum in their pants.)

I'll say it again: Yes, this essay is rooted in the author's personal biases and fond fuzzy memories of viewing the movie for the first time. And obviously, seeing it on TV, in two dimensions, is going to have considerably lesser effect. But it cannot be argued that *F13 3-D* is anything but a success, because it delivers on its promises, and there are a surprising number of exploitation films that fail on this scale. So I find myself irresistibly compelled to love it. I expect to remain alone on this island for the rest of my life, and that's okay.

LOVE OBJECT (2003)
Dir. Robert Parigi

Upon my first time viewing *Love Object*, I quite enjoyed it. The characters are certainly well written, the direction is competent, and the acting definitely above average. As a story of a man descending into psychosis and the woman who stumbles into his crosshairs, it's involving, disturbing and thought-provoking.

As a rather heavy-handed message movie, I suppose I can't say it doesn't have its heart in the right place. Men can never be encouraged to look at themselves and the way they view women enough. Sure.

However, *Love Object* does need to be taken to task a bit, not only for how far it goes with this message, but for the questionable and unintentionally ironic means it uses to get this message across.

Like the novels of John Skipp and Craig Spector, *Love Object* seems to view pornography and fetishism as mere pathology, with no therapeutic or cathartic value, dehumanizing both object and objectifier. There is no middle ground in this film: If you fantasize about control, you are a control freak, a misogynist, and above all, a man.

While the film may present itself as the story of *one* man's obsession with control and security and how this obsession takes over his love life, *Object* still portrays *all* men as total pigs and there is only one "real" woman to speak of in the narrative. Most of the other women in the film are viewed either in the background (and out of focus) or otherwise filtered through tinted windows and spy-holes, or heard as off-camera voices. If women other than our heroine appear unfiltered and up close, they do not speak. All of the men are in charge, and all of the women are either girlfriends or in the typing pool.

Sex, even at its kinkiest, is still an act of affection, but an act of violence is something entirely different. So if pornography shapes sexual behavior, rather than being shaped by it, then what in God's name does that say about horror films? Can horror films still be considered cathartic while porn is considered desensitizing? It just doesn't make sense. So if *Love Object*'s message is correct, than we should all avoid horror films like *Love Object*, just to be safe.

It may seem I'm on a bit of a soapbox about this film. I reckon I am, and I'll be the first to admit it's because *Object* seems to take a contrary tack to the entire philosophy of this book. And while the director has stated in the film's commentary that this is indeed the story of one man (a crazy one, at that), not *all* men, I must still take the film at face value, because no effort is made in the film to *emphasize* that this is the story of one man. As I mentioned before, all the sickness in *Object* lies in the men, and all the men have the sickness. Even Udo Kier's landlord character, who eventually tries to save the heroine, still checks the teeth of the women he has one night stands with, as though they were horses.

Linking porn or BDSM sexuality with violent behavior is certainly nothing new—TV crime shows have been doing it forever—but it simply doesn't equate to real life. And *Love Object* doesn't strengthen its case at all by resorting to these kinds of generalizations.

Further driving the nail into *Object*'s coffin is yet another stigmatizing association it relies on to make its point symbolically. The clerk at the porn store suffers from an elephantitis-like deformity, and the customers in the shop, as well as the deliveryman who brings Kenneth the doll, all have large birthmarks on their skin. It's a cheap shot on the grandest scale: using physical deformity to signify internal evil.

Diversity of any sort (except for the eating of ethnic food) does not make *Love Object*'s world go 'round. In its quest to be meaningful, it does quite a bit of stereotyping—*objectifying*—of its own, and subsequently buries itself with its own heavy hands.

THE PIT (1981)
Dir. Lew Lehman

I remember seeing the commercials for this one as a kid and being very intrigued. I remember the weird kid saying, "They eat people" and pushing an old, wheelchair-bound lady into the titular pit. This week I finally got around to checking it out and, damn me to hell, I liked it. I must say I got more out of it than I was expecting for some piece-o-crap film from the early '80s, directed by and starring nobody.

There's a neat mix of Freudian and Jungian imagery going on here, as well as a few seconds of cheap creatures and gore and mucho perversity. The weird kid in question is a 12-year-old boy named Jamie, who has a lot of trouble making friends. His mom seems a little too interested in him, if you know what I mean, as does the school

librarian. He talks to his teddy bear, and it talks back. He's in love with his housekeeper/babysitter. And he's the only one who knows about a strange pit in the woods, in which live several toothy, hairy monsters. Is this pit Jungian or Freudian? Is it the black pit of the subconscious, where the shadow self resides? Or is it a distorted, foreboding vaginal symbol, symbolic of his mother and the librarian?

His relationship with the creatures (which he names Tra-la-logs) intensifies after his relationship with the teenage object of his affections worsens. He begins to feed them: candy bars at first, then raw meat, and of course eventually, everyone in the town who is mean to him. At first he feeds the monsters because he's afraid they might get out. But soon enough, he grows to appreciate their presence a little too much. Eventually he decides he wants to let the woman he loves in on his secret. After she falls into the pit by accident and is torn to pieces, he loses whatever marbles he might've had. He throws a rope down the pit, allowing the creatures to climb out.

I love the dreamlike logic surrounding the notion that these creatures have been here for so long and he's the only one who knows about them. It's obvious that these trolls *belong* to him psychologically, and yet once he lets them out, it becomes obvious that they really exist. The whole thing is played so matter-of-factly that it takes on a quietly absurdist quality. And once the townsfolk catch on that people are being murdered, the men organize a manhunt, trap and kill the creatures in the pit, and bury them. In having this aspect of him killed by grownups, Jamie himself begins to grow up.

I also love the delirium with which *The Pit* explores Jamie's perversity. He spies on his babysitter in her bedroom and in the shower, sweet-talks her into bathing him, and feeds her boyfriend to the Tra-la-logs. He fakes the kidnapping of the librarian's niece in order to force the librarian to strip naked in front of her window. While she does this, he snaps pictures of her from the shadows outside. When he shows the pictures to his teddy bear, Teddy says, "I'm gonna look at these a *lot.*" He strips the tutu off of a girl his own age before he dumps her into the pit.

At the film's closing, Jamie is shipped off to live with his grandparents. There, he meets a little girl, the first child who will play with him. She leads him into the woods to yet another pit. There are, of course, Tra-La-Logs in this one as well. And the girl, of course, pushes him in. She's his first playmate in his age group, and yet it is she who sends him on a fatal trip back into the womb.

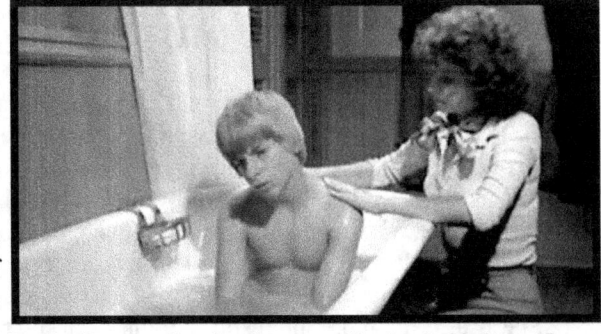

Jamie (Sammy Snyders) sweet-talks his babysitter (Jeannie Elias) into bathing him.

If we analyze this scene from a Freudian perspective, she's his last real sexual experience, assuming his mother went as far as we are led to believe. And this sexual experience is yet another violent one. Jamie's family and peers all behave violently toward him, so it's only natural that he would solve his problems with violence—by feeding his enemies to the Tra-la-logs. When his babysitter treats him with kindness, he falls in love with her, but she winds up in the pit anyway. His monsters will not let him have this perverse slice of happiness any more than Norman Bates' mother would let him have Marion Crane.

But if we're gonna look at in a more Jungian way, maybe this final destination of Jamie's—this idyllic country house where his grandparents live—is symbolic of his real death. Maybe when the townsfolk discovered Jamie's secret and killed his monsters, they actually killed him, too. Maybe *all* children have access to these pits. Some of us learn to "feed the monsters" in a safe way, some of us let them out, and some of us either suppress them or have them suppressed by real life. As a loner kid who didn't get along with my peers, talked to imaginary friends, and had a thing for one or two babysitters, perhaps I identify with Jamie a little too much. If you're reading this book, chances are you do too. But it's okay; we're all friends here. I won't tell the grownups your secret.

Chapter Four: Art With Guts

Give the people what they want. This is the ingrained motto of commercial art, which, in the world of American cinema, is composed of summer blockbuster fluff and exploitation. These two genres are distant cousins; there's certainly a formal resemblance, but the former is a well-dressed, wealthy tart that is welcomed to the family gathering with open arms because of her good looks and far-reaching influence. The latter is a black sheep, very grudgingly accepted into the party because she is family, but seated far in the back—you have to make a conscious effort to find her.

She is also the more interesting to talk to of the two, for she'll occasionally ask you about yourself in conversation. Little Miss Blockbuster only talks about what she's currently wearing, whom she's currently dating, and what she thinks about everything—including you. But Exploitation, she'll split a fifth of Jack with you, tell you how to get free dinner at the local steakhouse by sticking your finger down your throat and faking food poisoning, and ask if you want to skip the party altogether and go out shooting at nutria or something.

And if you look deep enough into Exploitation's eyes, you'll find that she resembles Great Grandma High Art much more than her bitchy cousin. There's something about creative filmmakers working not only in horror—the second lowest genre on the cinematic totem pole (only one step above porn)—but in *low-budget horror* that frees up their imaginations, that whispers in their ears, "Go ahead, do whatever you want. Nobody will pay attention otherwise."

And why is it that the low-budget horror films seem to work better than most Hollywood horror films? For one, there's the obvious: Their visions are not only usually wilder by nature than those of mainstream cinema, but said visions aren't tampered with as much by (gag) test audiences. I mean good fucking lord, the idea that a group of Santa Barbara mall-walkers are sufficiently representative of the film-going United States is scarier than anything I saw at the movies or on video last year.

Now, back in 1978, when the original *Dawn of the Dead* was pending theatrical release, producer Richard Rubenstein felt that it would make more money unrated then it would going through the MPAA and having all sorts of cuts demanded in order to receive an R. And of course, it turned out he was absolutely right.

Not only did the producers of *Evil Dead* feel the same way, they used their budgetary limitations to their advantage. Location shooting in a run-down cabin, on 16mm equipment, gave the film a stark immediacy and subjectivity. The look of a film is invaluable in creating mood, and mood is a very important factor in enhancing the subjective experience of film going. The graininess of 16mm film stock makes the viewer feel as though they've walked into the *Texas Chain Saw* farmhouse. We feel kinda dirty, kinda uncomfortable. We just don't feel safe the way we do in Lucasland. If there's anything that's holding modern low-budget horror back, it's that the video equipment used by the new breed of indie filmmakers lacks the richness of film emulsion. The look of video is simply too plastic and shiny to really make viewers feel uncomfortable.

Aside from their visual texture, the old-school indie classics are also filled through and through with shocking originality of vision: *Texas Chain Saw Massacre*, with its

"H.R. Giger meets Ed Gein" set design, *Evil Dead*, with its surreal, almost cartoon-like manipulation of camera and foley effects, and *Night of the Living Dead*, with its stark black-and-white photography, spectacular editing and composition, and emphasis on character interaction amidst all the "exploitive" gut-munching.

Jamie Lee Curtis once remarked on the irony in the exploitation films she made—she was the least exploited actress. Likewise the lowly horror film can often slip subversive and intelligent ideas into its packaging, because that's where intelligence is least expected.

PHENOMENA (1984)
Dir. Dario Argento

Dario Argento's work has been analyzed, perhaps as well as it can possibly be, by Maitland McDonagh in her book *Broken Mirrors/Broken Minds*. It's an amazingly in-depth work and amazingly enlightening. It's such a definitive text, actually, that it's quite difficult to write about Argento in the post-McDonagh world and not come off sounding like her. I am aware of this, and give Maitland kudos and apologies before I proceed.

It's easy to understand why a viewer would give up on a movie like Argento's *Phenomena*. It starts off weird enough and only builds in strangeness up until the straight-out psychotic climax. It's a lot to swallow, a lot of disbelief to suspend. Perhaps, like *Santa Sangre*, it requires you to be in a very receptive mood to allow its current to pull you along, muttering, "What? WHAT?!" with each new reveal in the story, each escalating step into absurdity. You'll either utter the "whats" in frustration or exhilaration, but like *Santa Sangre*, if we can just relax and let the story take us where it's going, you'll find some pretty great stuff lurking within.

I'm really surprised that a writer like McDonagh, one of the few in this world who would bother to dive into Argento's work with such intelligence and passion, would so easily dismiss *Phenomena* in almost the same tone that many critics dismiss Argento's entire body of work. *Phenomena* is, in my opinion, a beyond worthwhile film. Argento claims it to be his favorite of his own movies and, God help me, so do I.

In the setting of *Phenomena*'s eerie Swiss boarding school, we have a very strange cast of characters indeed: there's Jennifer, the pretty young misfit who can communicate telepathically with insects; Dr. John MacGregor, a forensic entomologist confined to a wheelchair; his "nurse"—the chimpanzee Inga, who "never forgets" an object (or person) once MacGregor points at it with his laser; and the strange Miss Bruckner, who works at the school. Lastly, there also happens to be a mutant killer of young girls, whom we soon discover is Miss Bruckner's son: a byproduct of a sexual assault by a lunatic. And those are just the *primary* characters.

Argento sets up a neat little circle of symbolic doubling in *Phenomena*. MacGregor is a sort of twin to Miss Bruckner, for starters. Both have had monstrously traumatic experiences in their lives, and both bear the burden of these experiences on their bodies. MacGregor is wheelchair-bound as a result of an auto accident, and Bruckner bears a scar (and of course the child) as a reminder of her rape. But it seems as though the mutant child's killer instinct is more a product of his mother's conditioning than his unfortunate genetics. Unlike MacGregor, who has lost none of his empathy after losing the use of his legs, Miss Bruckner's rage and bitterness seem to have manifested itself in her son.

And then there's Jennifer the telepath and Inga the chimp. Both are on the evolutionary forefront of their species—Jennifer with her telepathy and Inga with her capacity for compassion and bloodlust (not to mention wielding tools).

Jennifer, MacGregor, and Inga are also linked together by their ostracism. Jennifer and Inga have been separated from their natural habitats and relocated among creatures that are practically (in Jennifer's case) and literally (in Inga's) not even in the same species, and MacGregor has been ostracized by his fellow scientists for his strange (yet true) theories on insects and telepathy. MacGregor is friend and mentor to Jennifer, but out of shame, Miss Bruckner keeps her poor child apart from even his fellow misfits. She might love her son enough to kill for him, but apparently not enough to treat him with compassion. She confines him in the house, covering all the mirrors, never letting him forget that he is a monster in her eyes. He is denied the chance to become a mere misfit.

The most consistent theme in *Phenomena* is that evil is the result of fear of evolution. Evolution is symbolized in the movie by the ability to communicate across species: Jennifer can communicate with insects; MacGregor can communicate with Inga; and both Jennifer and MacGregor are better-adjusted human beings for their open-mindedness. Everybody at Jennifer's school is closed-minded and vicious, believing insects and animals—and by extension Jennifer and MacGregor—to be lowly and contemptible creatures. They have sealed themselves in an evolutionary box with their fear of the unknown.

Phenomena's outcasts—Jennifer, MacGregor, Inga and the Bruckner boy—either evolve or devolve, in relation to the level of fear and loathing in their lives. And at the end of the day, the two surviving misfits— evolutionary doppelgangers Jennifer and Inga—turn to each other with their compassion and sorrow after everything they have done and experienced in this most bizarre adventure. Both have lost people close to them, and both have killed. Both have been through a remarkable ordeal, and it is their ability to adapt and absorb, as well as their empathy for each other, that will help them to move beyond it all—to *evolve*.

I suppose it's my love for *Santa Sangre* that endears me to *Phenomena*. Both films go places you've never been before, both pile on the gore and the visual excess with maniacal abandon, and underneath it all, both have something cool to say about the human condition. Both the films also have at least one Argento family member lurking behind the scenes and soundtrack contributions by Simon Boswell. Weird, huh? I personally think it's the Iron Maiden songs that throw people off in *Phenomena*. Argento's use of cheesy heavy metal in his movies is always their most unintentionally discordant element, it seems. It threatened to completely destroy *Opera*, and it threatens *Phenomena* even more. You have to find a way to either accept it or ignore it in order to enjoy the film, but it's worth the effort.

TENEBRE (1982)
Dir: Dario Argento

Tenebre is fascinating and exhilarating for a number of reasons: the narrative cohesion normally lacking in Argento's films; the sheer volume of visual motifs that echo, or are echoed by, his other films (there are more links to *Tenebre* than any other Argento flick); and the idea that art can indeed kill.

Tenebre is one of the few Argento films (maybe his only film) in which even most of the surreal subconscious stuff can be interpreted logically. Indeed, this might have been the point all along, as *Tenebre* is flooded with harsh white light in every frame. Unlike the rest of Argento's oeuvre, *Tenebre* wants to be scrutinized—the light begs us to take a good look. So, let's.

There are loads of visual references to past Argento films in *Tenebre*, as well as references to it in his future films. You'll find my list of these references at the end of this essay, and I don't have the arrogance to assume that I caught close to all of them. The one peculiar thing I noticed is that I couldn't find a visual link between *Tenebre* and *Phenomena*. I don't know why this is, especially because in my opinion, the two Argento films that could be considered polar opposites are *Tenebre* and *Suspiria*. As *Suspiria* was a very feminine film, dealing with witches and comprising a mostly female cast, *Tenebre* is a film about twisted male sexuality manifesting as murderous impulse. Thus, as *Suspiria*'s cinematic composition and set design is filled with rich colors and curving lines, *Tenebre* is composed almost entirely of straight lines and corners, and the colors are largely bleached out (the standout colors being white and red).

The two killers in the film are men (which is quite unusual in Argento's world): Christiano Berti and Peter Neal. Berti, the film's initial killer, dispatches women with a straight razor and claims inspiration from Neal's writings. During the course of the investigation of Berti's murders, both Neal and police detective Giermani quote *Occam's Razor:* "When you have eliminated the impossible, whatever remains, however improbable, must be the truth." And of course, "Berti's razor" eventually draws out the "truth" that Neal, like Berti, is homicidal. Ironically, at the film's climax, a razor helps to fool Giermani into thinking Neal has committed suicide—it helps Neal lie (twice, if you consider that the razor was in fact Berti's weapon of choice, not Neal's).

Neal's first "act of annihilation" in the movie is to kill Berti (immediately after the axe replaces the razor, Neal replaces Berti). Once he has done this, his hidden self comes to light; the self that apparently killed a girl in red shoes when he was a young boy. And it is only now, after his shadow self has been set free, that Neal can finally sleep with his secretary Anne, with whom he has likely been in love for some time.

The flashbacks about the red shoe girl can easily be interpreted as memory of Neal's childhood and become the seed of his madness. In his dreams, she teases him sexually; he responds violently, slapping her. Sexual ambiguity is writhing under *Tenebre*'s surface, and of course any Argento fanboy worth his salt knows a transsexual (Eva Robbins) plays the girl. So is it possible that she is Neal's Anima in the flesh—a symbol of femininity that terrifies him (note that she's doing her striptease in front of the ocean—the ultimate threatening feminine symbol) because of his inability to accept femininity within himself?

In Neal's dreams of the past, the girl *steals* his masculinity by forcing the heel of her shoe into his mouth. And in the present, Neal's agent Bullmer (John Saxon) steals his masculinity by having an affair with his ex-wife Jane. Hence, Neal anonymously gives Jane a pair of red shoes as a gift (recreating the scene of the original crime, as so many of Argento's killers do) and kills Bullmer in exactly the same way he way he killed the red shoe girl—by stabbing him in the stomach. And it goes without saying that the way he kills Jane later on—chopping off her "gun hand"—is an attempt to rob her of *her* masculinity.

Most of the characters in *Tenebre* have a secret side that is exposed in the "light" of the film, with the exception of Anne and detectives Giermani and Altieri. Of these three, only Anne survives. The light in this film is a sort of merciless crucible, exposing dirty secrets left and right; however, Anne is saved not by her purity, but by blind luck at the film's denouement.

Early on in the film, Christiano Berti confesses to Neal that he is interested in the author's life as well as his writing, and later, detective Giermani also admits to being a rabid fan of Neal's work. Thus, these two characters appear almost to be outward manifestations of the two selves within Neal: the detective and the killer. Both of these facets of himself he indulges equally (and harmlessly) by writing murder mysteries.

But the murderous circumstances tempt him to become both detective and killer in the real world. Peter the writer vanishes; Peter the detective investigates openly with Giermani by day; and Peter the killer stalks around in secret (mostly at night, save for when he kills Bullmer, in broad daylight and full public view).

These "normal" (meaning narratively satisfying) elements help to make *Tenebre* Argento's most "abnormal" (meaning atypical) film. But there are still a couple of set pieces that keep *Tenebre* rooted in Argento's rubber reality. For instance, there are the two oddly similar scenes where a girl (the shoplifter at the film's beginning and later the landlord's daughter) is menaced by a seemingly random element (the crazy street person, and later the dog); in each scene the respective girl teases the menace to the point where it escapes and chases her straight into the killer's arms (is this perhaps an echo of the "red shoe woman" teasing Peter Neal as a boy, only to invite his rage at full force?).

And of course, there's the *almost random* element of the lethal sculpture, which wraps things up quite neatly by impaling Peter in the last scene. I say "almost random" because several times in the film we are treated to images of menacing metal sculptures, light glinting evilly off their edges. All seemingly benevolent things, from the act of flirting to works of art, are loaded to the brim with violent potential just waiting to be "brought to light" here.

Thematic Links in Argento's Films: An Incomplete List

Argento's Mother of Tears *seems to contain references to every film he made before it, so we'll only look into the films he made previous to it:*

Airport opening scene: *Tenebre/Suspiria*
Dog attack: *Tenebre/Suspiria*
Lethal sculpture: *Tenebre/Bird with the Crystal Plumage/Suspiria*
Staged suicide of killer: *Tenebre/Opera*

American stranded in Rome: *Tenebre/Bird with the Crystal Plumage*
Killer's flashbacks: *Tenebre/Opera/Deep Red/Four Flies on Grey Velvet*
Tracking shot of feet walking: *Tenebre/Sleepless/Cat o' Nine Tails*
Killer's photographing of victims: *Tenebre/Bird/Cat*
Taunting phone calls from killer: *Tenebre/Bird/Cat*
Close-up of killer's iris: *Tenebre/Deep Red/Cat*
Insect telepathy: *Deep Red/Phenomena*
Child-sized doll: *Deep Red/Phenomena*
Creepy boarding school: *Suspiria/Phenomena*
Weird fairytale-style opening narration: *Suspiria/Phenomena*
Maggots: *Suspiria/Phenomena*
Vengeful animals: *Phenomena/Opera*
Opera house with curtained hallways: *Opera/Deep Red/Four Flies*
Elevator decapitation: *Deep Red/Trauma*
Psychic sensing killer's presence: *Deep Red/Trauma*
Trapped lizard: *Deep Red/Trauma/Opera*
Evil mother: *Deep Red/Trauma/Opera/Suspiria/Inferno/Phenomena*
Killer driven by painting: *Bird/Stendahl Syndrome*
Gratuitous Iron Maiden music: *Opera/Phenomena*
Death by train: *The Card Player/Cat*

Argento and Feminism

Of all the horror filmmakers in the world, Argento is certainly one of the most flamboyant when it comes to stylized, sensualized murder sequences. Many of these sequences feature female victims. Yes, we've covered all this territory earlier, but I believe Argento is a case worth studying apart from all other slasher directors.

The cry of misogyny is perhaps less true of Argento than almost any other horror filmmaker out there. The proof of this is most clearly presented in *Deep Red*. And it's not merely because the female lead beats the male lead at arm wrestling (twice). For most of *Deep Red*'s length, everyone assumes the killer to be a man—even the eyewitness, as well as the psychic (who is gifted enough to sense the names of complete strangers). And because of the brutality of the murders, we the viewer also assume that they are most likely being committed by a man. In the end, Gianni and Marta (female investigator and female killer) prove to be smarter, stronger, more sadistic and more masculine than any man in the film. Marta shows us that a woman can indeed kill like a man.

In fact, in a vast majority of Argento's filmography, women have wielded the blades. So...does this mean that Argento's lady-killers, with their phallic devices, are suffering from penis envy? I don't think so. No more than a lesbian (or a hetero woman with an open-minded boyfriend) wielding a strap-on is, anyway. A knife, much like a strap-on, is simply a practical tool for the job at hand.

In *Deep Red*, a female killer wields the blade.

In fact, Argento will occasionally bend logic for his ladies, eschewing practicality in favor of symbolism. Case in point: *Trauma*'s portable motorized guillotine, perhaps as close to *vagina dentata* as a murder weapon can be. Doubly fitting, as *Trauma*'s killer seeks revenge for the accidental killing of her just-born infant son with a phallic scalpel. The offense, in this case, was practically committed against and witnessed by the vagina itself.

And of course, Argento's ladies meet comeuppances every bit as glorious and gruesome as any male killer you've ever seen. They are decapitated by elevators, slashed to ribbons by razor-wielding monkeys, and skewered with Art Deco peacock feathers. And it is here that Argento demonstrates belief in the feminist concept of "equal pay for equal work."

SANTA SANGRE (1990)
Dir. Alexandro Jodorowsky

Santa Sangre split the critics down the middle, half of them calling it brilliant, half of them calling it lurid, pretentious garbage. This is a reaction director Alexandro Jodorowsky (*El Topo, Holy Mountain*) is used to and enjoys.

In my humble opinion, *Santa Sangre* is far less pretentious then, say, Fellini's *La Dolce Vida*. Sorry, but Fellini's stuff, while often visually neat, is just too self-consciously highbrow for my taste. Jodorowsky's mission as a filmmaker seems to be to take the art film and bring it down into the gutter, investing in it a human quality decidedly lacking in the works of the art house elite. And with *Santa Sangre*, Jodorowsky takes the horror film and elevates it to high art.

Fenix (played in childhood and adolescence by Jodorowsky's real life sons Axel and Adan) grows up in a Mexico City circus with Concha, his trapeze-artist mother, and Orgo, his knife-throwing father. Concha is also the leader of a bizarre, heretical religious cult that worships an armless martyr: a young girl named Lilio, victim of a brutal rape and murder. Subsequent viewings of *Santa Sangre* have led me to believe

that Lilio was Concha's daughter. The cult builds their temple on the spot where the young girl was killed, and after the Monsignor condemns the temple, the place is razed to the ground, with Concha almost going with it. She clings to a statue of her *Santa* as the bulldozers approach. At the last minute, Fenix beckons her away from her impending martyrdom.

A tattooed woman comes into town, looking for a place in the circus act. In tow is a deaf-mute girl named Alma, whom the tattooed woman is half-heartedly looking after. Young Fenix and Alma bond almost instantly, and the tattooed woman makes a beeline for Orgo. Concha intervenes, locking Fenix in a circus trailer (probably so he can't again interfere with her quest for the martyrdom she craves). When Concha catches the two of them in bed together, she mutilates Orgo's genitals with acid. In retaliation, Orgo slices off Concha's arms, and, apparently unable to go on living without a cock, slashes his own throat. The expression on Concha's face after she is "disarmed" is beatific, as is Simon Boswell's music, emphasizing the ecstasy she has found in meeting the same fate as her beloved daughter/saint.

Fenix, a helpless witness to the whole ordeal, is committed to an asylum, where he grows to manhood. On a field trip one night, he spies the tattooed woman, which brings all the old memories flooding back. He escapes the asylum the next day and joins up with his armless mother. He gives her his arms to use as her own in a mime act; she subsequently uses them to extract revenge on the tattooed woman. Before long, she is using "her" arms to kill women to whom Fenix is attracted. One of these women is a decidedly masculine female wrestler named "Saint." Fenix seems attracted to "her" mainly because she looks strong enough to break his arms when he attacks.

Fenix' only hope for salvation lies in the now-grown Alma, who discovers what he is up to and tracks him down. She offers herself as a martyr to Concha's wrath, and Fenix' love for Alma enables him to regain control of his arms and "kill" his mother. And then the bottom falls out. Fenix is hit full-force with reality: He has been unable to let go of his mother's memory, and he must say goodbye to all his hallucinations and take responsibility for what he has done.

One of the great things about *Santa Sangre* is that it doesn't totally clear up upon repeated viewings. We watch for the second time knowing that Fenix lives in a largely hallucinatory world, but discrepancies keep popping up that blur the line between hallucination and reality:

Santa Sangre **makes us question everything we are seeing.**

Alma, who acts as Fenix' voice (no pun intended) of reason, bumps into a man on the street during a Dia De Los Muertos parade, who slowly peels off his ear and subsequently tries to force it into her mouth. Cryptic-as-hell symbolism aside, Fenix' warped perspective has nothing to do with this scene, so what the hell does it mean? Did it really happen? Does Alma, having seen the same horrors Fenix did as a child, suffer from hallucinations as well?

There's also Trini and her mobile Apothecary, where Fenix buys the elements he needs for his alchemical experiments. Trini and her drugstore-on-wheels seem extremely out of place, even in this film's world, and Trini's attraction to Fenix seems completely unmotivated and absurd. Yet both she and her attraction are apparently real enough at the film's climax; she shows up for a date that she set with Fenix (after watching him wrestle with an imaginary giant snake, no less), and it is she who calls the police on him during his final battle with the ghost of his mother.

During the film's final revelation, Fenix flashes back to "reality," seeing himself playing an imaginary piano, singing along with the life-sized puppet that he's been substituting for his mother. But we see *both* his hands playing piano as the puppet's jaw moves up and down; what is maneuvering the jaw?

And finally, Fenix' dwarf friend Aladdin, who is apparently a hallucination as well, is at one point seen shining the shoes of the soldier who tried to molest Alma.

The line between reality and vision is blurred to the point of erasure in *Santa Sangre*, so we begin, upon the third time viewing, to question *everything* we are seeing, which gives the movie a metaphysical bent. Can there *be* such a thing as a hallucination in this world? Is everything a mad dream in Fenix' head? Is there real paranormal activity going on? If this reality seems real enough to create the drama experienced by the characters, isn't that good enough? Do we as an audience suspend disbelief and immerse ourselves deeply enough into *Sangre*'s reality to care what happens? Well, as mentioned before, some viewers do and some don't. People seem to either love *Sangre* or hate it. For those who love it, alchemy happens with our suspension of disbelief.

In *Santa Sangre*, Jodorowsky collaborates with producer Claudio Argento, brother of director Dario. Claudio gives the film the bright, garish colors and splashy violence usually associated with Dario's work. Claudio also seems to have influenced the overall mood of *Santa Sangre*, convincing Jodorowsky to slow down in telling the story and not flood every frame of film with kaleidoscopic imagery. The film is most certainly Jodorowsky's, but the film's pace is deliberate and hypnotic and we never feel as though we're watching a new movie every 10 minutes, as we do in *El Topo* or *Holy Mountain*. This influence is most undoubtedly Argento's.

The collaboration, in the author's opinion, is wildly successful. *Santa Sangre* never feels like an art movie the way *Topo* and *Mountain* do, but rather it feels like a human story with horror underpinning (underpinnings of *Psycho* and *Peeping Tom* to be exact), and a myriad of artsy flourishes. There are still loads of eye-popping set pieces, possibly the best Jodorowsky has ever dreamed up: from the funeral and burial of the circus elephant; to the beautiful and brutal slicing-off of Concha's arms and Orgo's subsequent suicide; to the hilariously absurd, fever-dreamlike sequence where Fenix kills the Saint, the "lady" wrestler.

Through Jodorowsky's masterful direction of his sons, Fenix becomes an utterly human character, and we never lose empathy for him, even though he becomes a serial killer. This is the crux of the story: that while Fenix is committing monstrous acts, he is not a monster. He is a scared little boy in the body of a grown man, who cannot free himself from the grip of his childhood horrors and thus cannot take control of his own hands.

Jodorowsky's chance meeting with a serial killer in Mexico City allegedly inspired the story. In conversation with him, Jodorowsky learned that the killer had been apprehended, treated, and become a new man—a lawyer, in fact. "I realized then," Jodorowsky is quoted as saying, "that rehabilitation is possible."

And there it is—the axis around which the story evolves, as well as the very reason that we seek out shadow play in the form of horror films: to confront, understand, accept and heal the dark half of the human heart. It's the polar opposite of the themes Texas-based author Joe R. Lansdale has explored in his work. Lansdale posits the idea of a new breed of man—one that lives solely to inflict horror, pain, and death upon the innocent, a human cancer that must be cut out. This is surely a frightening concept—that of an inhuman human—but is it more, or less, scary than the idea that the people who commit these crimes are indeed 100% human? Under different circumstances, we might be no different from them.

Jodorowsky's take on the serial killer is indeed a frightening one for our culture to consider. We practically own the copyright on serial killers; they're as American as apple pie. To take Jodorowsky's viewpoint would be to look straight into the heart of American horror, recognize it as a part of us, and take responsibility for it. *Santa Sangre* is poetic, but it's also tacky, brutal, garish, and funny. In other words, it is human. One of the most human films I've ever seen, actually. Jodorowsky lovingly shows us the humanity in Fenix' violence, the poetry in his humanity, and by extension, the poetry in *all* humanity.

DELLAMORTE DELLAMORE (CEMETERY MAN) (1993)
Dir. Michele Soavi

I've tried to write this analysis three times now, and each time I seem to derail before I finish page one. This is, I think, because as much as I love this movie, I'm still not entirely sure what it means to me. There are 1,001 perspectives from which to approach it, but I suppose if I want to get to the heart of my own perspective, I should just start rambling and, when I've finished, stop. Sounds like as good a game plan as any. Okay, then: onward.

We open up in Buffalura Cemetery and are introduced to its caretakers Francesco and Gnaghi (Gnaghi is a little on the simple side—the only thing he seems capable of saying is "Nyah"). Francesco is talking on the phone to his only friend outside the walls of the cemetery ("I stop by his office sometimes, to remind myself what he looks like"), and, midway through the conversation, he encounters a shambling zombie, whom he dispatches with a revolver, as casually as you or I would swat a fly. It seems this sort of thing happens all the time in Buffalura Cemetery; the dead return to life seven days after their burial, like clockwork. And Francesco, who can't be bothered to report this weirdness and risk losing a job so cushy, just re-kills the "returners," as he calls them, and re-buries them with Gnaghi's help.

Francesco was born to a woman named Dellamore ("of love") and a man named Dellamorte ("of death"). And in his development as a zygote, all the male traits won out. He inherited the male name (which usually eclipses [kills?] the female name in marriage), as well as the male chromosomes. He also seems to adopt the very persona of the surname itself, living in a cemetery—a shrine to death—distancing himself from the townspeople, and killing the dead when they try to return to the world of the living. He has little interest in the "rest of the world," which, as far as he knows or cares, "doesn't exist."

In my perception of the film, it's precisely Francesco's apathy that brings the dead back to life in the first place. Since he has ensconced himself in this self-contained universe, conveniently free of the living (Francesco and Gnaghi pretty much live in a limbo-world between life and death), death loses all its meaning to him. And therefore, in his

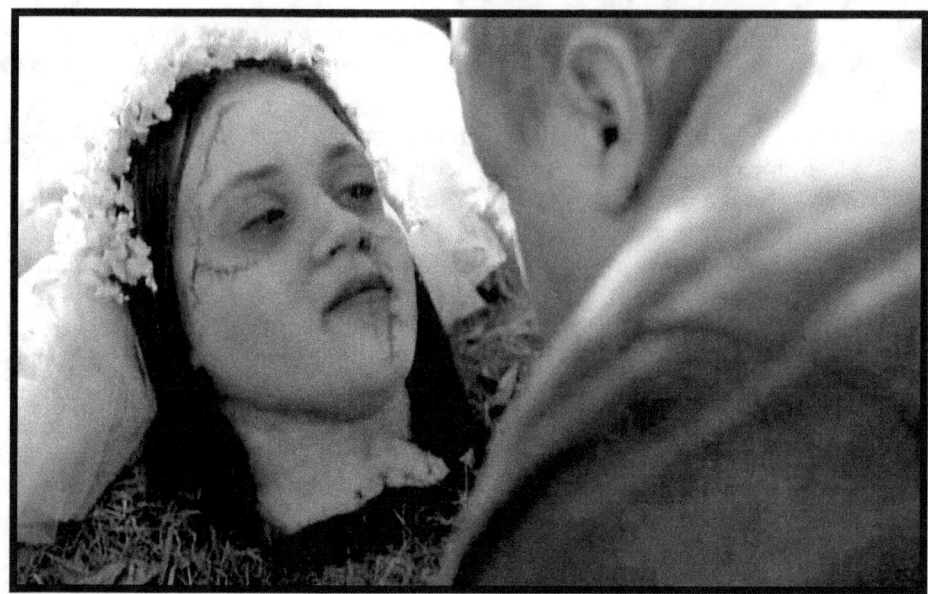

Gnaghi (Francois Hadji-Lazaro) falls in love with the severed head of the mayor's daughter.

world, death begins to lose its power on the dead themselves. He seems happy enough chatting with Gnaghi, killing zombies, and spouting dry Goth poetry (his voiceover narration makes the whole movie play like a Calvin Klein Obsession ad with splatter). And life, such as it is, goes on.

Until...

One day a gorgeous and busty widow comes into Buffalura to bury her husband. Francesco is smitten with the woman (known in the credits as "She") at first sight and makes an ass of himself trying to seduce her. In this one act—this push into the drama of the world of the living—Francesco allows the chaos of life to descend on the order of death that was his universe. For starters, the dead begin returning at more sporadic times, rather than the usual seven days, and unfortunately, the first of these is the woman's late husband, upon whose grave She and Francesco make love for the first time. The old bugger crawls out of his grave and chomps the woman to death, and thus Francesco is exposed to his first taste of life—the death of a loved one.

He takes it all relatively stoically; spouting his morbid one-liners while he waits for her to return so he can kill her again.

From here on out, things get weird.

It seems that even after her second killing, She isn't through with our hero. She returns to him three more times—as a zombie (he rationalizes that She wasn't really dead when he killed her the second time) and then in the forms of apparently different women. She returns yet again as the assistant of Buffalura's mayor (She breaks Francesco's heart in a *bad* way this time around) and then finally as a college student who forgets to tell him that She is a prostitute and that her telling him She loved him will cost him extra.

Gnaghi falls in love as well—with the severed head of the mayor's daughter. A busload of dead Boy Scouts return from the grave. A teenage girl pines over her dead biker boyfriend, and when he returns, she allows him to eat her. Poor Francesco tries to remain detached about it all and continues to make dry observations about how the living handle death. But finally, the Specter of Death Himself visits Francesco, challenging him to kill the living (daring him to venture out into the world and "get a life" as it were).

So, as Francesco is emotionally pulled out of the cemetery (his inner circle, his private fortress) into the town (the outer circle, the land of the living), he is overwhelmed by it all and decides to flee Buffalura, with Gnaghi in tow, escaping to the "rest of the world" (the third circle, the world no one really knows about, the death/rebirth afterlife). Francesco clambers into his car with Gnaghi and speeds off, past the town's city limits. The car dips into a long tunnel, and Francesco steps on the gas as they hurtle toward the light at the end. And then things come to a grinding halt.

Francesco slams on his brakes as he realizes that the road *ends* with the tunnel. His suspicions are confirmed: the rest of the world doesn't exist. Not only this, but Gnaghi appears to have suffered a fatal head wound in the sudden stop. As Gnaghi lies dying, Francesco realizes that his friendship with this weird little halfwit was his deepest connection to another living being. The strange lesson of love and death is now complete. And then, some unseen, mad clockworks begin to grind, and Gnaghi rises to his feet. He asks Francesco, "Could you take me home, please?"

To which Francesco replies, "Nyah."

The camera zooms out of a snow-globe as the credits roll, and the impression we are left with is that there is no afterlife to speak of; only a world of endless reincarnation. Francesco and Gnaghi are the only two real people in this world, destined to learn (and subsequently forget) the lesson of love and loss *ad infinitum.*

I was lucky enough to catch *Dellamorte* on its U.S. art-house run as *Cemetery Man*. A decrepit theatre in Fresno (!!!) was showing a different art-house movie every week, and somehow, miraculously, this one wound up on the bill. On the night I caught it, there were only two other people in the audience, and they both walked out halfway through. Apparently they wanted a *real* art movie. Something with Gerard Depardieu, maybe. I sat back, put my feet up on the chair in front of me, and enjoyed a bit of smugness in being possibly the only person in Fresno who got it. It's funny; this is precisely the kind of movie that exploitation fans find too dry and art-snobs find too wet.

But if only the Fellini-snobs would pay a bit more attention, they'd find a lot going on in every level of *Dellamorte*. It's perhaps the most extreme example of Art With Guts; if you don't have a taste for the lowbrow, no amount of film schooling is going to help you enjoy it. And at the same time, it's so blatant in its artsy-fartsyness that your average gorehound might balk at it much in the same way I balk at Fellini films. But if you're lucky enough to have taste that resides somewhere in between lobster bisque and Spaghetti-O's, you'll find that this flick delivers glorious goods. There are levels of symbolism that I haven't even yet begun to decipher; levels that have been perceived and analyzed by other horror geeks in magazines like *European Trash Cinema*. Stuff that's more purely cerebral.

But it's at that level in between cerebral and visceral that *Dellamorte* works for me. I see it as alternately witty and sophomoric, but it's never less than a pure cinematic experience. It gave me the thrill of not knowing what was going to happen next, kept me horribly interested in what was happening at the time, and gave me something to think about as I left the theatre. All that and a shitload of sex and gore, too. There really is nothing much else to ask for from the cinematic gods.

BUBBA HO–TEP (2003)
Dir. Don Coscarelli

A recurring theme in this book is the stoner/metaphysical conceit that the only reality is what we experience to be real. We applied it to the concept of suspending disbelief to accept the reality of movies, and thus to be moved by them. We applied it to dreaming world, real enough until we wake up and shrug it off. We applied it to paranoid schizophrenia, and the delusions that haunt many of the protagonists and antagonists discussed in these films.

A film that seems to relate too well to paranoid delusion is the remarkably faithful adaptation of Joe R. Lansdale's short story *Bubba Ho-Tep*, in which Bruce Campbell plays a present-day Elvis and Ossie Davis plays a present-day JFK. Both reside in a crappy rest home in East Texas. Elvis, as it turns out, switched places with an impersonator years ago in order to escape the spotlight, and JFK was dyed black and had his brain replaced with sandbags as part of a conspiracy headed by LBJ. Of course, the nurses and caretakers at the rest home patronize the two, believing them to be nutbags, but neither the short story nor the film take this low road. The two leads believe they are Elvis and JFK, and the film decides that this is good enough. The movie does not judge them and does not laugh at them, unless they say something particularly funny.

Also real enough to our two heroes is a strange creature that now roams the halls of their rest home at night. Through the deciphering of some hieroglyphic graffiti on the bathroom wall, JFK deduces that they are dealing with a mummy that is preying on the weak souls of the folk that languish herein—it sucks their souls out their assholes, to be precise.

Ho-Tep is a thousand-year-old mummy—the personification of age itself. Shriveled and shambling, he is everything the residents of the rest home are afraid of within their own bodies. Face to face with this creature (their shadow-self), most of the residents succumb to their deepest fear and allow Ho-Tep to take their souls. Most

of the victims meet their fate passively, having given up the will to live long ago. But our two heroes have a bit more piss and vinegar. Both hold fast to their identities—whether they are their real identities or not—and both still hold true to their old ideals, even if JFK does have to use a little of his presidential power to inspire Elvis to get the hell out of bed, to find the dying embers of his belief—the sheer arrogance that sometimes powers the human soul in its darkest hour.

Crass as the subject matter and dialogue are, *Bubba Ho-Tep* belongs solely in the Art chapter—it could fit nowhere else. It toured the art-house circuit during its theatrical run because the art-house theatres were the only ones that would touch it. *Bubba Ho-Tep* could've been played for mere camp, or for cheap thrills, but director Don Coscarelli plays it absolutely straight, utterly faithful to Lansdale's prose. He tells the story with all the humanity, pathos and yes, raunchy silliness, present in Lansdale's giddy short story. All of these elements can be combined successfully—as Coscarelli proves—if you don't play it too broadly and keep the lead characters sympathetic. The story is already outrageous enough; the filmmakers don't need much more than a sly wink to punctuate it. Coscarelli is not normally known as one with a penchant for sly winks—*Phantasm* and *The BeastMaster* were pretty over-the-top affairs. But he pulls this story off with class and wit, even as he's referencing *Phantasm* in the "giant scarab" scene.

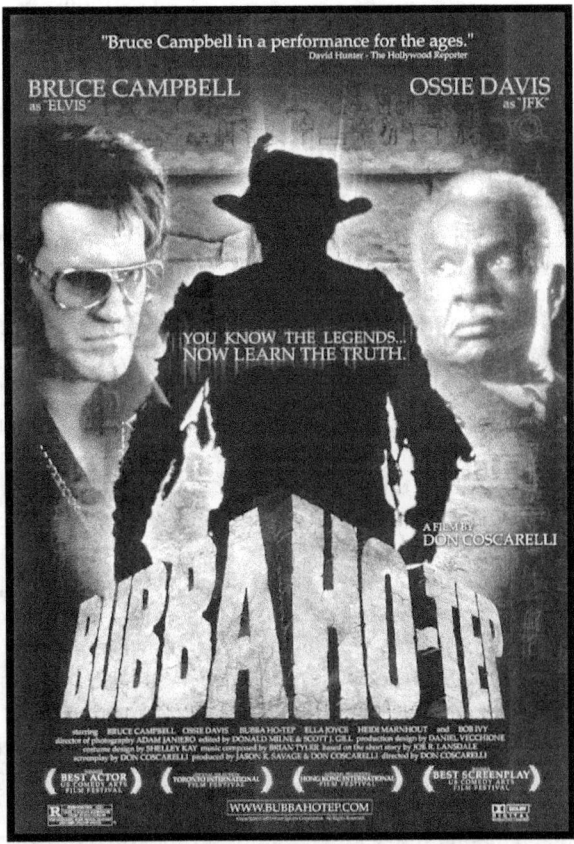

And he also gets the most layered performance of Bruce Campbell's career to date, presumably because Coscarelli allowed him some room to act. As Sam Raimi's whipping boy, Campbell was never at any time allowed to be subtle. Not that we don't love him as Ash, cavorting about in Raimi's Three-Stooges-on-PCP world, but seeing him as Elvis is a real kick in the pants. We just gawk at the screen, muttering to ourselves, "Holy shit, he's playing a goddamn *character* up there!" And Ossie Davis brings proper nobility to his role as JFK, assuming the air of a natural leader when it's necessary to inspire Elvis to take care of business.

Bubba has the distinction of being the first Lansdale story to be adapted for the big screen, as well as the last story any fans of his work would consider at all possible to adapt. One could easily see the cinematic potential in *Mucho Mojo, Cold in July,* or *Incident on and off a Mountain Road*. *Bubba Ho-Tep* is more of a head-scratcher on its own accord, as well as in consideration as a potential movie. The story is so wacked-out that, as a film, it would either succeed gloriously or fail miserably, depending on the director.

Bubba Ho-Tep has a bit in common with *Phenomena* in that it takes several elements that should not gel in theory, but its makers make them work via sheer belief in the material. And this is what secures its place as art. *Bubba Ho-Tep* is a film unlike any you have seen before, period. In this day and age, that is such a rare thing it makes me weep when I am exposed to it. *Bubba Ho-Tep* is a celebration of the stubbornness and consternation of the Old Geezer. If it had a moral, then indeed it would be: Do not go gentle into that good night.

MAY (2003)
Dir. Lucky McKee

May is the teen-slasher film's answer to Roman Polanski's *Repulsion*. It follows the mental deterioration of a young woman, symbolized not by a rotting rabbit, but by the ever-cracking glass case that houses May's doll (and best friend) Suzie.

As a small girl, May was saddled with lazy eye. Mom encouraged May to "cover it up"—to present herself as perfect, in order to gain acceptance from her peers. Mom's advice goes unheeded, and May pays the price by being shunned. As a consolation, Mom presents May with the first doll she ever made: Suzie. Suzie is porcelain and pristine (reminding me a bit of the masked girl in *Les Yeux Sans Visage*), locked away in a glass case. Mom gives Suzie to May, telling her, "If you can't find any friends, make your own." Suzie was apparently a friend of Mom's for an unhealthily long time, and according to Mom, Suzie must never be taken out of the case—she's too fragile.

This cements mom's earlier advice of "covering it up" deeply in May's mind. But, as we discover throughout the film, May is a very heart-on-the-sleeve type of girl. She sees what she wants, and she goes for it. First, she goes for the weird filmmaker Adam, whom she has a crush on (she has a particular attraction to his hands). Adam invites her to his house, shows her his shrine to Dario Argento, and stabs her in the belly with a retractable knife. "Does this stuff freak you out?" he asks her, and of course it doesn't. Neither does his short film about two young lovers at a picnic who wind up feasting on each other. But when she bites his lip as they are about to make love, Adam draws the line: May is too weird for him.

May is then seduced by her freaky coworker Polly, who actually lets May cut her with a scalpel and finds it kinda hot. Polly gives May her cat—*her* best friend as it were—to take care of, signifying that she trusts May enough to share everything with her. The one thing Polly cannot do for May, however, is commit to her. And though she shares this kink with May (she lets it slip that she is seeing the leggy Ambrosia on the side), May cannot handle it. Her jealousy turns to rage, and the first victim of her rage is Polly's cat.

May's physical imperfection (her eye) mirrors her inner imperfection (her fear of being seen a freak). She fears being perceived wrongly by others, and yet her own physical sense of perception is warped (clearly a case of Jungian projection if ever there was one). Whenever she is rejected, she takes her rage out on her eyes, scratching them to the point of making them bleed. And each attempt to reach out (and each subsequent rejection) also causes great stress on Suzie's doll case. Slowly, it begins to splinter and crack. May only sees herself as freaky because others do, and the first person to point out May's imperfection was her mother, who is now symbolized by Suzie the doll: Beautiful, untouchable, shielded from the prying hands of the world in a quest to appear perfect.

May is attracted to the freaks Adam and Polly for the same reasons she is attracted to the blind kids she sees in the park—because she believes they might "see" her as normal. But she inadvertently shows her dark side to all of them.

During the day care class she worms herself into, she shows Suzie (her fear in the flesh) to the blind kids. And like every other time she attempts to reach out, it ends disastrously. The kids swarm the glass case, knocking it over, cutting themselves to ribbons and tearing Suzie to pieces.

Though May mourns Suzie's loss, she quickly grows to find that Suzie's spirit is now *free* of the box, free to do more than haunt and taunt May, to possess her. May is now free to create her own best friend out of all the spare parts she likes best: like Adam's hands, Polly's neck, and Ambrosia's "gams." On Halloween night, May dons a homemade costume (care to guess who she dresses as?), collects some amputation equipment and a portable cooler, and sets out "trick-or-treating."

The clashing colors of red and white (rage and innocence) punctuate May's killing spree. Polly is killed on a red-and-white striped couch. Later, Ambrosia, wearing a red-and-white-striped skirt, is skewered in Polly's kitchen. Her blood splashes on the floor with her spilt milk; kind of an Andres Serrano touch. Nice.

Adam, dressed as Julius Caesar, has more of a maroon-and-white color scheme happening, which more matches the dark maroon "Suzie" dress May has on, and perhaps matches the darker tone the film is taking on as it reaches its conclusion. May dispatches Adam in the same way he play-killed her earlier—stabbing him in the stomach. Everything that Adam pretends to do or be, May does, and is.

When May has all of the parts she needs, she hauls them back home (in a red cooler with a white lid) and goes to work. Once she has all the parts stitched together, everything seems perfect. But May quickly notices something is wrong. Her creation (named "Amy") is incomplete. It won't move. And it won't "see" May. This appears to be the big problem for her—she screams for it to see her, and when it doesn't respond, the story comes full circle. She picks up a pair of scissors and cuts out her eye—her imperfection—to add to the creature's amalgam of "perfect" parts. Thus May learns the lesson that was passed on by Polly earlier in the film: "It's your imperfections that make you special." With a flawed part, the creature can now live. And its first act is to touch May's face, giving a first moment of comfort in the last moment of her life.

It's a tragedy that just edges in as a horror film with its slasher climax and little homage to Argento. One of those movies that the makers could claim is "not a horror film," as filmmakers afraid of being pigeonholed are wont to do. *May* is haunting, unique stuff. Not afraid to be a little exploitative or a lot weird, it shines as one of the most unique films to grace the genre in a very long while. Fortunately, director Lucky McKee does not, in fact, seem afraid of being pigeonholed.

MOJU (BLIND BEAST) (1964)
Dir. Yasuzo Masumura

Erotic horror is difficult territory to traverse without tripping, to be sure. And of course the Japanese excel at it. If you've ever seen an SM movie from Nikkatsu Studios, you know what I'm talking about. There's that feeling of, *There's a part of me, lurking in the basement of my brain, that's kinda turned on by this. Should I turn myself in to the police?* Neil Jordan's adaptation of *Interview with the Vampire* achieved a couple of soft-core moments of erotic horror, but American cinema is often too nervous about treading that taboo territory.

Not only does *Blind Beast* succeed wildly at outdoing William Wydler's *The Collector*, but it was made in 1964 and still holds up (and shocks) quite nicely today. Its technical brilliance, deliriously inspired art design, and breakneck perversity are, I think, just now beginning to look modern. I can only imagine what it seemed like in its day. I imagine if it were released in America back then it might have caused riots the way Igor Stravinsky's *Rite of Spring* did when it premiered.

Our male lead is a sculptor named Michio, blind since birth and obsessed with the female form. Friendless all his life, he is fully dependent on his mother, who, from his perspective, helped him to "live as a human being." In actuality, dear mother has probably convinced him that his disability makes him less than human, and that he would not have survived without her constant dotage. He's been sculpting giant female body parts in his warehouse studio, and the walls are covered with larger-than-life eyes, noses, mouths, breasts, arms, and legs. But he's heard rumors from adolescent boys about Aki, a bondage model with a "perfect body," and he's sufficiently intrigued to track down—and desperately fondle—a sculpture of her. Aki herself accidentally witnesses this molestation-by-proxy, and, as she watches him work, begins to hallucinate that she can feel his fingers on her own body. She freaks out and runs away. After copping his feel on her statue, Michio is convinced Aki's got the goods, so he convinces Mother to help him kidnap her.

He poses as a masseur to wedge his way into her life at first. She makes an appointment and he intercepts it. When he knocks on her apartment door, she lolls on her bed and calls out, "It's open, come in." This not only lets us in on Aki's self-destructive nature, but also symbolizes her *nether door*, which has been open to Michio ever since she "felt" his fingers on her body.

***Blind Beast* stars Mako Midori as a kidnapped model.**

Like the leads in *The Collector*, Aki and Michio spend most of the movie battling for dominance. She repeatedly tries to escape; he repeatedly recaptures her. He states that he will not let her go until she agrees to model for him, and eventually she gives in. This relenting on her part, this submission, is obviously trickery to anyone watching the film, but not to Michio. He swallows it whole and is crushed and infuriated when she tries to run. *Love is blind.*

Mom soon takes over, helping to keep Aki under control. Michio tells her, "I couldn't do anything without you, mother." He's obviously dependent on her, but she, too, is dependent enough on him to manipulate him in such a way. They are both holding each other prisoner, and it's this mutual dominance that Michio passes on in this new relationship with Aki, the first woman he has ever been intimately close with. He is her captor, but he is also a slave to his obsession with her. Michio, his mother, and Aki all struggle for control over each other: a bizarre love triangle indeed.

One of Aki's escape attempts results in a fight between Michio and Mom. Aki is playing them against each other now, professing her love for Michio, and feigning outrage when mother calls her bluff. But life for the mother and son has shifted drastically upon Aki's entrance into their world. Michio is growing up very quickly, and in Jungian terms, the *mother* is transforming into the *crone* now that son has discovered the *maiden*. And when Mom is accidentally killed, the shit really hits the fan. Michio now focuses all of his attention on Aki, and she begins her descent into futility and surrender. She relents to model for him; as he gropes her body for reference and slowly completes his sculpture, he also molds her into what he wants her to be—his artistic interpretation of her. The acts of creating and destroying (sculpting Aki's likeness and brainwashing her, respectively) become the same basic thing— transforming one thing into something else. *Manipulation.*

Slowly, Aki begins to go blind in the always-dark studio. And thus she begins to fall in love with Michio. Without sight, she overlooks his faults and grows dependent on him. *Love is blind.*

As Aki and Michio become more obsessed with exploring physical sensations and less concerned with self-preservation, they lose differentiation between pain and pleasure. They lose interest in sex in search of more intense physicality, and soon turn to teeth and claws, then to rope and whips, and finally to knives. Shortly into the knife-play, Aki begs Michio to slice off her arms and legs, which he does. He turns the knife on himself, and as they lay dying, we fade out on Aki's face, and the last things we see in the growing darkness are her blind, staring eyes.

The eyes are indeed the windows to the soul, and Michio falls for Aki and her tricks every time because he cannot look into her eyes. There are moments in the film where Aki is mocking him with her eyes and he is utterly oblivious. It is this lack of sight that takes away Michio's masculinity. For all his domineering attempts to tame Aki, he is helpless in her presence, as well as that of his mother.

On this subject, *Blind Beast* seems to comment on the nature of erotica itself. Men are very visual creatures when it comes to sex, and it is because of this that the porn industry thrives as it does. Women, conversely, are supposed to be the tactile ones. But here, Michio is obsessed with touch and it was Aki in the film's beginning who felt a masochistic tingle by *watching* Michio feel up her statue.

Michio's predicament also dictates that he doesn't have much power when it comes to observing women. Guys with the gift of sight sneak peeks at girls more often than they'd ever admit to any woman. Michio cannot be so sly. He cannot "observe" women without their knowing it. Perhaps it was this inability to obtain any kind of *voyeuristic release* that contributed to his madness as much as his mother's manipulation. Yet another argument for the merits of shadow play's visual catharsis, perhaps?

KAIRO (PULSE) (2001)
Dir. Kiyoshi Kurasawa
SUICIDE CLUB (*SUICIDE CIRCLE*) (2001)
Dir. Sion Sono

A lonely teenage boy, logging onto the Internet, in hopes of connecting with someone.

A lonely girl, obsessed with computers, terrified of connecting with someone.

A library that is virtually empty in the age of the World Wide Web.

A sprit world overflowing with souls—souls that are looking for a home on earth.

A country haunted by the shadows burned into its walls by the atomic bomb.

Polarities reaching out to each other, compelled to do so, even though contact will mean the end of the system they occupy.

The lonely boy stares at a computer program in fascination. The lonely girl informs him:

"If the two dots touch, they die, but if they get too far apart, they're drawn closer together."

"It's a model of our world," she elaborates, "but only the grad student who designed it understands it."

It's within this bit of dialogue that the key to *Kairo* lays. The grad student is likely a metaphor for God, but for all intents and purposes, he's also a metaphor for writer/director Kiyoshi Kurasawa. Kurasawa has set these dots in motion for us and is not too eager to divulge precisely what the program means. The dots are representative of, well, virtually every polar relationship in *Kairo*, and most all of the relationships in *Kairo are* polar: male/female; life/death; love/loneliness; Internet/library; spirit/body.

Kairo's vision of Tokyo is largely populated by computer-using teens, which makes the movie a classic "vengeful ghost" story updated for a new generation. Nice of Kurasawa to give them something more than the stalk-and-slash that's been spoon-fed to them for so long.

A strange, cryptic website seems to find computer users of its own accord, asking them, "Do you want to see a ghost?" In the real world, those who are haunted by the

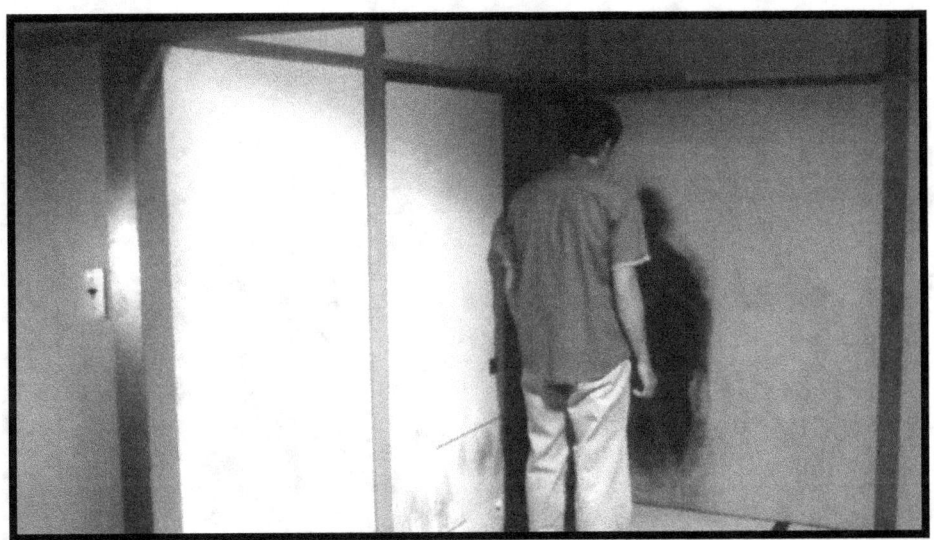

Kairo has the uncanny ability to be simultaneously spiritual and existential.

website eventually happen across a door sealed off with red tape. Those who enter this *forbidden room* emerge decidedly scathed; in fact, they become downright suicidal. They have, indeed, met a ghost on the other side of the door.

As the movie progresses, Tokyo becomes increasingly desolate. People, especially adults, grow scarce and suicide becomes commonplace. The batch of characters we are introduced to at the film's beginning are killed off or disappear by the midpoint, a la Janet Leigh in *Psycho*, and in the second act we take up with a new set of protagonists: lonely boy Kawashimi and lonely girl Harue, seemingly the last two souls left in the city. He is a hopeless romantic at heart, clinging desperately to life, going so far as to fantasize that mankind will one day find a cure for death (he doesn't take into account the overpopulation this would entail—and, of course, overpopulation is a big problem in the spirit world, where there is no death). Harue is scared of reaching out to Kawashima, afraid that she is doomed to be alone forever, and yet she is unable to seek an alternative. She is merely marking time though her life, observing it rather than experiencing it. It is she who posits the theory that displaced spirits are influencing living souls to suicide, "trapping them in their own loneliness for eternity," and making room for themselves on Earth. Indeed, it seems that the spirits have already defeated her before she is presented with her very own red-sealed door.

As the third act unfolds, these red rooms are presented almost as biblical trees of knowledge, and human hubris is too great to resist their morbid fruit. The virus spreads, the spirits multiply, the spiral widens. By the film's end, Tokyo is literally a ghost town. Not only is it utterly devoid of people, but its buildings are reduced to smoking husks. Shadows of the dead are burned into its concrete walls and floors. Military planes crash down in the heart of downtown.

Perhaps, with these allusions to World War II, it could be safely said that mankind's splitting of the atom is yet another example of the horror wrought by "two dots touching." Another example of polar opposites bound together in a dance where contact is the most desired, but least desirable, goal.

Suicide Club **is an enjoyable undecipherable thrill ride.**

A true puzzle-box of a film, *Kairo* has the uncanny and admirable ability to be simultaneously spiritual and existential. It's this conundrum, this balancing act, that makes *Kairo* not only so unique but so genuinely disturbing. Despite a number of stunning (and stunningly creepy) set pieces, *Kairo* is at times an almost unbearably slow and quiet film, a stove set so low it isn't until after you take your hand away that you realize you've been burned.

Suicide Circle is, if such a thing can be said, the cute counterpart to *Kairo*. *Kairo*'s suicides are bloodless but incredibly effective. But the set pieces in *Suicide Circle* are not only far, far bloodier but much more cheerful as well. The grinning schoolgirl suicide daisy chain at the beginning has become one of the most talked-about opening scenes in recent history. It is grand, shocking, and outrageously bloody, but it somehow still manages to retain the mood of a bubblegum girl-group pop song: cloyingly, surreastically over the top and giddy, but just sentimental enough to retain emotional reality.

A detective traces clues from the mass suicide to increasingly absurd sources. An obscure website seems to document the suicides (before they even happen) with dots, different colors representing boys and girls. Coils of sewn-together strips of human flesh show up at crime scenes in white bags, again seeming to foresee future deaths.

Soon the detective receives a phone call from a child who keeps asking him, "Are you connected to yourself?" He attempts to have the call traced but fails to take the question seriously, and his lack of peripheral vision in this matter defines his character. When he comes home from work one night, his daughter asks him for some help, and he puts her off. He doesn't even look in her direction, and this time his tunnel vision costs him dearly. He doesn't notice that she's covered in blood head to toe. He doesn't realize until too late that his wife and kids have joined the Circle without his ever suspecting. While his partners wallow through the aftermath at his home, trying to comfort him, the little boy calls him back, to scold him for being a bad parent and person. The poor guy then quickly joins the Circle himself, by way of a bullet in the head.

From here, things quickly go even further south. The film becomes nearly impossible to describe; events seem to make less and less sense (case in point: a woman commits suicide by sticking her head in an *electric* oven). But as we plunge along with the film, sifting though the red herrings, the final revelation *seems* to be that the children of the city are behind it all. They might be speaking through the girl-group Dessert (or Desert, or Desart as they're also called in the subtitles), but they appear to be the puppet masters. When they meet the film's heroine, who declares that she is, indeed, connected to herself, they seem satisfied and call off the next mass suicide. Dessert performs what they announce will be the last song they ever perform in public (a tune about living for today) as the credits roll.

Does this make sense? I *think* so. I came away from the movie thinking that the children were putting the adults to some kind of test, to see if they thought the world was worth inheriting. I could watch *Suicide Club* again tomorrow and decide that this idea is total bullshit. Perhaps what a lot of the fans say is true and *Suicide* is indecipherable. But is it enjoyable? Hell yes; suicide has never been this much fun.

SHAUN OF THE DEAD (2004)
Dir. Edgar Wright

I'm putting *Shaun* in the Art section mainly because I don't know where else to put it. My justification is that it's British. Okay then: onward.

The only thing I found more astounding than the avalanche of rave reviews *Shaun* received upon its release in the U.S. was the utter justification for every last one of them. It's one thing to create homage to an established cinematic masterpiece. It's still another to make said homage a "horror-comedy," a phrase most horror fans regard with a shudder. But it's still another thing—a rare, beautiful thing—for said comedic homage to be genuinely witty, thoughtful, and not the least bit pandering. *Shaun* doesn't feel the need to resort to irony; it knows that the right people will get all the jokes and geek references (I was the only person in the audience who laughed when Shaun didn't want to throw the Stone Roses' *Second Coming* at the zombies—trust me; it's funny) and trusts that the non-geeks in the audience will find pleasure in the rest of the film anyway.

As exquisitely droll as *Shaun* can be, it gives us more

Shaun of the Dead was genuinely witty but never pandering.

than we could've asked for by being a great drama as well. And, in an altogether unheard of flourish of generosity, throws us the first gut-munching scene in a theatrical release since *Day of the Dead*.

So much praise has been heaped upon this film that it's almost embarrassing to add more to the pile, but sheesh, how can you not want to sing this movie's praises from the rooftops of the world? It's a movie that even zombie-movie-hating girlfriends love. It's a date movie, a geek movie, a critic's movie, a movie with no discernible flaws. It's as carefully written a script as most any I've ever come across.

Like *Fight Club* before it, *Shaun* is preoccupied with the phenomena of the "30-year-old boy." Its protagonist is a slacker who's still living with roommates, playing videogames, working a dead-end retail job, and hanging out at his favorite pub every night. Quick-cut montages establish the patterns he repeats each day and the lack of attention to detail such repetition encourages (shades of *Requiem for a Dream*). And in the film's most talked-about scenes, long steadicam shots reveal how, even though the world around Shaun changes overnight, Shaun's world stays pretty much the same.

Repetition is the very essence of *Shaun*'s story, both in text and in subtext. Shaun's girlfriend leaves him because she doesn't want to fall into a rut by hanging out at the Winchester pub every night, and Shaun simply can't see past his routine to grasp her perspective. Even when he finally does try to take control of his life—he can reconcile with his stepfather, stand up to his enemies, and face down his own weaknesses—he still can't conceive of an ultimate goal greater than getting over to the Winchester.

And almost every scene and line of dialogue in the movie is repeated at least once. Every significant scene has a regular version and a zombie version, from the obvious (the steadicam shots) to the not-so-obvious (Shaun flipping through channels, coming across the news, wacky game show, and tabloid talk show).

And the dialogue:

"You've got red on you."

"Removing the head or destroying the brain."

"Who the hell put this on?" "It's on random."

"Player two has entered the game."

"Gay."

"Sorry, we're closed."

"Top left! Reload" "On it!" "Good shot!"

"How are you?" "Surviving." "Glad somebody made it."

"What do you mean, 'Do something'?"

And, of course, the "I'm sorry, Shaun" routine.

The irony, of course, is that a lot of this repetition will be caught mainly by people who watch the film over and over…people with lifestyles rooted in repetition. People like Shaun, in other words. The movie's target audience also happens to be its subject matter. I love that.

The final punch line of the film, of course, is that Shaun's life with Liz after "Z-Day" is pretty much the same, except that her posters are now on the wall, and Shaun now takes two sugars with his tea. Liz has adapted surprisingly easily to Shaun's lifestyle; it could even be said that he has "bitten" her.

Chapter Five: Visceral Horror

"Look At This"

What *is* it that makes us want to gawk at the car accident? We just can't help ourselves, can we? We know that if we see more than we bargained for, we'll take something away with us that we'll never get out of our heads. But the dread of seeing too much is sometimes not enough to keep us from wanting to look just a little closer. It's a primal urge, an instinct that's sometimes stronger than dread or apprehension, stronger than taboo.

Because we know it's silly to try to impose the concept of taboo on death in the first place, be it serene or ugly. It cannot be outlawed or made to go away, and it will knock on our door one day soon enough, so where, exactly, do we get off trying to impose a taboo on it? What's the worst that could happen if one takes an interest in the image of death? They'll die?

We're all kids at heart, and we wanna know how shit works. It's a good thing children are as small and weak as they are. They spend so much time pulling their toys (and sometimes insects) apart to see how they work that their size might be the only factor keeping them from taking Aunt Martha or the babysitter apart. No malice intended, just scientific curiosity: *What's in there?*

Older movies and TV shows lied to us about what happens to the body when it breaks. Somebody gets shot on *Hawaii Five-O*, and a neat little hole appears in their shirt, they grunt and fall, and they're dead. Subconsciously, watching these kinds of shows as kids, we knew better. We knew that everyday cuts and scrapes were far more bloody and dramatic, so there had to be more to this whole *getting shot* thing.

And eventually on our scientific quest, we happened upon horror movies, or maybe a couple of early Scorcese flicks. Movies that pull the body apart and show us what's inside. The body, once a holy and magical mystery, is now just a mass of multicolored organic stuff. Staring at a corpse, we are staring into certainty. Death is the one thing everyone on this planet has in common, and the one thing none of us will understand until it's our turn.

The stuff of life.

As we come across more and more images of broken bodies, we become more aware of the realities of pain and death, and we begin to understand why the grownups are so reluctant to talk about it. We begin to realize the reality of horror, and thus, we begin to grow up. But rarely does our curiosity ever go away upon realizing that death is horrible. Some of us embrace our curiosity and continue to explore death vicariously through horror fiction—some of the more ballsy ones among us explore it first-hand via forensic and mortuary science. And some of us feel guilty about wanting to look and try to suppress the urge. We flagellate ourselves internally, thinking we are wrong for having morbid impulses.

When the soul succumbs to guilt, the damage begins, and a potential monster is in the making, convinced of its own rottenness, ready to explode.

So let's look, shall we? Let's look long, hard, and without shame. Let's look at the corpse: the melting machine, the fast-decomposing glimpse of our future. Let's look at the human monsters, the ones who want to do more than look, the ones who truly do want to pull Aunt Martha apart. Let's look at how lack of light and love can turn human beings into terrible, terrible creatures, so that we might learn from their mistakes.

IRREVERSIBLE (2002)
Dir. Gaspar Noe

Not a traditional horror film, per se, but *Irreversible* is certainly horrific enough to be included here. There are only two acts of violence in it, but they own the movie, and if you can sit through them, you'll likely take them away with you forever.

Stylistically a sort of cross between *Memento* and Hitchcock's *Rope*, *Irreversible* consists of 10-minute takes that unfold in reverse order. *Memento*'s justification for its reverse order is to put the viewer inside the head of its memory-challenged protagonist, but *Irreversible*'s is a little more vague. At one point in the movie, Monica Belluci's character, the doomed Alex, is talking about a book she is reading, which states that everything in life "has already been written" and that knowledge of destiny can be gained via pre-cognitive dreams. The film seems to believe in this conceit (the film's centerpiece is that infamous nine-minute scene) as subconscious gestures and statements by Alex and her lover Marcus foreshadow Alex's rape several times. While they are frolicking on their bed, he covers her mouth with his hand and tells her, "I wanna fuck your ass," as Alex' rapist also does. In addition, Alex has a dream of being in a red tunnel that splits in two. She thinks she has the dream because her body is trying to tell her she's pregnant, but she's apparently, and tragically, pre-cognizant of her destiny. I suppose we can't truly call these events foreshadowing because, even though they occur chronologically before the rape, they appear afterwards in the film's narrative and serve more as incredibly cruel punctuation.

Another reason for the reverse narrative, I think, has to do with the manipulation and exploration of our perceptions of violence. The opening murder scene seems, at first glance, unbelievably brutal and quite senseless. If it were presented after the rape (and had Pierre in fact killed the right guy), we might derive some morbid satisfaction, not only from the killing, but also from the sheer brutality of it. As it is, the killing is presented on its own, apart from any justification, amidst the sexual chaos taking place at Club Rectum, and it disturbs us no less than the rape scene.

And, as we learn more about the motivation for the murder, we realize that Marcus' blind quest for revenge is spurred not only by the brutalization that has befallen Alex, but also by his own unwitting participation in it. He's out to avenge himself for his irresponsibility at the party Alex left him at to meet her fate.

A more legitimate form of foreshadowing occurs at the film's beginning, as Marcus and Pierre (Alex' ex-boyfriend) stumble through

Irreversible. starring Monica Bellucci as the doomed Alex, is a direct view into the abyss.

a club called Rectum, looking to kill a man who goes by the name of Tenia, or "tapeworm." Given that Tenia anally rapes Alex, this becomes perhaps the sickest symbolism I've ever seen in a movie.

Probably the only character who can be saved at the end of the day is Pierre. Alex has been beaten into a coma, and Marcus, witness to this most horrible of nights while tripping, has presumably lost his mind. After seeing Alex carted off, he loses every shred of his humanity, sinking down to equal footing with Tenia.

In the end, however, it's Pierre who commits the irreversible deed. Pierre, the voice of reason, begging Marcus to call off the hunt, murders the man they think is Tenia. Perhaps he's merely trying to save Marcus from suffering Alex' fate at the hands of the Rectum's patrons, or perhaps he's still in love with Alex and overcome with rage at the last second. At any rate, he's the only one in the movie who retains any shred of sanity, and it appears that he has saved Marcus from Alex' cruel destiny, only to bring it upon himself. As he is being led away in handcuffs, he's mercilessly taunted that he's going to be butt-fucked in jail.

In fact, *Irreversible* might be the most anally fixated non-porn movie I've ever seen. Virtually every line of dialog is about sex or penetration—mostly anal. Aside from the aforementioned Club Rectum and the nine-minute rape scene, everyone in the movie, at some point, is called either a "faggot" or a "fuckass." And while the opening murder may not necessarily be a penetration, the fire extinguisher is certainly phallic and forceful enough to suggest rape.

And it was certainly director Gaspar Noe's intention to violate and penetrate the audience. Except for two reels in the film, the camera lurches and spins crazily from scene to scene. On the soundtrack we hear noise loops used for crowd control by riot police, harsh industrial beats and swoopy, nauseating drones. As the narrative regresses, however, the sounds become less blaring and shrill, segueing into nicer, more generic techno for the party scene, and lush, dramatic string music for the last reel. The film's color palette also turns warmer, and the camera movements become more graceful. It's the last shot that sticks with me now, probably because it's rendered more poignant by the film's "punchline"—that Alex is pregnant. The camera starts off upside-down, gazing at Alex' prone form. It then slowly lifts up into the air, looking down on her, all the while spinning faster and faster, until it careens up into the sky, the shot fading to white. We're bathed in white for a minute before the screen starts to strobe, slowly at first, getting more and more intense. I couldn't tell you if the outer-space images I saw in between flashes were real or my imagination. And then, we're snapped out of the trance. The final title card reads, "Time destroys all things," and then the house lights come up, leaving the audience in the most uncomfortable of silences.

I could watch this last scene over and over and be completely enraptured. And we have to sit though the ultimate in ugliness to get to this one slice of beauty.

Irreversible represents precisely what this chapter of *Shadow Play* is all about—a direct gaze into the abyss. And in playing with the form the way Noe does, he achieves the ultimate irony for a film like this: a happy ending.

THE DESCENT (2005/U.S. 2006)
Dir. Neil Marshall

This was the film we'd been waiting for in the '00s: a horror movie made for real horror fans. A film that pulls no punches (with one minor exception in the case of Lion's Gate's handling of its US theatrical run), *The Descent* is bold, bloody and fearless.

One year after Sarah (Shauna MacDonald) loses her daughter and husband in a car crash, she joins up with five female friends in the Appalachian Mountains for some cave exploring. Freudian symbolism here is certainly meant to be taken at face value; these women—especially Sarah—are exploring *themselves* as literally as possible.

Rounding out the rest of the troop are: Juno, the alpha female of the group, who has some unresolved issues with Sarah (more about that in a minute); Beth, the best friend who was rafting with Sarah and Juno on the day of the accident; Sam and Rebecca, two sisters living out a slight mother/daughter dynamic; and Holly, the newcomer obsessed with extreme recreation. These women have one night of revelry and reunion, and then it's down into the depths for them.

Little by little, all hell breaks loose: the cave collapses behind the group; it is revealed that Juno has led them all into a cave system that has not yet been charted, and that nobody knows where they are; Sarah begins to mentally unravel; Holly suffers a compound fracture; tensions flare among the internal dynamic; Rebecca has the skin of her palm ripped open by rope. And then the shit *really* hits the fan.

Saskia Mulder and MyAnna Buring enter a journey of terror and madness in *The Descent*.

Much like 2005's *Wolf Creek*, the film takes its sweet time getting to know the characters and their situation before the real horrors kick in. In fact, the pasty, bat-like creatures don't say hello until near the middle of the second act. But when they do—courtesy of an infrared camera's viewfinder—it's one of the greatest monster reveals in horror history. I went back to see *The Descent* four times in the theatre just to take delight in observing the heart attacks of my fellow patrons during this scene. The second time I saw it, indie horror film director Dan Gildark practically jumped into my lap. (I'm sure he'd want you to know that.)

At its core, *The Descent* is the story of Sarah's journey into madness. Having lost her daughter, she ventures into a rocky, barren womb, re-experiences birth trauma in a squirmingly claustrophobic cave-in scene, and finds the place crawling with monsters. And the monsters don't begin to wreak havoc until Sarah starts seriously losing her grip; their presence and their dangerousness increases on a direct parallel with Sarah's mental deterioration, driving home the notion that these creatures, in some way, belong to her. If the cave is Sarah's womb, are these creatures her children?

Once the creatures are officially on the scene, they attack and consume everyone around her, viciously and horribly. Holly is the first to die in an arterial geyser; she is later ripped apart and eaten while Sarah watches from the darkness. Juno kills one of them in a fever-pitched fight scene, and then immediately after, she mortally wounds Beth by accident. One believes Juno probably didn't intend to do it, but nevertheless she leaves Beth lying on he floor, choking and bleeding to death, and there is likely some deep-seated motivation for it. Beth was the keeper of a terrible secret: that Juno was having an affair with Sarah's husband. And it's likely that Juno, somewhere in the pit of her soul, is happy to be rid of her.

The girls get separated. Sarah is trapped in a pit filled with bones both animal and human, where the creatures dump their prey. It is here that Sarah stumbles upon the dying Beth, as well as the secret about the affair. Beth begs Sarah to kill her before the monsters get to her, and this last act of mercy is what finally drives Sarah completely out of her mind.

Juno discovers markings made by other cavers, who were likely there around a hundred years ago (never to find their way out again), and realizes they can use them to find their own way out. But first she is determined to find Sarah and bring her with them. One wonders about this decision: if it is truly selfless, than it means that Juno has experienced as valid a character arc as Sarah. But it's possible—even likely—that Juno wants to find Sarah to appease her own ego. It would be not only another accomplishment for her, but a chance for her to redeem herself in her own mind.

After the rest of the cast has been mercilessly whittled down in a series of grueling set pieces, Sarah and Juno are the only survivors. They find themselves face to face with three creatures, and, with much spurting and spraying, dispatch them. It is after this that Sarah wordlessly confronts Juno with her knowledge of the affair…and wounds her, leaving her to die the death that Beth would've suffered without Sarah's mercy.

And it's here that the original ending of the film is absolutely crucial (chances are, if you're reading this, you know that the ending was softened for U.S. distribution). Juno had a piece of knowledge that was vital for escaping the cave: the markings on the walls, leading to the exit. If Sarah had found it within herself to forgive Juno, they both would have escaped the pit. But as Juno committed the uncharacteristically selfless act of going back for Sarah, Sarah commits the uncharacteristically *selfish* act of sacrificing Juno to the creatures. Thus, at the film's conclusion, her escape turns out to be a dream, and she is still trapped inside the pit, hallucinating her dead daughter, completely mad. She surrenders to her evil side, and therefore cannot get out of the pit she has consigned herself to. Purgatory transforms into Hell.

Many of my friends concluded that Sarah would likely be discovered by the creatures and eaten, but I want to suggest an alternative: Sarah will devolve to live down in the dark, and become one of the creatures herself. I like that ending, and that's the one I take home with me at the end of the day.

Much has been made of *The Descent*'s use of a 99% female cast, and the revolutionary aspects of it. I completely agree with it. Some critics argue that Sigourney Weaver's Ripley set the standard for strong women in genre film with *Aliens*, but I must argue that Ripley in that film was too flawless to be believable. The women in *The Descent* are strong, yes, but not perfect. They make decisions—not always the correct ones—and live or die with the consequences, much like the character of Ben in *Night of the Living Dead*, and I believe that *The Descent* will have as much to do in the fight against sexism in the film industry as *NOTLD* had to do in the fight against racism, because these characters are treated like human beings, with all the nobility and all of the flaws that come with being a human being. Humanity is given preference over gender or color in any film that *truly* wishes to make prejudice a thing of the past.

So, here we are. With a film that horrifies, grosses out and enthralls while it goes to work on changing the depiction of people in film. Could it be we're looking at the new *Night of the Living Dead* here?

SEVEN (1995)
Dir. David Fincher
AUDITION (2000)
Dir. Takashi Miike

Even I have limits, I guess. I personally love over-the-top screen violence—the more gratuitous, the better. Severed limbs, exploding heads, sentient intestinal tracts that slither and strangle; it's all candy to me. I'll even sometimes go for the grim-as-hell, doom-laden puke-fests like *Aftermath*, *Maniac* or Takashi Miike's *Audition*. Movies that make you want more than a shower afterwards; more like a de-lousing.

But I'll be goddamned if *Seven* didn't cross my threshold. *Seven* is perhaps the most gratuitously disgusting movie ever made by Hollywood. There is nothing holding this film up other than the sheer hideousness of the murders. So, given the fact that I rank some of the goriest, trashiest, and, yes, most gratuitous films ever made as personal faves, why do I hate *Seven* so much? For hate it I do.

Alright, I'll try to get to the crux of it as expediently as I can.

First off, I'll state that I don't mind being disturbed. I'll rate *Henry: Portrait of a Serial Killer* and *Audition* as films that are as amazing as they are hard to watch. What makes them disturbing is not so much the violence, but the fact that characters we're very interested in are embroiled in it.

Like Shigeharu Aoyama, the protagonist in *Audition*, for example. He doesn't *come up* with the idea of the audition—examining unwitting actresses for the real-life role of future wife—but he doesn't exactly kick and scream in protest to the idea, either. After having been married for so long—and widowed for yet a few more years—he finds himself completely lacking in flirting and dating skills. Therefore, he allows his movie producer friend to set up the bogus auditions for him.

He isn't necessarily a terrible guy; he's just a *guy*, given to typical guy selfishness and typical guy weaknesses. And if we read the back of the box before renting the movie, we know that this poor guy is headed for a very nasty fate. But we never wish it on him. And because we have grown to know and like Aoyama, the last 20 minutes of *Audition* are fucking excruciating.

One of my favorite scenes in the movie is where Aoyama and his producer friend sit talking at a bar. They are in the background, and in the foreground is a woman, framed on the right side of the screen, her face just out of frame. She has nothing to do with the scene, and yet she takes up most of our attention. With her facelessness, she is a kind of Everywoman in *Audition*, unknowable to any of the men. I also see her as an unintentional foreshadowing of the "faceless" female ghosts that would invade Japan and America in the wake of *Ringu*.

There is another amazing moment right before the nightmare climax of the film, where our doomed hero is about to succumb to the drug he's been slipped. As he's falling to the floor, we are subjected to a series of flashes of Asami's childhood, and all the traumatic events that have supposedly made her what she is. These events seem, in the cinematic language Miike is using, to be Aoyama's visions, as though he is seeing the events of her life from her point of view. It's as though he's inexplicably (psychically, one could suppose?) connected to her.

And then, when he's drugged and helpless, about to be tortured within an inch of his life, Asami chastises him for being yet another conniving, exploitative male chauvinist pig, which we of course know he really *isn't*. So, here at the end of their relationship, he has grown to understand her, while she has completely failed to understand him. And it's this misunderstanding that is almost more tragic and hard to take than the torture Aoyama endures at Asami's hands.

The message *Audition* seems to drive home is one we've known forever: that men are pigs and women are fucking crazy. And that sometimes a man can't help but be drawn to what's bad for him, especially where women are concerned.

Amen, brother Miike, amen.

Now, all of the murder victims in *Seven* are introduced post-mortem, so they aren't really even characters. We can't care about them without knowing them, so the only way the filmmakers can disturb us is with the utterly foul nature of their murders.

And sure, it does work; in fact, I can't dredge up the "Lust" murder in my mind without having my face, fingers, toes, stomach and soul scrunch up tightly in a seizure of pure eeeeEEAAAAGH!! But it's an empty disturbance, devoid of any human weight. There's no real humanity in *Seven* (the three characters that are *supposed* to represent humanity are too stereotypical to give a damn about), and though that might be the point of the film, it doesn't give us a reason to watch it. It takes itself far too seriously, which destroys it from a "gratuitous gorehound" standpoint, and at the same time, it alienates those looking for good drama by its cynicism and detachment from humanity.

From beginning to end we are pummeled with ultra-noir photography, editing and art design, and agitated into fits by jittery, splicey title cards and slithering, sputtering Bowie and Nine Inch Nails music. (I am going to digress for second here in regard to the film's title, while we're on the subject of the over-the-top art design. Let it be known that I will not refer to this movie as *SE7EN*, as it would like me to do. This is fucking stupid. How are we supposed to pronounce that? "Sesevenen?") All this serves to remind us that *Seven* is slick! And edgy! And fucked up!

And while the Rob Bottin–designed corpses might disturb us while they're onscreen, they will not genuinely haunt the mind after the film is over, because there aren't any personas, any people that we can attach to the faces of said corpses, much less remember when we leave the theatre. Every character that we *do* get to know in *Seven* is pure stock: from the grizzled, jaded veteran police detective doing "one last job

before retirement," to his brash, gung-ho rookie (to the big city, anyway) partner, to the partner's cloyingly cherubic wife, whom by the nature of her purity telegraphs herself as dead the first time we see her.

The city *Seven* takes place in is every other *noir* city: dingy gray buildings spattered with neon, rainy fire escapes, crummy apartments, too many people and not enough room. This, if anything, might be some sort of message: overpopulation drives people homicidal. There are friends of mine who believe that the film is a slam against religious fundamentalism, which would enable me to get behind it more, but the discussion between the detectives and John Doe in the car near the end of the film has more to do with being remembered in pop culture than making religious statements.

Seven is an exercise in flashy filmmaking and unflinching brutality for their own sake. And unlike the grindhouse flicks of the '70s, this one has no fun with itself or its audience whatsoever, and there's not even the sleaze appeal that could be present had this film tried to revel in its own excess, rather than trying to be so damn heavy.

So apparently there is such a thing as bad gratuitous violence after all. Who knew?

28 DAYS LATER (2001)
Dir. Danny Boyle

28 Days Later is not only an open love letter to Romero's *Dead* trilogy (as well as his lesser-known classic *The Crazies* {1973}), but a refreshing renewal of the conventions of horror cinema itself.

28 Days Later opens with an animal rights activist group's liberation of a monkey, whom we learn is infected with the virus of "rage." And then, after the carnage that accompanies the monkey's release, we fade in on a fellow named Jim, and follow him out of a hospital (where he has lain in a coma for almost a month). London appears to be completely deserted, as we and Jim discover to the music of Godspeed You Black Emperor (the only choice for music in this scene, wouldn't you agree?). Eventually Jim wanders into a church, and quickly learns that the house of God will offer no solace or enlightenment in this strange, dark time. And, just as quickly, we as viewers learn that there will be no relief or solace for us anywhere in this film. And as grueling as that fact is, it is also exhilarating and welcome to those of us who are begging the modern horror film to knock us off our jaded asses.

Under the surface, *28* is obsessed with the concepts of *restraint* and *release*:

The scientists release the virus into the monkey's bloodstream, dooming it for the "good of humanity" ("Before you can cure, you must understand," the scientist whines, trying to rationalize his actions), and then they restrain the monkey. The activists restrain the scientist and release the monkey, unwittingly dooming humanity for the "good of the monkey." Neither the scientists nor the activists have seriously considered the consequences of their actions, and it is this thoughtlessness that causes the downfall of England.

Once Jim wakes from his coma and ventures into the deserted streets, several rules of past horror films get sequentially upgraded. The first new wrinkle in the movie is that the zombies are *fast* (a fact that is excusable since these aren't really zombies, but rabid people; I will, however, call them zombies with a clear conscience in light of all the *Dead* references the film makes). The second rule is that the zombies can strike at any time. The third rule—the one that would make Joe Bob Briggs proud: *Anyone can die at anytime.* As we watch Selena, one of the last remaining humans in London, kill Mark, her survivalist partner (and possibly lover), with a machete on grounds that he *might* have been infected, we realize that no lead character is safe in this film. These rules are set up pretty early on, and keep the viewer from relaxing entirely at any point.

Everything about the pacing and dynamics of *28* is designed to keep you in a constant state of unease, and then jar you horribly, even from within your tension. There is no real rhythm established for when the film shifts from quiet to loud, and when it shifts, it shifts drastically.

If there is any reliable rhythm in the pacing, it's that the movie just keeps ratcheting up to new heights of dread every 10 minutes or so. I actually can't recall being this tense at a movie since my first time watching the original *Texas Chainsaw Massacre*, and I think this was worse.

Each act of the film seems to pay homage to each consecutive installment of Romero's *Dead* films, in increasingly obvious ways. Act one is expository and, eventually, housebound, with the discovery of corpses upstairs and the eventual home invasion sequence. Act two has a spirited shopping spree and a refueling/zombie-kid-killing scene that mirror the same in *Dawn of the Dead*. And as for the military assholes and the zombie-on-a-chain in the third act, well, *come on.*

It's this third act that is the most excruciating, because the depths to which some of the humans sink are as believable as they are horrifying. Not so hard to imagine it happening in real life, should such a crisis occur, which is also what gives the *Dead* films their power; they're not so much about death as they are about life in the midst of death.

In both *28* and the *Dead* movies, killer zombies are merely a new situation for human beings to react to.

And, as also in the *Dead* films, the more things change, the more they stay the same. Innocent civilians are still at the mercy of both the criminal element *and* law enforcement, and one is seldom more civilized than the other. The world is still a tiny pocket of humanity amidst a sea of brutality, exploitation and betrayal. And unthinking humans are still experimenting on "lower life forms" out of scientific curiosity and latent sadism.

However, it is very important to note a significant change in human behavior at the film's climax. Jim has decided to take on the Establishment, to try to save Hannah and Selena. In order to do this, he makes two conscious decisions: to surrender to his primal side, and to release the tethered zombie. He is fully aware of the consequences of these actions, and follows through with them because he knows they're absolutely necessary. And it's this awareness—this *consciousness*—that sets him apart from the scientists and activists in the film's beginning. He releases the "monkey," symbolized by the tethered zombie, and also symbolic of his own primal side, knowing that both will tear the soldiers utterly apart. And he does this out of love.

It is also important to note that as Jim releases his primordial side on the soldiers, Mother Nature finally *releases* the cleansing, unforgiving rain that it had restrained since the epidemic was released. The rain pours down as Jim and the zombie lay waste to the last bastion of civilization that fought to control Nature, almost as if She were applauding this shift in the balance of power. (Jung also posited in *Memories, Dreams, Reflections* that rain "showed that the tension between consciousness and the unconscious was being resolved.")

Once the soldiers are dead, Selena comes face to face with Jim, and she too acts consciously, restraining her killer instinct—her inner monkey—restraining herself from killing Jim (who might or might not be infected) *out of love for him*.

28 Days Later is a movie with a shitload on its mind, and no shortage of talent with which to express it. Every shot is framed as exquisitely as Sascha Vierny's work for Greenaway's films, and every scene bursts with creativity and passion. New perspectives on horror itself give new life to the conventions of the genre. There's Jim's walk through the desolate streets of London, his discovery of the bodies of his parents, and their note to him ("…we left you sleeping. Now we're sleeping with you. Don't wake up"), and Major West's revelation to Jim that he promised his troops women to keep them from killing themselves and each other.

These scenes hit secret places in our hearts, trapdoors that send them plummeting into pure horror. They make death—both personal and apocalyptic—seem new again. And thus, along with the "no rules" rules imposed on its narrative and rhythmic structure, it allows us to re-experience horror cinema's power as though it too were brand new.

CANNIBAL HOLOCAUST (1980)
Dir. Ruggero Deodato
EVIL DEAD TRAP (1988)
Dir. Toshiharu Ikeda

Ahh, *Cannibal Holocaust*. The stuff of legend. One of the most profoundly fucked-up films of all time, and a surprisingly influential one at that.

The plot might sound a tad familiar: A group of young filmmakers disappear while shooting a documentary, and we discover what happened to them via their found footage. Said footage consists of the crew fighting with each other (albeit a bit more brutally than in *Blair Witch*) and falling prey to the subject of their documentary (except this time you get to see *everything*). The sights we see in the found footage are sick as hell: a woman impaled vagina-through-mouth on a wooden stake; a cannibal adulteress' punishment by her husband (genital mutilation); the delivery of a stillborn fetus; and loads of animal violence.

There is also a rather heavy-handed message herein: the documentarians are the real savages, staging a war between rival clans and killing many of them for the sake of interesting footage. In the end, they get their comeuppance for fucking with nature. The message seems like it was injected into the script in order to justify the carnage: the film is loaded with depravity, but depravity is the subject—the very *essence*—of the film.

The only issue I have with this film—and really the only issue *anyone* seems to have—is the animal violence. The film was modeled after (and perhaps supposed to be a satire of) the "*Mondo*" films of the 1970s, made by the duo of Jacopetti and Prosperi. These faux-documentary films featured some hokey, staged material, combined with real footage of violence and the abasement of indigenous Third World tribes. But if director Ruggero Deodato had intended *Holocaust* to be a satire, he failed miserably by killing animals on camera. My viewpoint is not one of a PETA activist, nor even a vegetarian, but of a movie lover. Horror films are supposed to scare or shock us with illusions; that's what makes them special. Anyone can kill an animal and film it. Considerably less people have the talent to fake it and make us squirm.

I find it remarkably ironic that writer Chas Balun walked out early during a screening of Nacho Cerda's short film *Aftermath,* yet lauded *Cannibal Holocaust* in his earlier writings. As insanely disturbing as *Aftermath* is, it's all done with prosthetics. That's simply how well made the film is. *Holocaust* takes the low road by choosing to film real death, and even though people are still talking about it (and throwing up over it) after all this time, it will never be taken seriously, never be seen as an *important* horror film, in spite of all its influence.

What makes it retain its popularity is that it's one of those films that dare you to watch. That's the way I felt when I finally got around to renting it: "Let's just do it and get it over with." There are a couple more of those films that I still haven't gotten around to renting—more on them later.

Cannibal Holocaust made more money in Japan than *E.T.*, so it's no surprise that the Japanese are responsible for many of the most disturbing films of all time. Over the years, Japan has produced a cavalcade of cinematic perversity, from the *Guinea Pig* films (one of which Charlie Sheen thought was an actual snuff film) to the *Atrocity* video series, to their extensive and jaw-dropping catalogue of SM porn, to remarkable and twisted horror fare like the *Evil Dead Trap* flicks.

Trap is a prime example of what the Japanese excel at: absorbing foreign pop culture, field-stripping it and reassembling it in their own image, eschewing any iconic importance (and often literal meaning) in favor pure aesthetic. In *Trap*'s case, it borrows heavily from the hyper-stylized ulraviolence of Dario Argento, *Friday the 13th*'s stupid-ass teen stalk-and-slash, Cronenberg's visual essays on bodily transformation, and maybe a little De Palma–style misogyny and second-rate Hitchcockisms. And in glorious Japanese fashion, *Trap* spews all these influences back out in an eye-popping potpourri of shiny sleaze.

Trap is so simultaneously beautiful and ugly it must be seen to be believed. Several camera tricks, including a time-lapse speeding-demon point-of-view, and a scene in which the only light comes from a popping flashbulb, are simply breathtaking. The more grotesque scenes—including a grueling rape in a van and a scene involving a very, very long tripwire hooked to a doorknob—are equally stylish, and produce ridiculous tension.

More importantly, *Trap* takes the care to one-up every director it pays homage to in sheer visual audacity—a task that perhaps only the Japanese are up to. Japan has spent a lot of time on the cutting edge of horror, for they seem to have no inhibition. And God bless them for it.

"TORTURE PORN"

In 1931, producer Carl Laemmle Jr. talked his father, the owner of Universal Studios, into greenlighting his production of *Dracula*. Laemmle Sr. initially balked at the idea of making a horror film, but changed his tune once *Dracula* became a smash hit, and soon a wave of monster movies crashed upon the shore of the American consciousness, taunting our decidedly Christian sensibilities with sacrilegious, supernatural threats.

In the 1950s, in the wake of mankind's splitting of the atom, movie monsters moved out of the realm of the supernatural and into that of the scientific. Scientists became cinema's villains, and the military became its heroes, cleaning up the messes left by unchecked scientific arrogance.

In the 1980s, the collective American unconscious was brought up to speed with the times yet again; John Carpenter's 1978 classic *Halloween* had made the "monster next door" the newest archetypal icon of horror cinema, and exploitation filmmakers of the following decade were more than happy to milk this new archetype for all it was worth.

Having grown up in this era, the serial killer had been a part of my world since I first became self-aware. The grownups of the day were largely appalled that youth culture found such high entertainment value in wonton bloodshed; in fact, Gene Siskel went so far as to give out Betsy "Mrs. Voorhees" Palmer's address in his column, urging his audience to write Ms. Palmer hate mail for betraying America by participating in such garbage as *Friday the 13th*.

Which brings us to today.

It's weird enough to me to think that the generation after mine wasn't around for life before the Internet, much less before the constant threat of terrorism. 9/11 officially marked an end of an era for us; America had undergone a cruel initiation from world police to world citizens. We no longer lived on an island. The political waves we had made in the world for so long were now coming back to us as tsunamis.

In our new heightened, frightened state of consciousness, all too aware of the way we were perceived by most of the world, and able to view footage of our soldiers and journalists being beheaded on the Web, it was only natural for the youth culture of the '00s to gravitate toward the horror subgenre known as torture porn. And it is of course equally as natural for the previous generation to fail to relate to it, as I do.

I can't really cite the lack of cinematic "quality" in films like *Saw* and *Hostel* as a reason for disliking them; even in my less discerning youth, I knew that the slasher films I loved were largely total crap. In fact, their shittiness would become one of their more endearing traits to me and my generation. So I can't justify my dislike for torture porn, because it's simply a matter of aesthetics. Slasher films, and the people who love them, are preoccupied with violence and gore, death and the fear thereof, whereas torture porn, and the generation who love it, seem to have more of a preoccupation with suffering.

In the era from the '50s to the '80s, our bogeyman was the USSR. In the '80s, we were our own bogeyman. In the '00s, terrorists became the new Russians. We're more afraid of traveling abroad now than we are of going into the basement. And in the wake of Guantanamo Bay, as well as the fate of many an American in the Middle

Hostel is difficult to accept as entertainment.

East, ultraviolent, creative torture replaced ultraviolent and creative murder as the prurient adrenaline rush of choice in exploitation cinema.

As of this writing, my gestalt has not yet shifted to accept these films as entertainment, and honestly, I don't know if I'm in any hurry to bring myself around. To my perception, the motto of torture porn seems to be, "How bad can things possibly get?" There doesn't seem to be any interest in hinting at solutions; rather, these films delve down into grottos of pure nihilism that no light can penetrate. The rule of horror cinema as shadow play of course applies here: filmmakers are taking situations utterly devoid of hope and light and *containing* them on screen, allowing viewers to explore them in an arena removed from reality, usually alongside a socio-political narrative that touches a nerve for the film's country of origin. The *Hostel* films certainly reflected the anxieties of American tourists, and the French films *Frontier(s)* and *Inside* (both 2007) take place during the race riots the country experienced in 2005.

Torture porn arguably began with David Fincher's *Seven*, of which James Wan and Leigh Whannell's *Saw* was practically a remake—from the notion of a preaching serial killer who's always one ludicrous step ahead of his pursuers, to the fact that the torture-murders are presented post-mortem, to the "everybody dies horribly and the killer wins" ending. In the ensuing *Saw* sequels, whenever a chance is presented for something remotely positive to happen, we know it isn't going to, if for no other reason than their target audience would likely start booing. No amount of unbelievable plot twists can distract us from the inevitability of their endings.

Torture porn films had their precursors in the sexual horror flicks of the '70s grindhouse subculture. These films took audiences down into the same grottos, but they were intended to completely devastate said audiences emotionally. *Last House on the Left* (1972), *The Candy Snatchers*, *I Spit on Your Grave*, *Being Twenty*: these films were pure cinematic electroshock. They were cheap, obvious, gratuitous, and grudgingly effective. These, along with the Italian *Mondo* and cannibal films, were made because their directors had neither the talent nor the resources to get audiences' attention in any other way. While the films of Eli Roth and Rob Zombie do not have nearly the impact the aforementioned flicks have, I believe that they make them for precisely the same reason.

It's easy for those of us who are one generation removed from torture porn to imagine its surge in popularity as a sign of the apocalypse, but one must take into account that the adults of the '80s once felt the same way about our precious *Friday the 13th*. Whether or not I come around to experiencing torture porn films as anything other than completely depressing, I know one thing in my heart: The kids are alright.

That was a reference to The Who, by the way—a rock band that old people like.

HIDEKI: EVIL DEAD TRAP 2 (1991)
Dir. Isou Hashimoto
INSIDE (2007/U.S. 2008)
Dir. Julien Maury/Alexandre Bustillo

I don't know if the sequel is really bloodier than the first *Evil Dead Trap*, or if the mood is simply a bit less "popcorn" than *Part 1*, and therefore the violence hurts a little more, but in any case, *Evil Dead Trap 2* is utterly remarkable and remarkably disgusting. It reminds me a bit of *Eraserhead* with its pervasive fear of sexuality and its consequences. It's a very oppressive, doomed-feeling movie, living in the mindset of its tormented protagonist. Her name is Aki, and she works as a projectionist in a movie theatre. Surrounded by few real people but plenty of fake ones, she works an ideal misanthrope's job.

Alienated because of her plus size, afraid and hateful of everyone in the world (including herself), she avoids men like the plague, and viciously butchers pretty young women, cutting their stomachs out with film scissors. She's trying to remove (or "edit," in keeping with the film scissors) what is, in her eyes, the root of all evil: reproductive equipment. Tormented by an abortion she once had, Aki takes out her hatred of her own body on the bodies of more desirable women.

Her only friend Ami is such a girl. She's a newscaster, and reports on the new series of gruesome murders, unaware that Aki is behind them. Thin, pretty, extroverted and famous, Ami is also vain and shallow. On the surface, her fears appear to be different from Aki's; she used to be a singing star and is terrified of losing her fame and beauty. So Aki is terrified of people, and Ami is terrified of being alone. But at root they are both afraid of the same thing: their bodies rebelling against them, be it in the form of age, obesity, pregnancy or love.

Into their lives comes a man named Kurahshi, and the girls' downward spiral really begins. He gets Ami pregnant almost immediately. He hides his wedding ring in her presence. He goes home every night to his decidedly insane wife and their child, a strange and dead-looking little boy named Hideki.

Aki is simultaneously attracted to and repulsed by Kurahshi, and he seems to be attracted to her as well. He is at first goaded by Ami to try to seduce her, but his interest seems to be genuine, if not a little predatory. He barges his way into Aki's sacred space—the projection booth—and marvels at how clean it is. He asks her out and she blows him off, but the clockworks have been set in motion.

Aki sits up in her booth, a warm, meditative place amidst the glaring neon chaos of the city, watching the audience watching the movie, when she spies the little corpse-boy staring at her from the seats. Kurahshi has gotten inside her head (the booth) and now there's a malevolent child in her body (the theatre). Aki tells her boss about the kid, who cannot be found. Her boss senses her anxiety and suggests she go to visit a white witch, who also happens to be the boss's ex-wife. The witch goes into a trance and tells Aki she has a great evil in her body. Aki is overtaken by the witch's ritual and falls into trance herself, screaming the name "Hideki" over and over again.

At this point, the world of every woman in the film begins to unravel and explode. The witch is overtaken with cancer. Aki sleeps with Kurahshi, and Ami becomes insanely jealous. The roles reverse: Aki becomes desirable, and Ami becomes homicidal. The two women collide in a maelstrom of psychosexual (and I mean *psycho* sexual) fury, slashing at each other (and anyone else in their way) with their tiny knives. The third act of *Trap 2* is unbelievably bloody and brutal. Aki and Ami are each other's shadow-selves, each other's own worst fear in the flesh, and they desperately slash each other to bloody ribbons in the climax, before we're treated to yet another monstrous birth scene—the only thing this film seems to have in common with *Trap 1*.

The city that *Trap 2* takes place in—garish, loud and densely packed with people—is the true father of all the evil that germinates in the minds and bodies of the women in this film. In this film's overpopulated society, where another mouth to feed is the last thing needed, pregnancy is on a direct parallel with cancer: an organism living inside (and feeding off) its host. The men are indifferent, childish caricatures who only care about spreading their seed. Aside from Kurahshi, there's also the witch's ex-husband, who apparently left her because she couldn't bear children.

Original, disgusting, and like its predecessor, genuinely scary in some parts, *Evil Dead Trap 2* may well be my favorite in the series. There's a lot more narrative substance this time around, as well as a lot more pulpy red substance splattered on every available white wall.

Inside is weirdly similar to *Trap 2*; it's the story of an epic, bloody, ridiculously brutal battle between two women who have nothing to lose, and pregnancy is the motivating force. But where *Trap 2* isn't remotely believable, *Inside* is going for claustrophobic intimacy and unflinching suffering that take it far beyond simply "disturbing" and straight into "depressing."

Inside begins with a news photographer named Sarah waking

up after a car crash. She looks over to the driver's side and realizes her husband is dead. The camera then pans down to show us that Sarah is very pregnant. Before the opening credits have even begun, our protagonist is in the darkest place in which a human being can be. Or so we think.

Sarah decides she is going to spend Christmas Eve alone in her house, making arrangements for her editor to take her the hospital the following morning, where she will undergo labor-inducing procedures. But as it turns out, there is a mysterious and maniacal woman (known in the credits only as "La Femme") trying to break into her house and steal her baby, with the aid of a large pair of scissors. The majority of *Inside* focuses on the battle between Sarah and La Femme. Several secondary characters, including Sarah's mother and editor, stumble into the melee, only to die the most horrible deaths imaginable.

Those last five words seem, to me, to be the main thrust of the screenplay. If *Inside* could ultimately be said to be about anything, it's about the most horrible deaths imaginable. It might be the best torture porn film made up until this writing, but it's still torture porn.

There might be a subtextual theme implying that La Femme is Sarah's shadow-self; that Sarah is suicidally depressed and succumbing to madness. After all, Sarah inadvertently commits the first murder of the film: she slashes her mother's throat, mistaking her for La Femme. It's possible that Sarah completely breaks with reality after committing matricide (the most horrible of all crimes—especially for the person who commits it, as the psychiatrist in *Psycho* once informed us), and subsequently imagines that the ensuing murders are being committed by La Femme. Unfortunately, this would not make *Inside* a better film, merely a more derivative one. (*High Tension*, anyone?)

But *Inside* doesn't really seem as interested in exploring subtext as it is in putting Sarah through a Job-like gauntlet of unadulterated agony. Again I find myself compelled to bring up my imagined motto of torture-porn: "How bad can things possibly get?"

Evil Dead Trap 2 is certainly as dark a film, if not darker, than *Inside*: its vibe is sick, sleazy and grim from frame one, it features not one likable character, and at the end of the day, it contains no light or humanity whatsoever. Thus, nothing that happens in it feels gratuitous; these characters are simply behaving the way their environment dictates, like animals in the jungle. This, coupled with the supernatural element, as well as the twisted parallel *Trap 2* draws between pregnancy and cancer, place it in a completely unreal context, rendering it easier to watch objectively.

Inside, however, features a very believable and likable protagonist, and is set against a backdrop of real-life events: the Paris race riots of 2005. And *Inside* doesn't even offer up the political commentary about racism and classism that *Frontier(s)* (also 2007, also set against the Paris riots)—a decidedly more grindhouse movie—gives us. There doesn't really seem to be a reason for its setting, other than to make the cops less available to Sarah in her hour of need. Indeed, *everything* in the movie seems to exist solely to make Sarah's life hell.

Inside wants you to be as emotionally involved as possible, so that it might repeatedly sucker-punch you for 80 minutes. This, for me, is where the film crosses the line into "bad" gratuitousness. Like *Seven*, it gives the impression that its writer began his first session by asking himself, "What is the most awful thing I could do to my lead character?" The plot followed shortly after: "She's pregnant! And her husband's dead!

And it's Christmas! And a crazy bitch wants to cut her baby out! And she kills her own mother by accident! And the crazy bitch stabs a dude in the kneecap and the dick! And despite the hellish arc the protagonist goes through, and despite the fact that she finds the strength to fight back, and the will to live, the crazy bitch still cuts her baby out while she watches! Dude!"

Yes, I realize that the writer probably spoke to himself in a far more refined and French manner, but if you change the dialect over to that of an American death metal fan, it's not so hard to imagine *Inside* being made by Jim Van Bebber, is it?

NIGHT OF THE LIVING DEAD (1968)
DAWN OF THE DEAD (1978)
DAY OF THE DEAD (1985)
Dir. George A. Romero

Many conclusions have been drawn about what George A. Romero's *Night of the Living Dead* is meant to be an allegory for—most of them relating to late '60s uprisings: the counterculture movement, the Watts riots, etc.

All and none of them are correct, in my opinion. *NOTLD* deals with massive social upheaval, and the world turning into an unfamiliar place overnight, which was what was happening on almost every level at the time of its release. The world was changing drastically, and the establishment and counterculture had little or no idea how to relate to each other on an aesthetic, racial, political or spiritual level.

NOTLD was filmed in 1968, when racial tensions were a bit more on the forefront of the collective American consciousness than they are today, and Romero is a filmmaker that, if we had to classify him as one or the other, is definitely counterculture. Whether he intended to or not, Romero classified the concept of racial tension as a quaint tradition that was now obsolete. He not only cast Duane Jones, an African-American, in the lead role, but he never once brought up the issue of race in the script.

The idea suggested by Romero's writing and casting decisions was that when the pressure is on and everything counts, racial prejudice is a "luxury" that the world simply can no longer afford, and subsequently doesn't think about. In *NOTLD*'s world, the notion of "us and them" becomes very black and white indeed: those that are trying to eat us, and those of us trying not to be eaten. Most traditions that the old world held dear to itself (like comfort, freedom, and respectful rites of mourning for dead loved ones) become instantly irrelevant. Nothing but survival matters, and if the living do not work together against the dead, they do not survive.

Ben and Harry's relentless arguing has nothing to do with racial tension, but with stubbornness; both of them think they know what's best for the rest of the group, both refuse to compromise, and both pay a price for it—ironically, not at the hands of the enemy. Ben kills Harry in a fit of rage (Harry tried to lock him out of the house), and subsequently learns that Harry was right all along: the basement *was* the safest place.

I personally see a bit of allegory in Ben and Harry's feud. Ben wants what liberals want: freedom. Harry is a symbol of the Establishment or Republicans in that he wants security for himself and his own, and damn the rest. The youngest people in the film, with the exception of the almost catatonic Barbara, side with Ben; they want to be able to run in any direction, but in their freedom they remain vulnerable to attack from the

Night of the Living Dead **deals with massive social upheaval.**

outside. Harry is practically agoraphobic in his obsession with protecting his family—so much so that he doesn't see that his family is actually his greatest threat.

Ben's death, of course, is infamous now. It very well might imply that some of the living are trying to keep a few of the "old ways" alive. The rednecks have taken control of the sticks, and no longer have to fight quite as hard to stay alive—they have the guns. Being a bit more "comfortable" then the rest of the poor shmoes trying to fight off the zombies with tire irons, they perhaps have a bit more room to entertain their traditions. The question remains: Did the rescue party shoot Ben because they truly thought he was a zombie, or because he was black? Did Romero intend at all for them to *have* a motivation?

I like the question unanswered, myself. Maybe Romero talked about it in an interview somewhere, but I don't really want to read it. The simplicity of *NOTLD* makes it a sort of Rorschach test on film. The ideas expressed are basic, almost primitive, and any embellishments imposed on the narrative reveal more about the viewer than they do about the film.

The characters in *Dawn of the Dead* are more three-dimensional.

In *Dawn of the Dead*, we take up with a new set of protagonists and follow them in a stolen helicopter in search of the greenest possible pasture they can find. It takes place presumably a few weeks after *Night*'s events, and the zombie epidemic has spread exponentially. America has once again become an untamed wilderness, and our heroes are its settlers, taking what they can to survive, and fighting off "savages."

The settlers luck out and happen upon a shopping mall. Romero has a bit more clout this time around, and is perhaps freer to make bona fide social statements. Hardly anyone will argue the meaning of Romero's "shopper-zombies," compelled to endlessly mall-walk, lacking the ability to question why they're doing it. No one who has seen *Dawn* can walk into a mall, observe the shambling shoppers, and resist the urge to quote, "This was an important place in their lives."

The characters in *Dawn* are also more three-dimensional. We know them much better than we knew Ben, Harry and the *NOTLD* gang—Roger and Peter especially, as we get to see the dramatic circumstances under which they meet, and the strength of their bond afterwards. Steven is a weasel, but not without a soul. His weaknesses are clearly defined and humanized, and though we may not like him, we believe in him for the time he's onscreen.

Fran is perhaps the least fleshed-out character in the ensemble. She's certainly given the cheesiest dialogue. She's kind of a Madonna; the one character that sees the way the mall has "hypnotized" the men. She states "I'm not gonna be den mother to you guys," but she certainly is enough of an earth mother archetype; she wants to live a more natural existence, and she's pregnant. And unlike the men, she doesn't have any visible character flaws.

Romero's gift for drama shines here, and it must be stressed that it's his ability to make these films as much dramas as they are horror films that makes them so special.

The TV broadcasts where "Mr. Logical" is preaching the gospel of detachment—and losing his cool when his audience reacts with emotion—give *Dawn* the final touch that makes its human struggle all the more important. And the way his speech coincides with the shooting of Zombie Roger ("We've got to remain une*motional*!" – BANG!) is one of my favorite moments in the history of cinema.

The *Dead* films succeed in combining both the *apocalyptic* horror of the 1950s with the *intimate* horror of the modern age; the monsters are man-sized, but there's a shitload of them. And if you die at their hands, your death will be quite intimate indeed—can murder get any more personal than eating someone alive? We're talking about our loved ones becoming our enemies in death, and about a restoration in the balance of nature, where the species with no natural predators has slipped to the bottom of the food chain. In the Industrial Age, few things are as horrifying as the loss of our control over nature, the loss of our "right to comfort."

Day of the Dead was a failure in many ways—the reason most often cited being that budget cuts prevented Romero from making the film he wanted. I do wonder how much of this undermined Romero's vision, for the piece of his vision that made it on screen is philosophically interesting, but oftentimes it's the screenplay and direction's limitations, and not those of the budget, that stand in *Day*'s way.

The characters in *Day* are written and directed so broadly as to cross over the line from melodramatic to absurd. Basically, the scientists are the good guys; the military men are the bad guys. It's a reversal of the morality of 1950s monster movies, but every bit as simplistic.

The film's opening scene, a wonderful and surreal exposition of the dire state civilization is in, is almost ruined by one of the rescue workers braying, "Hellooooooo! Is anyone theeeere? Helloooooo!" incessantly and pointlessly into a megaphone.

The workers find no one living and hightail it back to their camp—an underground military base. Once there, we are introduced to the characters. Among the good guys we've got Sarah, the tough-as-nails female researcher; Miguel, the medal-kissing Catholic basket case; McDermott the whiskey-drinking Irishman; Dr. Logan the oddball scientist; and John the laid-back, *ja mon* Jamaican. The base is located on the coast of Florida, and it could possibly be read into the film that the zombies this time around are standing in for Cuban refugees.

The major bad guys are a military grunt named Steel, and the leader, Rhodes. The characters are all over-the-top, but Rhodes is so ridiculous it's impossible to take him seriously as a genuinely threatening villain. The first two acts of *Day* are filled with histrionics and caricatures. For example, Sarah is supposed to be tough enough to handle herself in the company of these depraved men, but since she doesn't show any fragility until her breakdown in the third act, she comes across as a bitch for most of the film, and if we see no humanity or likability in her, we can't identify with her drive to *save* humanity. Dr. Logan's experiments and mannerisms are absurd even to us, so it's impossible for us to see why anyone had faith in his work to begin with (there's also a minor plot hole in Dr. Logan's rewarding of Bub the zombie; it is stated in *Dawn* that the zoms only feed on warm, living flesh, so Bub shouldn't be interested in the scraps Logan feeds him). The dialogue is full of weak attempts to convey characterizations, like, "You're collapsing from stress," or, "Can't you get that through your thick skull?"

However, in *Day*'s third act, things get interesting, and fortunately not just in the gore department. It's in the last third of the film that what might be Day's underlying

Day of the Dead gets interesting in the third act.

philosophy lies. Sarah and John have an argument about whether or not civilization is worth saving. She wants everyone to try to work as a group for the common good, and John counters with, "People got different ideas about what they want outta life." It might seem nihilistic of John to write the cause off so easily, at least because we've spent so much of the movie with Sarah.

But as the film nears its climax, this idea solidifies itself neatly. Everyone conforms to their "type": Miguel martyrs himself, sacrificing his living flesh as a lure to bring the zombies into the base; the military men die in combat; and the self-preservationists John and McDermott live to see another day. Sarah grows to understand the belief that the idea of everyone working together is more or less impossible, and learns to give up on the more stubborn factions of humanity and, subsequently, save herself. And John finds some selflessness within himself after all, fighting to save his newfound friends from the military goons.

It works, sort of. And as far as exploitation movies go, it's intelligent. But against the legacy it has to live up to, *Day* is a thundering disappointment.

LAND OF THE DEAD (2005)
Dir. George A. Romero

Sitting in a movie theatre, watching the title "George A. Romero's *Land of the Dead*" fade in on a huge screen was one of the biggest kicks in the ass I have ever received in my horror-junkie career. I was doubly impressed (not to mention relieved) to find that the *movie* kicked ass to boot. A perfect movie? Far from it. But none of Romero's *Dead* films are perfect. To expect *Land of the Dead* to live up to the legendary status of the first two films is to take *Land* out of its own context; times have changed, and a Romero zombie movie is no longer the taboo-busting watershed it was back in the '60s and '70s. We all have the image of the flesh-eating zombie (an archetype *invented* by Romero) firmly imbedded in our subconscious by this point. So, knowing that audiences know what they're getting into with a new *Dead* film, Romero decided to let the politics, rather than the gore, be the radical element of the new film.

Calling *Land*'s political agenda "subtext" would be underkill. *Land*'s politics are bold and in your face—every bit as much as *They Live*'s. Both films state, pretty overtly, that Republicans are the root of all evil. I find it hard—nearly impossible—to believe that anybody interested in horror films would disagree with this notion. Few horror fans aren't at least subconsciously preoccupied with social concerns. We may not all be political activists, but these issues hold at least some slight interest for us: *What makes humans turn on one another? What are our stumbling blocks? Are there any solutions?* These questions are, let's face it, decidedly *liberal* in nature.

Land of the Dead takes place a few decades after the onset of the Official Romero Zombie Plague, and times have changed on both sides of the fence. Many humans are trying to resume life as it once was, pretending that nothing has changed, and the zombie hordes are not only increasing in number, but also evolving.

In the essay about the previous three *Dead* films, I mentioned the notion of humanity dropping down on the food chain. *Land of the Dead* drives this notion home thoroughly, reinforcing the idea that humans and zombies are truly different species. Humans are still as bumbling and prone to in-fighting as they were in the original *NOTLD*. Zombies are learning—not only intellectually, but also emotionally. Big Daddy—the zombie that leads *LOTD*'s revolt—learns not only how to use a machine gun, but also how to organize troops, how to feel rage and sadness, and how to euthanize his wounded (how to express *mercy*, not to put too fine a point on it).

Also capable of these emotions is the film's hero Riley Denbo, the leader of the human "revolutionaries" of the film. Both Big Daddy and Riley rally their troops against their common enemy: Kaufman, who is clearly a stand-in for George W. Bush. Riley is a reluctant hero, trying to keep to himself at the outset, but eventually drawn into the good fight by both circumstance, and by his nature. Every step of the way he tries to convince himself that his motivations are completely selfish, but he can't lie to himself. He betrays his human nature again and again: rescuing Slack from the zombie cage in the casino; pulling his sidekick Charlie "out of the fire"; and trying to save the citizens of the Pittsburgh ghetto from the encroaching zombie horde. Thus, he earns his right to live alongside the zombies, who are fast becoming more human than us.

Euthanasia embodies a strong subtextual theme running through the film. The first time we witness it is when Big Daddy stomps on the severed (and still living) head of the machine-gunned zombie. Later in the film, Riley tells the story about having to put his brother down, after which Slack kills the terminally bitten Manolete. Big Daddy puts the burning zombie out of his misery with his machine gun. And last, Riley fires missiles at the doomed and screaming townspeople at the electric gates of the city. Riley and Big Daddy never find this choice easy to make, but they do it anyway. It is this strength of character that puts them at the evolutionary forefront of their species, and why they so easily assume leadership roles.

Evolving right along with the zombies is the zombie virus itself. Back in the days of *DOTD*, a human who found himself bitten could be expected to last only three days. But now, in *LOTD*'s world, the bite only takes an hour to turn its victim into the enemy. Viruses are mutating, species are evolving, but many of the humans

seem to be de-evolving. And these, largely, are the ones that get chomped in the film's denouement. *Survival of the fittest*. And I absolutely love the idea Romero posits here: that "fittest" means "most capable of emotion." *Land of the Dead* reminds us that compassion—not strength—is the pinnacle of evolution.

The three leaders of the zombie revolution are Big Daddy, the hockey zombie and the butcher zombie. Big Daddy is black, the hockey zombie is female and the butcher zombie is on the far side of middle age. In terms of their human symbolism, they are a kind of holy trinity of oppressed minorities: race, gender and age. And in *Land*, the zombies are standing in for virtually every oppressed minority group we've got: the homeless, immigrants, the HIV positive, etc.

The strangest aspect of the film comes at the end, when Riley dissuades Charlie from killing the remaining zombies led by Big Daddy. "They're just looking for a place to go, same as us," he says. Romero has implied in interviews that this means zombies and humans are arriving at a *détente*. So does this mean, in the evolutionary scheme of the *Dead* films, that the zoms are evolving beyond the need to eat? This, to me, is the hardest aspect of the film to swallow, but at the same time, it's intriguing as hell. I do hope he fleshes this idea out one day. As it is at the end of *Land*, it's simply cryptic.

As per usual in these films, the characters—both human and zom—are painted with a pretty broad brush. But *Land i*s a romp on par with *Dawn*, as opposed to a claustrophobic melodrama like *Night* or *Day*. There's a serious sense of humor in this film, and I do mean a *serious* sense of humor. It has a lot of fun with itself (case in point: The ultra-cheesy fireworks display at the end), while at the same time absolutely skewering the Bush administration as being the source of the problem. When Big Daddy punctures the windshield of Kaufman's limo with the nozzle of the gas pump, filling up the interior of the car with gasoline, the symbolism is perfect: *George W. Bush being killed by oil*. And of course, the ultimate goal of the good guys is to get the hell out of the U.S. and high tail it to Canada. With *Land of the Dead*, George A. declares war (or is it *jihad?*) on George W…and wins.

"SOUTHERN DISCOMFORT"

The only real fear is fear of the unknown, when you boil it all down. It manifests in many ways, from physical pain (the body's built-in fear-of-death alarm system) to subtle neuroses like shyness, religious zealotry and bigotry.

Bigotry is nothing more than a fear of unknown culture, and back in the '70s, director John Boorman tapped into the sneakiest, and least often acknowledged, sect of bigotry in our culture:

Deliverance was perhaps the first film to explore our fear of rednecks.

Of course, the bad guys in *Deliverance* are a bit more extreme than your typical chaw-spittin', "Yer not from 'round here are ya?" stereotypes. They're a self-sufficient, willfully isolated breed, the Amazonian Lost Tribe of the Appalachians. Inbred yokel elevated to modern American mythos. Films like *Texas Chainsaw Massacre*, *The Hills Have Eyes* and Walter Hill's *Southern Comfort* all share similar traits with *Deliverance*. The moral of most of these films seems to be, "Don't mess with the locals. They'll kill and eat you and have their way with that pretty little husband of yours." And while the family in Wes Craven's *The Hills Have Eyes* may not be Southern in origin, their way of life reminds us of *Deliverance* a bit. Even the Sawney Bean clan, upon whom *Hills* was based, fit the Killer Hick stereotype: isolated, inbred, and murderously hateful of city folk. Perhaps it would be safe to call them Scottish rednecks?

Since the directors of all these films are Anglo themselves, perhaps they have more leeway to claim "dark satire" rather than "bigotry." Or perhaps they're really trying to tap into an inherent bigotry in all of us, fear of a culture beyond our comprehension. God help me, I know I fear the redneck, even though the big cities have produced comparable—if not greater—horrors. I think of the state of Alabama, and the first image that pops into my head is that of a Klan rally. I hear a name like Thelma-Lou or Bobbi-Sue, and my mind plays a sick word-association game: Uncle Dad. I hear a banjo and I think of anal rape.

And then I think about the Redneck Monster mythologized in these films, and I find I am forced to confront my own shadow.

Jon Voight learns not to mess with the locals in *Deliverance*.

PET SEMATARY (1989)
Dir. Mary Lambert

As a movie, *Pet Sematary* was doomed from the beginning. To faithfully recreate the tone of Stephen King's book would be to make one of the most depressing and unmarketable films of all time. George Romero had originally claimed the rights to it, and King himself said that Romero would be the only director in the world he trusted with it, the book being so personal. Sadly, Romero and his producer Richard Rubenstein parted ways before the film could be made, the rights stayed with Rubenstein, and the directing job wound up going to Mary Lambert (of the interesting *Siesta* and a Madonna video or two). The end result is flawed, to say the least.

This sad truth also serves to drive home the masterpiece of horror the book is.

Louis Creed moves his family to a new town where he has been hired as a doctor. Their new house lies on a very dangerous stretch of road, and across said road lives a kindly old man named Jud, with whom the Creeds instantly bond. When the road claims the life of Church, the Creed's family cat, Jud tells Louis of a piece of land beyond the town's "pet sematary." Louis buries the cat in this ground, and of course, the cat returns to the household, albeit a bit more ornery than usual.

When the road claims the life of Louis' toddler son Gage, Louis begins the journey into the shadows of his own heart, with the least desirable results.

The subject matter here is the heaviest stuff imaginable. The atmosphere of reading (quiet, meditative, and most importantly, alone) lends itself wonderfully to the aura of impending doom the story weaves. Romero might have been able to pull the film off because, if for no other reason, Rubenstein made for a great marketer of his visions. If Rubenstein could market a film with no rating—tantamount to an X rating—he could certainly have sold a film as dark as King's book.

Aside from the obstacle of the book's mood, Lambert's film suffers from severe miscasting, as well as an uneven film score that relies too heavily on what

Joe Bob Briggs refers to as "Squealy-violin-*Psycho*-slasher-stuff." This is not a typical, "booga-booga" horror yarn, but a dark-as-hell tragedy with horrific consequences.

In the story, King gives Louis a tragedy that no one would be able to deal with, and then piles on the temptation of the burial ground. As bad an idea as we know it is, Louis knows it too, and cannot help himself. And we as an audience cannot fault him. We know that if we were in his position, we would make every stupid move he makes and not think twice about it.

The villain in *Pet Sematary* is neither the burial ground, nor the malignant Gage-thing that returns from the grave, but the folly of a human heart that cannot cope with loss. It's a ramped-up version of *The Monkey's Paw*, to be sure, but it's even more effective because, in this case, the folly is unstoppable. Its inevitability pulls us along with Louis and, though we might hate King while we're reading it, we can't stop. No more than Louis can stop himself from burying his wife—murdered and mutilated by the Gage-thing—in the cursed burial ground. We sit with him as he plays Solitaire on his kitchen floor, waiting for Rachel to come home to him. The last line of the book—

'Darling', it said.

—is horrible, crushing, and perfect.

The ending of the film leaves us with that last line, coupled with the image of Zombie Rachel (whom the filmmakers never should have shown to us in the first place) reaching for a butcher knife. This is slasher-movie garbage. Too many times the film takes this horror movie cop-out. But if the movie were as dark as the book, would anyone want to see it? Would a major studio know what to do with it?

To their credit, the filmmakers did get a couple of things right. The funeral scene is pretty right-on, and the flashback in which Rachel remembers Zelda, her spinal-meningitis-inflicted sister, is utterly bone chilling. The tone of these scenes is quite faithful to those in the book, and the image of Zelda was one of the few that has ever kept me up at night. But as a treatment for a movie (at least without Romero), *Pet Sematary* should never have received the green light.

Sometimes, dead is better.

ORGAN (1996)
Dir. Kei Fujiwara

Organ starts off with a sweaty, bloody bang. From the get-go we can practically smell the funk of a city teeming with bodies both live and dead, baking in the ozone-less night. Grimy, grainy and grotesque, *Organ*'s first 20 minutes can be summed up in the image of a guy's face being pushed into the open wound of a cadaver.

Organ's opening set piece is 20 minutes of absolute gore-drenched chaos. It's boiling over with ugly, slimy characters all trying to kill each other, and apparently one or two of them are supposed to be cops, but it seems they are too deep undercover to try to stop the black market organ traders from doing their thing, or even from killing other undercover cops. All hell breaks loose, everybody struggles with everybody else. The bad guys inject Numata—the cop in charge—with something, and everybody except Numata and the head bad guys get splattered all over the place.

Numata subsequently suffers from hallucinatory flashbacks about his partner being skinned alive with acid and spirited away by the organ-sellers. He's soon kicked off the force and wanders around vomiting, cleaning toilets and hallucinating some more. Apparently there was something potent in that injection they gave him.

We then cut to a school for teenage girls in sailor suits, and we begin to harbor hope that *Organ* might just be a movie that has everything. Not long into this new scene, the camera leers at the violated corpse of a schoolgirl, blood streaked across her thighs. We cut to another student who walks into her biology professor's office to whine about how bad her grades are. She then tells him of a decidedly Japanese kinky nightmare she had and drools slime all over herself while, outside the window, a gardener watches it all as he's dry-humping a rake. Yes, we can now relax, it seems *Organ* will indeed be a movie with everything.

The professor takes the girl into the backroom of his office and injects her with something. Here we see that this is where Numata's partner has been shipped off to. His arms and legs have been amputated, and he is being repeatedly injected with the stuff as well. He is also, apparently, beginning to sprout a little forest of fungal greenery on his skin. The professor shoots himself up and hallucinates a woman emerging from a chrysalis. He then rapes the schoolgirl with a great deal of bloodshed, leaving us to wonder just what the hell he's packing down there.

The film now begins to swing back and forth between grim, sweaty reality and slimy drug-trip stuff. People are shooting up this stuff that the organ-sellers manufacture, and it is slowly turning them into vegetable-y things—cocoons, maybe? There are flashbacks in which the professor and the female organ-seller (who we discover are brother and sister) are mutilated by their mother in childhood; she castrates him and pokes out her eye. Hence, their obsession with harvesting organs, I guess. Maybe the drugs are made from the collected organs? Hell, I really can't tell much of what all's going on in this movie. I tried, really I did; I wanted to be complete in my analysis, because I think there is some twisted sense to be made of *Organ*…but I just don't have the patience today, and I kept getting distracted by the flying viscera.

Organ is slathered in blood, bile, shit, piss and snot. It's truly amazing. Every frame of this movie teems with violence. During the film's half-hour-long climax, every main character gets to be mortally wounded, moan in stoic agony, bleed like stuck pigs, and drag themselves off to *even more mortally* wound one of the other main characters. It's like *Hamlet*, *Naked Lunch* and *Tetsuo* thrown into a blender. Toss in a few extra gallons of grue into that blender, turn it up to high, and then take the lid off, and you've got the gist of this movie. Say what you want about it, but you cannot accuse it of failing to deliver the goods.

JUST BEFORE DAWN (1981)
Dir. Jeff Leiberman

I just watched this one on a 20-year-old VHS copy, recorded on SLP. There were previews for *Funeral Home*, *One-Armed Executioner* and *Gates of Hell* at the beginning. Man, that really took me back.

Just Before Dawn is an incredibly atmospheric flick that wears its influences on its sleeve, but definitely reinterprets timeworn formulas regarding *forest horror*. There's a brilliant opening set piece, accompanied by the cool, moody score of Brad Fidel (who would later compose the soundtrack for *The Terminator*), in which two drunken hunters take refuge in an abandoned, desecrated church. One of them props up the toppled pulpit and offers praise to a hole in the church roof. The drunkard at the pulpit offers thanks to the lord for making him such a good shot. He and his partner argue for a few minutes about who the better shot actually is, and then…a round, large, dark face peers down at them from the hole in the roof. Is it the lord? Well, for all intents and purposes it might as well be. And these poor drunken louts are sinners in the hands of an angry God. The lout doing the praising gets away, the other fellow is much less lucky. The Mountain Man appears before him, grunting and squealing like a boar. The hunter gets skewered by a serrated machete in a very unfortunate place. The sword of God has smote the first infidel.

The fascinating thing about this opening sequence is that it takes place in broad daylight. The deep woods and high mountains, the dense and claustrophobic foliage, is acting very nicely as a stand-in for night. And I'm sure the grainy, washed-out videotape I was watching didn't hurt matters either.

We now join up with the next batch of infidels, foolishly winding their way up into God's Country. A camper van trundles up the dirt road, carrying would-be mountain climbers inside: we've got Warren, the alpha male driver/leader/landowner; Connie, the timid, innocent one; Daniel the photography nerd; Megan the redheaded nymph, and Jonathan the practical joker. Stock slasher-movie characters, to be sure, but Lieberman actually throws us a bone here in *Dawn*, directing these kids as a true ensemble. They act and interact naturally, their dialogue isn't hokey, and we do find them likeable.

On their way up the mountain, the kids spy a lot of inbred families, and the number of twins in these families seems to be very high. Yes, it is safe to call this foreshadowing.

One of the hints Warren gives to his novice buddies about climbing: "The trick is to become part of the mountain. Try and find its soul." Little does he know that several folks up here have beaten them to it, in a much more committed fashion than he has ever dreamed of.

The kids come across forest ranger George Kennedy, who warns them to stay away from the place to which they're headed. Warren shows him the deed that makes it his rightful land. "That deed don't mean nothin'," Kennedy tells them, "That mountain can't read." It's a great line, and also a bit of foreshadowing, for he might as well be talking about the *living mountain* that will soon be stalking them. The kids ignore the ranger's warnings (of course) and head deeper and higher into the wooded mountain.

Along the way they are set upon by the surviving hunter from the opening sequence, who begs them to pick him up. The kids fail to do the Good Samaritan thing, and leave the man by the side of the road (you would've too, admit it). The hunter is heartbroken by the sight of the RV driving off without him…until he spies the Mountain Man jumping onto the back of their vehicle. The Bad Samaritans will receive the sword of God as well, it seems.

The cinematography in *Dawn* does a magnificent job of utterly dwarfing the kids against the mountain's cliffs and waterfalls. As the kids set up camp, they hear ethereal singing off by a waterfall, and decide to investigate. They spy a feral mountain girl named Mary-Cat and unwittingly scare her off.

The waterfall in *Dawn* becomes symbolic of the forceful desire of nature to keep to itself. It's designed to cleanse, to carry away all that which is not rooted into the earth. It's seductive and terrifying. Megan the nymph loves to frolic in it, but her boyfriend Jonathan can't swim, so he finds it a bit overwhelming. Always the waterfall is an imposing, omnipresent, godlike force that cannot be ignored. And when Megan's back is turned on the waterfall, that's when the Mountain Man fades in from behind it and wades out in front of it, slipping under the water to "play" with Megan—feeling her up a bit before letting her go. This scene foreshadows another image in the film, in which Warren is standing in the river with a huge fish he caught barehanded. With much begging from Connie, Warren lets the fish go. Same principle here: catch and release. The Mountain Man is a good sport at first.

But once night falls, it all becomes a different story. The kids are hitting the bottle a little aggressively, and they've got some loud New Wave music blasting out into

Constance (Deborah Benson) deals with an inbred mountain man in *Just Before Dawn*.

the night air. Both the drink and the pounding beat begin to exhibit their influence on the campers—even the sweet, repressed Connie. She gets up and starts to dance, and her moves become less and less inhibited until she is grinding against her boyfriend. Everyone is surrendering to his or her primordial nature. The whole thing seems liable to escalate into an orgy, until a couple of shotgun blasts split the night. The father and mother (who is also the sister) of the feral girl warn the campers that they've raised the devil, and demand that they leave immediately. Indeed, the kids have raised something primordial. They're getting deep into inner nature, raising their own inner ids, and they've completely pissed off the Mountain Man with all the noise.

But have they raised the devil, really? What exactly have they awakened within themselves and within the woods?

Jeff Leiberman is—dammit, I'll say it—positively Hitchcockian in the way he manipulates the viewer via his set pieces. Particularly in the second church scene, where Dan and Megan are shooting pictures in the graveyard outside—sexy, kinda necro pictures. Dan realizes he left his glasses inside the church, thus they become a Hitchcock-style MacGuffin. Dan sees a blurry, shadowy figure approaching them, and assumes it must be Jonathan. They decide to make him jealous by getting all friendly-like in front of him. The shadowy figure approaches the two. "It's working," Dan says, "He looks really pissed."

And of course, it turns out that the blurry figure is not Jonathan. Dan gets skewered, Megan runs into the church, looking out the window to keep an eye on Mountain Man. It's not her fault; there was no way she could've known that Mountain Man had a twin, much less that he's in the church, standing right behind her. No way she could've guessed that...unless, of course, she had been paying more attention to her surroundings at the beginning of the film, heh heh heh.

Last survivors Warren and Connie are out searching for their friends when they stumble upon the half-breed house. As they approach the front door, all nature sounds stop, as if scared of them. The family warns them off the mountain one last time.

And now, it's night. Warren and Connie are alone, harboring only the barest hope that Dan or Megan might come back. They are nearly impossible to see in the grainy, wooded night, and, miracle of miracles, we identify with them. We believe in them, and we are scared for them. When Warren makes the decision to try to find Jonathan's corpse so he can fish the keys to the camper (another MacGuffin) from its pockets, we do not feel like yelling, "Retard!" at the screen. We know that it's their only chance to survive. He tells Connie that if he gets lost or needs help, he will blow on Jonathan's hunter's whistle (hello, MacGuffin). And as he ventures off into the dark, the dark becomes darker than ever.

In an agonizing set piece involving lantern light against virtually complete darkness, Warren finds Jonathan's body. It's been moved, and the whistle has been *re*moved. Meanwhile, back at the camp, Connie hears the sound of…you guessed it. She gets up to investigate, calls out for Warren, and Fat Boy is now chasing after Connie through the brush, relentlessly taunting her with the whistle. She climbs a tree for refuge, and he mercilessly hacks it down with his machete. But before he can do her in, Mountain Man is brought down by Ranger George Kennedy's shotgun.

By this time, Warren has lost most of his cool. He is gibbering in denial about the fact that Dan and Megan are dead. He is not much comfort to Connie as they prepare to leave their campsite and get the hell out of there. And once Mountain Man Two makes his appearance, Warren receives a machete wound to the stomach and is rendered pretty much ineffectual.

Connie now has to fend for herself; the girl who "couldn't even pick up a knife" before is now going against Mountain Man Two *mano-a-mano*. And a stellar job she does of it; she forces her arm down Mountain Man's throat all the way up to the elbow until he stops breathing. She is now queen of the mountain. At the film's conclusion, she can only communicate in grunts and growls; Warren only in wounded bleats. They have definitely become part of the mountain now, and as the sun rises over the trees and the credits roll, we doubt they will ever leave.

In his rewrite of Mark Arywitz' screenplay, Leiberman took out all the obvious religious underpinnings, but they're still definitely there under the surface. The Mountain Twins seem to live in the abandoned church—the house of God. They are certainly forces of nature: symbols of the mountain itself. And in their eyes, they are doing the Old Testament Lord's work: killing heathens and sinners.

In the outdoor dance party sequence, the inbred family believes that the nubile teens have awakened the devil, symbolized both in their carnality and in the two Mountain Twins. But it was perhaps the location of the woods themselves—nature unbridled—that brought out this lust in these kids, not just the evil music. In their orgiastic dancing, the campers were losing their fear of nature—learning to become one with it, even. Possibly the first step on the road to loving mother earth, only to be mowed down by Old-Testament–style fear and fundamentalism. These kids, these nymphs, innocent in their revelry, become nothing more than the blood of the lamb for the sword of God. Even the survivors are very drastically changed. Innocence has been sacrificed to quell God's wrath.

PREY (ALIEN PREY) (1978)
Dir. Norman J. Warren

I remember seeing the box for this one when I was a kid. The front cover gave away the ending—naked guy with a snout and black eyes eating the throat of a naked woman. It disturbed and mesmerized me. Today I've rented a copy from that very same pressing. In fact, I'm not sure it ever got reprinted.

An alien lands in the England countryside, killing a guy named Anderson and taking on his likeness. He immediately shacks up with Jo and Ann, a couple of lesbian cuties. Jo's an icy bitch with a jealous streak and a switchblade; Ann is seemingly nicer, but viciously teases Jo that she wants to take other lovers. It's hard to tell whose behavior inspired whose.

Anyway, "Anders Anderson" pops into this already tense dynamic, and hilarity ensues. The trio paces the floors of the house and back porch, struggling for dominance. In its minimalism, *Prey* feels like a stage play. There are only three sets, three characters to speak of, tons of dialogue and bizarre situations.

The girls are vegetarians, domestic to the point of agoraphobia, and hysterically bitter. Anderson is a carnivore, freely hunting when the urge takes him. He's an alien, but a lot more at home in the eat-or-be-eaten ecosystem than the earthling girls are. When he hunts, his face transforms into something kind of cougar-like. Sex and killing are considered one and the same in *Prey*, and so Anderson can be seen as taking multiple "partners," whereas Ann is only "taken" by Jo. Anderson is a hedonist, as Ann wishes she could be. Instead, she's coerced into the veggie domesticity thing; a bird caged in her own house. This is rather obviously symbolized by the, well, caged bird in the back yard, which Anders eyes hungrily every five minutes or so.

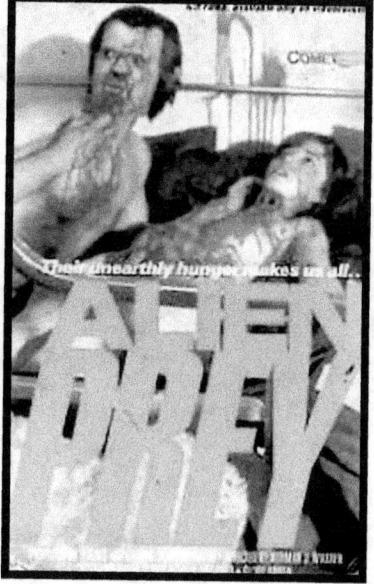

The sex/hunting parallel is not exactly subtle; when Jo and Ann have sex, Ann screams as though she's being killed. When Anderson hunts and kills a fox that Jo presumes was responsible for killing her chickens, she tries to maintain dominance by dressing him in drag at the celebratory party that night. The descent into animalism has begun for the girls; not only are they celebrating the death of the fox ("A memorial to something that tried to harm us. Now we get to eat it"), but Jo and Anderson are battling for position of alpha-male. At one point Ann leaves them alone to dance together, and they circle each other like animals about to go for each other's throats. The party climaxes with a game of hide-and-seek, in which Jo elects to be "it." She immediately finds Ann and Anderson hiding in a closet together (she's a closet heterosexual?), and tags Anderson it. He hunts the girls down by smelling them.

When Jo finds the fox carcass half-eaten in a garbage can, her suspicions of Anderson not being what he seems are confirmed. And he is only too good at being a

hunter; he hides the fox before Jo can show it to Ann, making her look even more hysterical than she really is. Jo is trapped. Ann tells her she's going to leave with Anderson, and Jo immediately storms off to begin literally digging Ann's grave. And here Anderson moves in for the kill. He beds Ann, and bites her throat out mid-coitus. Jo catches him in the act, and is chased into the very grave she had just dug moments before. Anderson radios his mother ship that planet earth is more than weak enough for a hostile takeover.

Made in 1979, *Alien Prey* asserted the notion that men and women are from different planets long before that whole "Mars and Venus" thing became fashionable.

Sorry; I couldn't resist. Hey, stop groaning. At least I didn't say, "Earth girls are easy."

Chapter Six: The Bottom

Chapter Five explored the lowest shelf in the chasm of cinematic taboo; we've dealt with cannibalism, ultraviolent gore, torture, rape and the like. But it's time to step off this last ledge, go down to the bottom, and observe the pale, bug-eyed films that feed there.

These are the films that revel in effects rather than causes—one of them is appropriately named *Aftermath*. No surprise, then, that the most common subject that pops up in the bottom-feeding films is necrophilia. It is perhaps the deepest, darkest taboo in the collective unconscious. The filmmakers who delve into this subject are well aware of its taboo power, for they all seem to dive into it with a gusto that's almost unnatural, each film trying to be the definitive one on the subject, and therefore the most hardcore.

I've decided to tack the bottom-feeder films after the Visceral section rather than the Crap section, though arguments could be made for putting them there as well. These films are certainly not out to win any awards at Cannes, but neither are they trying merely to fleece the viewer of his/her money. No, these flicks are out to *earn* their status as exploitation, as the acme of sleaze. They want your respect, and they want to be remembered.

NEKROMANTIK (1987)
SCHRAMM (1993)
Dir. Jorg Buttgereit

Jorg Buttgereit's films revel in the duality of sex and death, of art and exploitation, and his results have provoked some of the most violently mixed reactions from audiences thus far. He went so far with his imagery that *Nekromantik*, his breakout film, was called "the first erotic film for necrophiles" by John Waters. It's the story of a young man who works for a crime scene cleanup crew, who tries to keep his girlfriend happy by bringing body parts home for the two of them to play with, but she never seems to be satisfied. When he brings home a corpse, she takes more interest in it than in him.

Artsy touches abound in *Nekromantik*, but they are so blunt and heavy-handed that they practically become exploitative themselves. No symbolism is left to the imagination here. I personally "enjoyed" *Nekromantik* as much as I could, and saw the makings of a beyond-decent filmmaker in Buttgereit. The one scene that proved to me that he was actually able to *direct* as well as dream up the most disgusting spectacles imaginable, was the movie theatre scene:

Rob, our hero, whose woman has just left him for—and with—the aforementioned rotting corpse that was sharing their bed, decides to take in a movie. It's a terrible slasher film in which a blonde bimbo in a miniskirt is chased by a guy with a stocking over his head. The bimbo finds a bunch of dead bodies, screams a lot, and runs from Mr. Slasher. Eventually, Mr. Slasher catches her.

Next thing we see, he has her, arms tied above her head, teasing her with his knife, making her hold it between her teeth as he undresses her. This scene is shot in extremely intimate close-up, and the actress has suddenly become rather adept at showing emotion. She seems to enjoy, or at least to have surrendered to, the inevitability of what's happening. The look on her face is decidedly sexy. We cut back to the audience, comprised of couples except for Rob the necrophile, and they are snuggling closer together, nuzzling and kissing each other as the slasher cuts up the bimbo's breasts and she begins to scream. This scene marks the first time Buttgereit actually achieves a modicum of eroticism, and it is indeed uncomfortable, perhaps nailing the whole "intimacy between killer and victim" thing better than Argento ever has.

If Buttgereit had wanted to make us *truly* uncomfortable, he perhaps would have tried to achieve some kind of real eroticism with Rob and his girlfriend's acts. Don't ask me how one would achieve this in a love scene with a decomposing body, but that *is* the whole raison d'etre behind *Nekromantik*, isn't it? Perhaps there *is* true eroticism in it, and I can't see it because I'm not into that sort of thing, but I doubt it. Buttgereit plays the slimy ménage a trois to the hilt for shock value, and it works like a champ. The corpse is obviously where a vast majority of the film's effects budget went, and it's convincing enough to put us off our lunch. I'm actually a tad relieved that there wasn't enough money to convincingly pull off the blood-spurting penis at the film's end; it looks pretty ridiculous. But despite the film's subject matter, it's well made enough for us to want to see it through, and that's quite a testament to Buttgereit's potential.

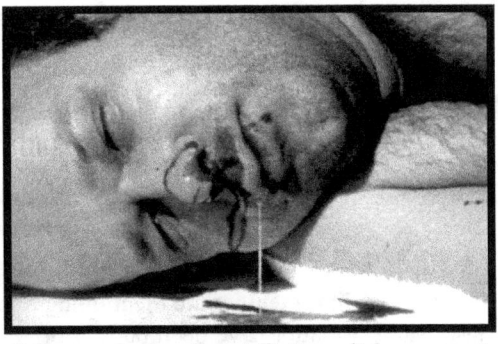

Schramm is the closest Buttgereit has come to sublime.

His last film, *Schramm*, was perhaps the closest he ever came to sublime. *Schramm* is a quiet, enigmatic little movie, but only in comparison to the outrageousness of the *Nekro* flicks. Buttgereit still manages to treat us to many heartwarming sights of the title character's pastimes, including but not limited to: fucking an inflatable female torso (no arms, legs or head); jerking off in front of his prostitute neighbor (whom he has drugged, stripped and photographed); prepping the bodies of his victims to be fucked (Jehovah's Witnesses, no less); and nailing his dick to a table (and this dick is a bit more convincing than the one in *Nekromantik*).

But Buttgereit also shows remarkable improvement at handling a camera, editing, and creating genuine, believable characters here. We actually do sort of accept the protagonist as such, though it's probably going too far to say we identify with or like him. We do grow to like his neighbor, though. Monika M. plays the self-destructive hooker with quiet vulnerability; it almost seems that she likes and is coming on to Schramm, but it later becomes apparent that she is just a bit desperate, that she needs someone to help protect her from herself, and that he is simply handy enough. She asks him to drive her to a couple of her appointments, and on the one day she needs him most, he becomes indisposed: while painting over a little blood splatter on his wall, he falls off his stepladder, and accidentally kills himself.

This bit of the film is shown at the beginning, and the fragmented narrative that follows seems to be his life, or at least the last week of it, flashing before his eyes, mixed in with a couple of ghastly hallucinations. Things end up back where they started, with the hooker knocking on Schramm's door, waiting for him to answer, and eventually, and resignedly, leaving to meet her appointment alone.

Inside his apartment, Schramm makes his exit from this world as she makes her exit from his front door. He apparently goes to some cockeyed version of heaven, and meets the Savior (played by Buttgereit), who whacks him upside the head. He ain't getting into heaven, this scene tells us, and perhaps as a sort of extra punishment (if the final shot of the film can still be linked to Schramm's perspective), he is allowed to see the last death he inadvertently caused—his hooker friend, without his vigilance, at the mercy of some not very nice clients.

Schramm is interesting as hell, and surprisingly sophisticated for all its sleaziness. It boasts a narrative that messed with the chronology of events before *Pulp Fiction* or *Memento* came along, its camerawork dazzles like the work of a Skid Row Barry Sonnenfeld (read: Sam Raimi), and the characters are quite fleshed out. Schramm was certainly a high note for Buttgereit to go out on, and it makes one wonder what might have happened had he kept going.

"BOTTOM DAY"

You might remember me mentioning a few films that, because of their incredibly nasty subject matter, I've been putting off watching for quite a while, because I was never really in the mood to see them. I realize that I probably never will be in the mood, and should just get them all out of the way as soon as possible.

So, I've decided that tomorrow will be Bottom Day for me. I'm going to rent them all, and watch them in one sitting. As these are not films in which I am expecting to find any kind of real subtext, I'm not going to write about them in the same way I'm tackling the other films in this book. Rather, I think it'll be more interesting to just sort of write about them stream-of-consciousness as they're onscreen, making notes on both the films and my mental state as the day wears on.

Funny that two of these films were made by Aristede Massacessi, or Joe D'Amato, as he is also known. Believe it or not, Movie Madness—one of the hippest video stores in the world—doesn't have *Porno Holocaust* at the time of this writing, so I'm going to have to settle for *Anthropophagus* and *Beyond The Darkness*.

So. Onward. And downward.

FILM NUMBER ONE: *BUIO OMEGA (BEYOND THE DARKNESS)* (1979)
Dir. Aristide Massacessi

Our hero Frank is a taxidermist. His girlfriend Anna is dying in the hospital. She wants makeup. A sort of taxidermy for the living (or dying, in this case). Frank and girlfriend kiss as she dies. Planting of the necrophilia seed, if it wasn't already there.

Iris, Frank's housekeeper, puts voodoo curse on girlfriend. Manipulation, surrogate mother. Apparently he's got a thing for his dead mother.

He breaks into the funeral parlor, and some guy sees him injecting formaldehyde into Anna's corpse.

After he steals her body from the graveyard, he encounters cops and a stoner hitchhiker. I don't think these are supposed to symbolize much; merely to act as obstacles for Frank, make us want him to get away, establish him as protagonist. Hitchhiker passes out in his car; he takes her back to his place.

Frank rips out nails of hitchhiker while she's alive; Iris paints nails of dead Anna. Duality, Iris and Frank as polar opposites.

The guy from the funeral parlor comes calling to Frank's house, posing, I guess, as a "baboon collector," asking Frank about his taxidermy.

Aah, the hitchhiker gets an acid bath. I saw this on *The Sopranos*.

Wait a second. So nobody embalmed Anna before she was buried? Plot hole. Major plot hole. Suspension of disbelief is totally blown for me now, ha ha.

Iris eats; Frank vomits. Another example of opposite behavior in the two.

Okay, so they've shown virtually everything else, but they can't show Iris jerking Frank off in front of his dead girlfriend? Not that I'm complaining.

The movie is surprisingly well made. Lots of soft focus, like *The Story of O* or something. Goblin music is great.

Victims seem to be drawn to Frank by fate. Hitchhiker practically forces herself into his car; female jogger injures herself in front of him. Maybe he's just a very lucky guy.

Wow, they got a dolly track and everything for this movie. A high class affair all the way. Oh yeah, and the zoom-in on the jogger's nipple while she burns up in the oven, very tasteful.

Is Iris wearing Frank's mother's clothing?

Iris and Frank's engagement dinner looked kind of like the dinner scene in *Freaks*.

Y'know, I'd heard this was a movie about necrophilia; is D'Amato showing some restraint in that department?

The villa Frank and Iris live in really is remarkably beautiful. And the whole movie looks like it was shot with a wide-angle lens.

Were any of Iris' friends real? Perhaps only she and Frank could see them? Iris never leaves the house, how could she have any friends?

Okay, he just smooched Anna's corpse; that's something, I guess.

An old lady passes by Frank and Iris on the street, muttering some bizarro death poem. Was she the voodoo lady from the beginning?

The climax is actually pretty interesting. Anna's twin sister Eleanor sneaks into Frank's house, looking for evidence of grave robbing. Sister as doppelganger, nice use of light and dark—reminds me of *Homicidal*.

Iris and Frank battle it out at the end here. Holy shit, she stabbed him in the dick!

The two pairs of opposites (Frank and Iris, Anna and her sister Eleanor) form a cross? No, that's stupid; never mind.

Great last scene: the sister waking up in the coffin screaming bloody murder. That's a memorable fucking shot, actually. I feel dirty, but not in the way I was expecting; it's well made enough to draw you in a bit, and that's actually the most disturbing aspect of it. This is the guy who made the zombie porno movie? Maybe I actually oughtta track that down.

FILM NUMBER TWO: *LUCKER THE NECROPHAGUS* (1986)
Dir. Johan Vandewoestijne

. Hospital corridor is kinda *Suspiria-y*. Here's this necro-rapist-killer guy, in a hospital, under heavy sedation supposedly. Inexplicably (but obviously), he wakes up. The nurse and her boyfriend are toast, of course.

Can't tell if this was shot on video or not; the VHS transfer is so bad.

Weird comedown from *Darkness*. Completely artless.

Lucker skewers the boyfriend. The screwdriver handle protrudes from his eye socket like a cock.

Looks like grainy 16mm transferred to video. And copied many, many times.

Um, I guess he killed the nurse…somehow. By lethargically knocking her head against the window of the car several times, I guess? Did I miss something?

Now there's a blue tint over everything as he humps her corpse. Was this intentional? I wouldn't be surprised either way.

Lucker now walks. And walks and walks and walks. The music sounds like Carpenter. No one will be seated during the infamous "walking scene." Man, can this guy walk. Oh—now he pulls out a knife to reassure us that something is going to happen eventually.

The TV news reports that Lucker has escaped, that Kathy, one of his past victims, was the only one who survived his attack, and even graciously reports where she lives! Jeez, the news is helpful.

Now the music sounds like Tangerine Dream.

He stalks a girl into an underground parking lot and disembowels her. At least the intestines aren't that realistic.

He follows a slutty girl to a club—he reminds her of the one that got away, maybe?

She's apparently turned on by freako pasty dudes who rake their nails across their faces. Ah, of course, she's a hooker.

I think maybe this movie was edited on a camcorder.

My, she's a sassy whore. She doesn't like being called "babe," buster.

Lucker beats the crap out of her drug dealer and rubs salt into his wounds. Just like *Grand Theft Auto*.

This hooker chick is doomed. She conveniently tells him how deserted her apartment building is, so no one can hear loud screaming.

Now everything's blue again. He cuffs her to the bed and stabs her in the throat…and seems to fuck her with the knife? Jeez, the sounds she makes. Just like in *GTA*.

Exposition from Lucker's psychiatrist: He can't love another human being, so he has to resort to this shit. Thanks, Doc.

Hm, I think the filmic quality of *Darkness* made it far more disturbing than this one. This is sleazy as hell, but impossible to take seriously. Not that I don't feel a *little* nauseous.

He's spent a week waiting for his hooker to rot sufficiently. Okay, here we go. He rubs the rot off her carcass and licks his fingers clean. Can you do this in *GTA*?

Hm. Artless, but effective, this "love scene." I am reminded of Bill Hicks talking about hotel room porno: "That's a hairy, bobbin' man-ass; I don't know who that's for."

Now she appears to be in garbage bags. He strangles neighbor who tries to help him carry bags down to the basement.

Two of the hooker's friends come to check on her; he kills one and kidnaps the other, tying her arms to an overhead pipe in the basement. He rubs dead hooker's severed head in her face, watches her struggle and scream. As predicted, I'm having a hard time finding subtext in this.

So finally he finds Kathy, the girl that got away from him that one time. He ties her to a chair in the basement, facing the other girl. They both won't stop screaming, so he disembowels the girl tied to the pipe.

Kathy stabs Lucker with a hidden knife, and the chase is on. Bunch of basement corridors with locked doors. Where the hell are we?

She could run for the staircase, but instead opts to hide under it, remaining *in the pit*, as it were. But she pushes Lucker down an elevator shaft, into an even deeper pit. *There's* some symbolism, maybe. But wait; aren't they already in the basement? Maybe the elevator goes to the center of the earth or something.

FILM NUMBER THREE: *MANIAC* (1980)
Dir. William Lustig

Okay, I'm in a 42nd Street grindhouse in 1980. The house lights go down. A roach skitters across my popcorn-eating hand. The movie begins.

Actually, I'm in my apartment and the all too rare Oregon sun is shining down outside, a sight I miss sorely. Alas, to said heavenly orb my shade is drawn, so that I might imagine I'm watching *Maniac* in Times Square back in the day. That is how dedicated a film fan I am. You're welcome.

Pretty slick going so far. Nice red credits and a Goblin-esque score. A poor doomed hooker (déjà vu) needs "one last trick to pay the rent." Joe Spinell offers to help her out. Spinell's pretty convincing as a sleaze-ass.

Ah, the golden days when hookers kissed on the mouth. Why oh why wasn't I of legal age back then?

What a face this guy has. The last thing the poor hooker sees is Spinell leering down at her. Almost worse than being strangled and scalped.

Helicopter shot over freeway as Spinell (don't know his character's name yet) prowls the streets in his car. Then the sound of a helicopter on the soundtrack. Perhaps suggesting that the perspective comes from a real helicopter? Police chopper or something? Like William Lustig is saying, "We wouldn't pull no fancy shots with cranes or helicopters just to be all cinematic-like." Or maybe I'm reaching. Ya think?

He kills a couple that are making out in a car. The guy is played by Tom Savini. Spinell blasts his head off with a shotgun. Savini's exploding head is one of the foulest things I've ever seen. Nice job, Tom.

The scene where Spinell stops the kid in the park, putting his hands on the kid's shoulders, is straight outta *Halloween*. Sheesh, and so is the music for the scene when Spinell is chasing a girl through the subway tunnel! And the way Maniac casually walks after the girl, very reminiscent of Michael Myers. I am reminded of *The People Versus Larry Flynt* where Woody Harrelson says, "Gentleman, *Playboy* is lying to you." Lustig is Flynt, *Halloween* is *Playboy*, and *Maniac* is *Hustler*. Damn, though, the end of this scene, where he kills the girl in the bathroom, is very intense and real. *Maniac* is as well made as *Beyond the Darkness*, but almost as sick as *Lucker*. It's kind of making me itch.

Frank Zito is the maniac's name; okay. He meets up with a beautiful female photographer. Her place is a reverse polarity of his…there are pictures everywhere, just like the room in which he lives. They engage in a debate about preserving beauty. They are yin and yang. Does he recognize this? Is she his ticket to salvation? Perhaps.

He stalks a model from the photographer's shoot, and ambushes her in her apartment. Ties her to the bed. She gets to struggle a bit while he explains to her (and us) that he was neglected by his prostitute mother when he was a kid. This whole scene is *extremely* fucking dark. He's projecting his mother onto this bound and gagged model. He mounts her, stabs her intimately (and phallically), then he dry-humps her corpse. So this is quite a combo: Oedipal-necrophile-surrogate-phallus-rape.

Now, back at his place, he plays with toys, listens to a music box, and shoots at the walls. Kind of Elvis meets Michael Jackson.

The photographer chick likes Zito a little too much. Maybe it's true after all that beautiful women are actually shy and like a man who takes initiative?

Jesus, I guess so! She even accompanies him to a graveyard at night!

Okay, so in your typical drama, the "hero" has a choice to make when offered redemption. Did he really have a chance to make this choice? I don't think so; he's a full-blown whack-job.

Regardless, here come his demons to rip him to pieces. Jesus, that's foul.

It's an incredibly depressing and confrontational movie, but I can't necessarily call it pandering. It wallows in its subject matter, like *Henry: Portrait of a Serial Killer*, although of course it's not quite as well made. But it's better than an exploitation film like this has a right to be, and that almost makes it worse.

FILM NUMBER FOUR: *ANTHROPOHAGUS (THE GRIM REAPER)* (1980)
Dir. Aristide Massacessi

The cat just took a fresh dump in the litter box, so it's a nice olfactory accompaniment to the beginning of Massacessi/D'Amato's *Anthropophagus*, I'd reckon. This film is infamous for the scene where the villain eats a fetus freshly ripped from its mother's womb; of course I had to save it for last.

We open with a chick swimming naked in the ocean. And the killer's under the water, like *Jaws*?

There's Tisa Farrow from *Zombie*, with a boatload of Greek island tourists. And here's a nice vomit scene right out of the gate. I imagine D'Amato wanted to set the tone for us.

It sounds like it was dubbed in a racquetball court.

This is the same guy who made *Beyond the Darkness*? The difference is amazing: crappily shot, shittily dubbed, and very boring. Far too much exposition from such a notorious master of bad taste.

Holy shit! Here we go! Chick with a knife, popping out of a barrel of wine and screaming. That's a pretty impressive image, slightly reminiscent of the last shot in *Darkness*.

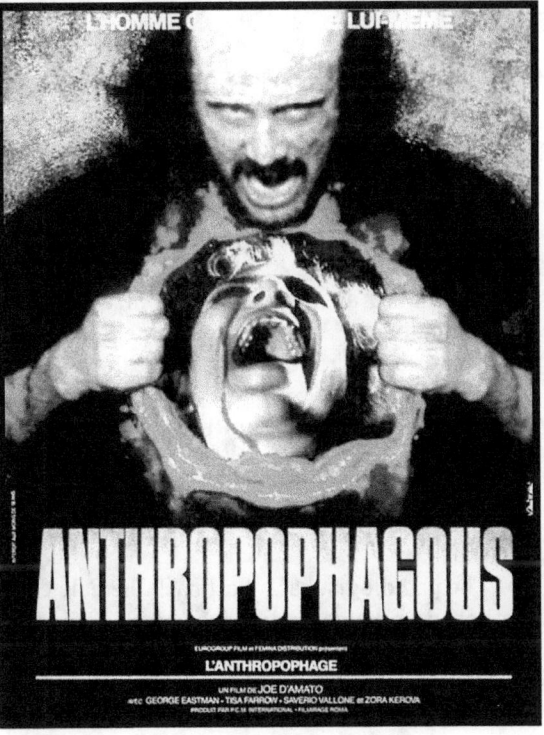

Well, you know, it has moments. Sometimes just the notion of the guy lurking about does generate tension. And when he shows up, he is a pretty creepy-looking bastard. But then the crappy music, dubbing or editing destroys any hope of sustaining atmosphere.

I have a feeling this beautiful blind English girl with the huge gray eyes (the girl from the aforementioned wine barrel) is going to die horribly. She's just too sympathetic and too beautiful.

Okay, maybe the graininess of the videotape I'm watching this on made the fetus-eating scene a little easier to digest (no pun inten...oh, fuck it), but it's still pretty fucked up that he did it in front of the dying father.

The English blind cutie gets it horribly. Damn, I'm good.

He gets stabbed in the belly. His intestines come slithering out here at the end. Ah, memories of *Darkness'* embalming scene. And he *eats his own guts.* The end.

Okay, well, that was…hmm. A few neat moments, a lot of shitty pacing, not enough gore to justify its infamy. Or am I just getting jaded? But hell: for both of the scenes that this movie is notorious for, the killer barely puts the fetus and the intestines in his mouth, and then the camera cuts away. I'm fairly sure this wasn't a cut version; I just think these scenes play better in the mind when one reads about them in *Horror Holocaust.*

But damned if some of the images from this movie aren't going to be in my head for a while. Mainly of the killer's face and the gorgeous doomed blind girl. Her and her death are gonna haunt me more than anything else in this movie, kinda like how watching Iris eat in *Beyond the Darkness* was sicker to me than its embalming scene. Are my priorities out of whack?

"BOTTOM DAY TWO"

As of last week, my relationship with my girlfriend of five years imploded. I've been drinking myself to sleep every night since then. I am currently on my way to drunk again. It is three in the afternoon. Let Bottom Day Two commence.

FILM NUMBER ONE: *AFTERMATH* (1994)
Dir. Nacho Cerda

Well, here we go: six minutes of opening credits and out comes the bone saw. A pathologist is alone in a morgue with a couple of corpses. I have a feeling hilarity is about to ensue.

I can't get over the notion that I've actually been waiting until this film's DVD release to see it. I just had to have it letterboxed and in five-point-fucking-one. Every sound is crystalline: those rib spreaders, the squishing of organs.

The pathologist washes the corpse's heart. Anubis. Oh. Wait, that's *weighing* the heart. Oh, whatever.

He shoves all the organs—even the brain—back into the gutted torso rather unceremoniously.

The scene at the beginning where the doctor handed the grieving couple the rosary (which obviously belonged to the deceased) sets up the idea driven home by the lack of reverence in the autopsy: Religion and ceremony are for the living, not the dead.

I'm gonna need more wine.

There was a tiny flicker of movement in the eyes of the second dead man. Does this imply that the pathologist is seeing him as a human being? Is it a shock for him to do so?

The pathologist has a flashback. Female corpse. The pathologist knows her? Was she linked to the second male corpse? Perhaps both the pathologist *and* the corpse? Love triangle?

The scissors he uses to cut away her underwear have an *extremely* phallic head on their tip. It goes without saying, it's so bloody obvious. Anyway.

The camera zooms into the drain of the autopsy table. *Vagina.*

Weighing of the brain. 1.203 lbs. Unless the scale is metric. Which it probably is. Never mind.

Again, the camera cuts away as he fucks her with the knife. Not that I'm complaining.

Oh. But to make up for it, here's a loving, lingering medium close up of him fondling her organs.

And the masturbation scene is also decidedly tasteful. He keeps it in his pants.

Holy fucking shit.

He fucks the dead girl while the camera's snapping away. *Love triangle.*

Nikon must've paid a fortune for the product placement.

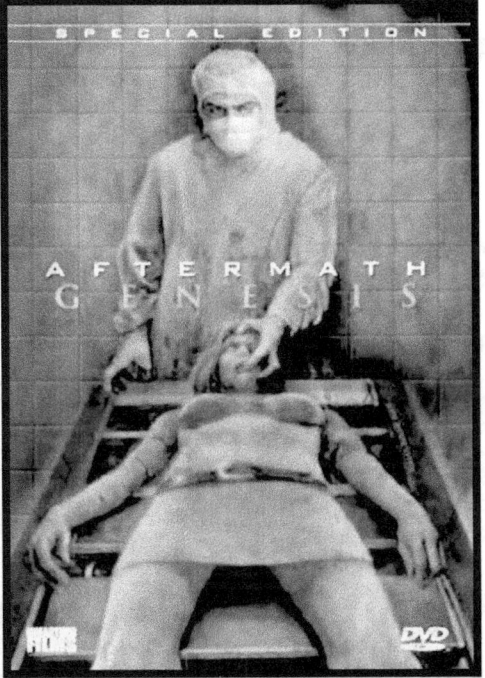

Her brain was on the scale the whole time. Did he not want her to have a brain while he had his way with her? Did he not want her to *remember* it? Or was that simply his idea of the perfect woman?

Bottle of booze. Faucet. Knife. Hose. The phallic symbols are winning out here in the end.

The kitchen where he feeds the heart to his dog (the same dog that gets splattered in the beginning of the film? Implying that he himself will learn the lesson of loss one day soon?) is all white, as are his pajamas. His house is as antiseptic as the morgue.

The female's name is listed as an obituary in the newspaper upon which the dog's dish is sitting. In death we are nothing but a name in a newspaper. A sex toy. Dog food.

FILM NUMBER TWO: *GENESIS* (1998)
Dir. Nacho Cerda

Same lead actor from *Aftermath*. Same character?

He's making a sculpture of his dead wife. Sculpture here is practically the same thing as the corpse in *Aftermath*: a three-dimensional representation of a soul. Sculpture begins to bleed. Sculptor begins to turn to clay. A bit heavy-handed, but it works.

The sculptor is always off-center in the film's framing. Very nice touch.

I can't get over how good this movie looks. It's as well photographed as anything I've seen.

Flashback. Car crash. For a split second, it's him in the wreck and her looking down at him. *Is he the dead one?* It would make sense—him being here in this solitary space! Limbo!

It's reminding me now of *Blind Beast*. The image of a person becoming a sculpture—surrender, dismemberment.

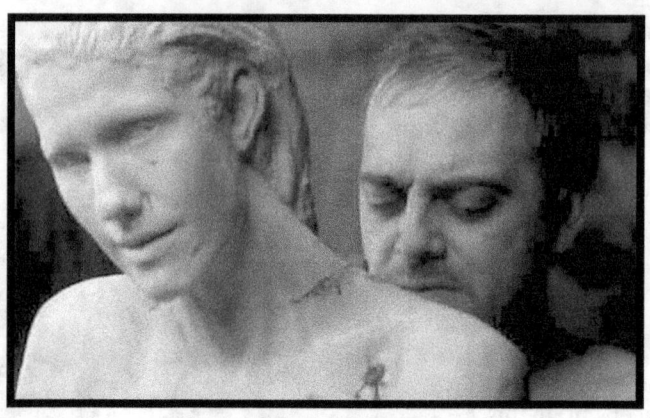
Genesis is beautifully filmed.

He gives everything to bring her to life. And by "bringing to life," I could mean giving her the strength to go on without him, if he is indeed the dead one. She becomes flesh; he becomes stone. God, I'm too fucking depressed for words now. I had to rent this fucking thing *today*.

Well, actually, yes, I suppose I did.

FILM NUMBER THREE: *LAST HOUSE ON DEAD END STREET* (1977)
Dir. Roger Watkins (credited as Victor Janos)

This is the Roger Watkins film I'd read about in <u>Sleazoid Express.</u> As I popped it in, I realized it's the Sun Video version, and is probably pretty drastically cut. Oh well.

Terry Hawkins, a pimp and drug dealer, is released from jail, intoning in voice-over about how he's going to repay all his "friends." He looks like a cross between Jack Black and a Bay City Roller.

Great line: "All that time gave me time to think."

Decent composition. Windows framed like guillotine blades. Flash-forwards of the horrors to come.

The absurdity of the dialogue is enhanced by the outrageously out-of-sync dubbing. Guy with a handlebar mustache babbling something about bananas and leather. What the fuck?

Terry says to him, "Nobody's interested in sex anymore." Great line. And this time I'm being serious.

Now the guy's talking about fucking a dead calf while the film shows us a cow being slaughtered. Jesus. The blood's jetting out like *Lone Wolf And Cub*, only it's real.

Two homely girls are talking themselves into being in Terry's new porno films. They are both terminally bored. This movie seems to take place in the same cinematic universe as Argento's *Tenebre* and *Opera*. Love and intimacy do not exist. People are looking for new kicks. Everyone's done it all.

A porn director is showing his producer his new "erotic art film." The producer hates it. The producer says, "This country's built on innovation." The porn industry is standing in for America here.

Terry drops in on the director's wife Nancy, who appears in her husband's movies. Terry tells her he's the mailman, and she sees that he's not, but lets him in anyway. *Just like in a porn movie.* And they immediately get to fucking. Well, there you go.

Several little tricks like this are used to imply that the line between movies and reality are blurred. And also throughout the film (especially toward the climax), the line is blurred between porn and snuff. They tie Nancy to a table and slowly cut her to pieces while keeping her conscious. The entrail removal scene I read about has been excised, except for the bits that were shown at the beginning.

Drills, branding irons, knives, deer hooves, tin snips, and cameras are the new phalluses. Not the most profound revelation ever made. The nihilism has more of an impact that any of the gore in this movie. It definitely feels like it was made by someone with a grudge against the porn industry, a taste for hard drugs and not much to lose.

FILM NUMBER FOUR: *FLOWER OF FLESH AND BLOOD* (1985)
Dir. Hideshi Hino

My first movie from the *Guinea Pig* series. Aw.

Cheapo cheapo video production. The stark, brittle quality of the video format makes this one feel more like a porno than any of the films I've watched today, which is actually more than a little unnerving.

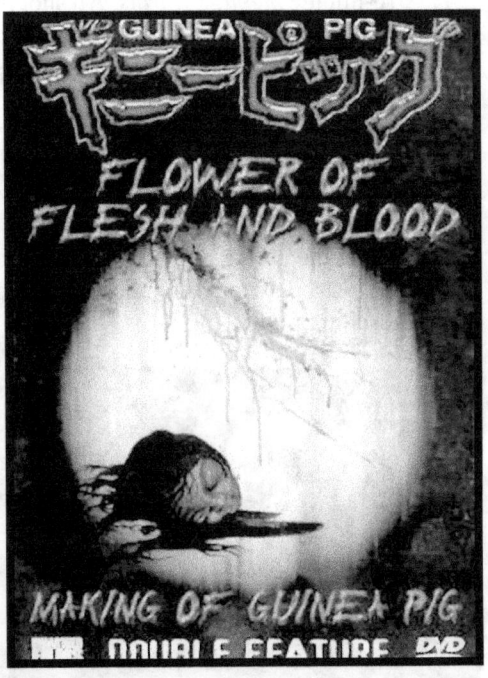

Guy chases and catches girl. She wakes up tied to a bed, with this guy in a medieval Japanese helmet sharpening a sickle a few feet away. He beheads a chicken above her, telling her, "This is your fate." I am already much more uncomfortable than I was while watching *Last House*, and I know the chicken wasn't real. Maybe because this one's panning out to be every bit as artless as I imagined it to be.

I can't help but think of Darth Vader when I look at this guy in the Samurai helmet. But then, *Star Wars* was based on *The Hidden Fortress*, so that makes some sort of sense, I guess. Darth looks into the camera and tells us that he is going to show us "the ideal of beauty" by shooting this girl up with opiates and cutting her up. He cuts off her hand. Looks like sweet and sour chicken in there. She doesn't seem to notice.

Out of all the films I've seen in both bottom-feeder festivals thus far, this is the only one I'm having problems with. Even though the girl I love broke my heart, I'm just not feeling this misogynistic. *Lucker The Necrophagus* was impossible to take seriously, but this one just has a skeezy tone to it. Trying to look like a snuff film for the sake of trying to look like a snuff film. Even though the limbs he's hacking off look a little bit rubbery, this one pulls off the sick vibe extremely well.

Jesus fucking Christ.

He guts her, beheads her, tongue-kisses the severed head. Spoons out her eyes and sucks on them. There is no point to this, other than to make death-metal fans slap each other on the back and say, "Dude!" Fuck this movie.

FILM NUMBER FIVE: *EROTIC NIGHTS OF THE LIVING DEAD* (1980)
Dir. Aristide Massacessi

We're back in Joe D'Amato territory. This isn't the one about the radioactive zombie that rapes women to death; it's D'Amato's *other* zombie porno movie. There's Luigi Montefiori from *Anthropophagus* getting it on with a nympho nurse right out of the gate. We're off to a wonderfully hilarious start. I'm so glad to be watching this after *Flower*. And shit, the nympho nurse is *hot*.

Ha! Dialogue! A story! This movie is so cute!

This is what I call a porno: bad sex puns, bad Tom Selleck mustaches, bad music. And the zoms are old school cheapo Italian zoms: wearing flimsy burial shrouds, with wet modeling clay stuck on their faces to pass for makeup. They just don't make 'em like this anymore.

A 10-minute *ménage-a-trois*. All shot in one take, with Joe's camera just bouncin' around in there, filling up the screen with pubic hair. We started off today with autopsies and disembowelments and corpses getting stabbed in the vagina. It accompanied my mood, I suppose. Now, as the sun sets and the bottle has been drained to dregs, it's nothing but naked, hairy '70s people rutting and getting their throats bitten out by cheap-ass Italian zombies. Suddenly I think it's all gonna be okay.

A girl squats down on a champagne bottle, performs a few up-and-down thrusts, and the cork pops inside her pussy. Does this mean that she *excited* the bottle? Or that she removed the cork with her vaginal muscles? 'Cause if it's the latter, that seems to imply she's strong enough to pop the head off a guy's dick, which doesn't sound like a sexual selling point.

Our hairy heroes arrive on some kind of Voodoo Island inhabited by zombies and a magical cat that apparently transforms into Laura Gemser. So basically this is the porno version of Fulci's *Zombie*.

Rather hot lesbian coupling on the shore here. Is this girl that's frolicking with Laura Gemser the nympho nurse from the beginning? I'm all confused.

Pretty slow going from that point up until the 1 hr 20 min mark. Now we've got some zombie carnage going on again. About time, too. It's almost like you can divide the movie into acts: act one is hairy sex, act two is tedious dialogue, and act three is—holy shit! She bit his dick off!

And finally, some ludicrous gut munching. And zombies rising out of graves that appear to be nothing more than a six-inch-deep layer of cat litter. Well, there *is* a cat running around on the island, so I suppose that makes sense.

A zom steals Luigi's rifle; a nod to *Dawn of the Dead?*

We go back full circle to the beginning, with Montefiori and the nympho nurse. It's a truly great, possessed ending: cackling, madcap sex. I'm suddenly in a really good mood. I realize the absurdity even as I write this, but for whatever reason, *this* is the movie that has made me a Joe D'Amato fan.

"THE BOTTOM LINE"

So. After this little cinematic spelunk, I suppose the question is: Do I feel I'm a better, more evolved person for having seen these films? Have I learned anything? Do I understand humanity any better than I did before?

Not really. But, in truth, I am asking myself questions I wasn't asking before. Mainly: What exactly is the root of the necrophiliac urge? Is it violent or sexual? Is it the ultimate violation—taking advantage of a body in the ultimate state of vulnerability, a body that cannot consent? Or is it truly, if morbidly, affectionate? Is it a manifestation of grief and mortal fear—a desperate attempt to beat death with the procreative act? An inability to let go of—and truly lose—the dead? I don't have the answers for these questions, and it is this uncertainty that poses another, darker question in me:

Do violence and sex have more in common at the root of it all—at the *bottom*—than we would like to believe? Is the line between sex and violence drawn only in the civilized mind? Is it all just *contact*, as far as the id is concerned?

Hell, don't ask me; I only watched these flicks because I have a book to write. And probably also to satisfy some subtly masochistic urge that lies within the mind of any horror buff. Going out of our way to make ourselves uncomfortable is, after all, the name of this game.

Mission accomplished.

Chapter Seven: Paranoid Horror

As I mentioned in the autobiographical segment of the book, home video has provided easy access to virtually the entire world of cinema, and at the same time, has killed off most of the social culture associated with horror films—drive-in theatres, grindhouses, midnight movies and the like. Throw in the advent of the Internet, not to mention delivery services for everything under the sun, and we're pretty much on our way to killing off *all* social culture.

Not only does your average Joe no longer have to leave the house, save to go to work (if that), but news and reality shows, from *World's Scariest Police Chases* to the forensics docu-drama *The New Detectives*, bombard us with images of a world populated by degenerates and psychopaths.

If one were paranoid (and who could blame ya?), one might assume that the powers that be were not only capitalizing on, but encouraging, agoraphobia. More and more Americans can work from home, or receive home schooling; they can communicate without ever having to speak to, or see, the other party involved.

Marketing techniques used by TV only drive this notion home a little further; the Fox network used to promote a lineup of its programming by calling it "Safe At Home Sunday," or some such thing. Fox, incidentally, is perhaps more earnest than any other network to present us with footage of our fellow humans behaving badly.

Hell, in my more paranoid moments, I think that xenophobia's boundaries of definition are getting more vague by the day. On *The New Detectives*, a majority of the homicides depicted are inter-familial. My girlfriend once remarked that *The New Detectives* "should be renamed *Women Who Poison Their Husbands*." "Fear of foreigners" could very likely, in a paranoid mind, extend to a parent, child, sibling or spouse. One no longer has to be a horror film fan to be inspired to ask the question, "Does anybody really know anyone?"

Every day the media brings us images of loved ones betraying, hurting, killing loved ones. One does not have to be a paranoid soul to question not only who to trust, but to wonder if we can trust our own hearts to properly judge anyone. This is the world we inhabit. And more and more of us are choosing to inhabit it behind locked doors, safe at home.

DAGON (2001)
Dir. Stuart Gordon

According to Darwin, life began and evolved in the sea. Slowly, select organisms began to adapt forms that facilitated their crawling out onto land.

Once on land, organisms began to move as far away from the ocean as possible. The creature that would become man began to deny his origin, to look away from the sea and up to the sky.

Religion, especially Christianity, painted water in a light almost as negative as fire. Fire became a symbol associated with the Devil and eternal suffering, earth became a symbol of original sin (be *in* the world but not *of* the world, they tell us), and of course, water had a knack for killing infidels: the great flood, the Red Sea, even Jesus' curing of a possessed man by driving his demons into the bodies of some nearby pigs, who were then compelled to drown themselves.

And that leaves us with only air, ether, the intangible. The realm of faith. The space where the Christian God lives. Our reward for accepting and having faith in him, we are told, is ascension into this intangible kingdom, into the ether, to live forever. On the bad side of the coin, it seems the surest way to earn this reward is to suffer on earth—to martyr yourself.

On the island of Imboca, a change has been made. The denizens of this island, save for one man named Ezequiel and one very special mother, have rejected their Christian trappings in favor of a new god. A god named Dagon. A god that seems to fulfill its promises more quickly and expediently than Jehovah.

In John Carpenter's *Halloween*, Laurie Strode relates a difference between the beliefs of two philosophers: "Costaine felt that fate was somehow related only to religion, whereas Samuels felt that, well, that fate was like a natural element, like earth, air, fire and water."

After waking from a recurring dream about a mermaid with sharp teeth, Paul snaps back into what is brand new reality for him. Paul and his girlfriend Barbara are vacationing in Spain, with their friends Howard and Vicki in a yacht. We quickly have their characters laid out for us: Paul is a very recent millionaire, uncomfortable with the money and its sudden appearance in his life. He cannot enjoy the moment, constantly worried about the future of his stock. He prefers to stay down below deck of the boat, away from the sun, sort of half underground and half

Barbara (Raquel Meroño) finds herself in a pagan nightmare in *Dagon*.

underwater (vague foreshadowing here). He is definitely in the world but not of it. His preoccupation with the future, with "programming" the "binary system" of life, almost removes him entirely *from* life; he might as well already be dead.

Barbara begs him to relax, to enjoy their vacation and their wealth, trying to plow him with a little oral sex, which he cannot concentrate on. Barbara storms off topside, while Paul follows nebbishly. Up here, we meet Howard and Vicki, both lying on the deck, working on their tans, obviously content to be rich, to enjoy their life. Lurking ominously on the shore behind them is the isle of Imboca.

Once Paul follows Barbara topside, he has joined in this mini-Pagan festival. Barbara throws Paul's laptop over the side and into the water—a last-ditch effort to lure Paul into the present. But somewhere down inside, Paul knows that the present is the last place he wants to be.

After these cute few minutes of banter between the foursome, the movie decides it's through fucking around, and the Imbocans butt in. The natives begin to sing in a strange tongue, and the singing seems to inspire the very elements themselves into action.

The elements take control in the form of a storm that seems to stream forth from the island itself, slamming the yacht into a reef. With Vicki trapped in the wreckage, Paul and Barbara row in a raft to shore, and try to appeal to the locals for help. It becomes quickly apparent that the Imbocans are a little different. They're a tad pasty, they don't seem to blink, and some of them have strangely altered features. They're evolving to better suit the water, you see. Barbara, Vicki and Howard soon disappear, and not long after, the entire town is hunting for Paul. From this point on, the film becomes a non-stop chase scene with very little relief, and a steadily mounting inevitability.

"Two possibilities" is a catch phrase Paul utters a lot during the movie, almost like a mantra. Almost as if he's trying to deny what his subconscious is certain of: that his arrival on the island was no accident, and that the certainty of his fate is so strong it's almost elemental.

Dagon feels very much like a nightmare, and every aspect of the production contributes to the overwhelming atmosphere of the film, which descends on the viewer like a black storm cloud. The direction, art and production design, makeup effects, editing and pacing are in full cooperation here, producing the most faithful-in-tone adaptation of a Lovecraft story I've yet seen. This is director Stuart Gordon's proudest hour, eclipsing *Re-Animator* or *From Beyond*, in the author's humble opinion. Fun as those movies were, they certainly didn't give one the creeps the way Lovecraft at his best does. *Dagon* brings the atmosphere in spades.

Brilliant tricks are employed to enhance frustration on the viewers' part and turn it into tension. Half the film is spoken in Spanish (or Gallego, a mutation of Spanish that the Imbocans speak among themselves), and no subtitles are provided. There is also very little music to speak of. For most of the film, the soundtrack is the steadily pounding rain, which becomes as teeth-grittingly reliable as Carpenter's percussive score for *Halloween*. 99% of the movie is shot with hand-held camera as well, which gives everything the immediacy of a documentary.

We're playing with a lot of fears here. There's the Christian fear that Darwin was right, that we evolved from the sea, and can evolve back *into* it if we so choose (of course, Paul never really has a choice, but once upon a time, the Imbocans did, and in choosing, sealed Paul's fate). We've also got the horror story of the local boy who made good and got out of the small town, only to be thrust back into the family business (a sort of twisted take on the Prodigal Son story). We're playing with the fear that any choice we make will bring us to one pre-destined fate, and that this fate may not at all be pleasant. And of course, we're in serious xenophobe territory.

The snake-handlers, the Mennonites, the Witnesses, those wacky Mormons, the Heaven's Gate comet-hoppers, whirling dervishes, and fundamentalists of any sort show us that there's a fine line between *cult* and *culture*. The Imbocans are a cult to the uninitiated, but a culture unto themselves. And they don't care what outsiders think of them. They're not out to proselytize, not out to convert anyone; they just wanna kill as many humans as necessary to please Dagon, sprout some gills and split.

When Paul and Ezequiel are captured, Ezequiel vehemently rejects Dagon. "I will die like a man," he says, before the Imbocans go to work on him. As they begin to peel his face from his skull, Paul tries to lead him in the Lord's Prayer. As the agony takes over and Ezequiel can only scream, Paul keeps going: "My cup runneth over, surely goodness and mercy will follow me all the days of my life," and as the butchers finish off the job, we wonder if any of the irony can be lost on Paul.

It would appear so. Paul fervently accepts the same fate—"Do it!" he screams—only to be saved by his long-lost sister (the mermaid from his dreams). It would seem that martyrdom is the only fate open to those holding onto human (read: Christian) ideals.

Though he tries to fight the Dagonites with fire (God's wrath), he is quickly subdued, and Barbara plunges into the water, to be consumed by the dark denizen that lives in it. And, as it was Paul's fate to be ushered back into the life his mother tried to save him from, perhaps it was also Barbara's fate to be drawn to him, and ultimately betrayed (he breaks his promise to kill her if she were to meet Vicki's fate) by him and martyred by the Imbocans. Paul makes one last attempt to choose his fate—self-immolation (choosing fire over water)—only to be "rescued" one more time by his tentacled sister. At the end of this blood-drenched road, this road of sorrow and suicide, the only choice Paul has is to succumb. Once submerged in the water, his flames extinguished and his gills kicking in, he resigns himself to his fate and swims off with his mer-lady.

At the end of the day, it appears to be nothing particularly supernatural afoot; it's just biology beyond our comprehension. A sort of Cronenbergian "new flesh." With no moral impositions upon all of this, it does sort of seem like a biblical description of heaven; dying, being reborn into new skin, and ending up where you belonged the whole time. Back in the water that gave you life.

Perhaps, as the man said, "Hell ain't a bad place to be."

DEAD AND BURIED (1980)
Dir. Gary Sherman

Potter-n: *craftsman, artisan, one who woks in clay*
Bluff-n: *lie*

Dead and Buried is one of those magic exploitation films; those ponies prancing proudly through Shit Mountain, but at the end of the day, it belongs here, in my opinion, rather than the Crap section. Like *Christmas Evil, Martin, Alone in the Dark* and others, it's that too-rare gore flick that doesn't underestimate its audience's capacity for an original story. It's a sort-of riff on H.P. Lovecraft's *The Shadow Over Innsmouth,* and a morbid satire of the American fetish for nostalgia.

Potter's Bluff is one of those quaint little seaside towns that the evil hand of Progress seems to have passed over. Suspended in time, Potter's Bluff carries on with its own little Norman Rockwell way of life. And the residents of Potter's Bluff are intent not only on preserving their town, but also on keeping their town to themselves—tourists are being quite nastily murdered by the townsfolk. Dan, the local sheriff, can't make heads or tails of the killings at first, but as he stumbles upon the clues that put him on the right trail, he begins his descent into the deepest darkness knowable to the living.

Dead and Buried posits the mortuary arts as the ultimate in nostalgia—the mortician as a preservationist *freezing* the dead in time for the viewing pleasure of the living. Mr. Dobbs, the local mortician, embodies this notion in the extreme. With his old-fashioned suits and his Big Band 78s spinning away on his Victrola, he is nostalgia personified. (It's important to note here Mr. Dobbs' resemblance to *Dead and Buried* screenwriter Dan O'Bannon, who has a similar predilection for vintage clothes. The name Dobbs is a clumsy acronym for Dan O'Bannon, as well.) And he meticulously preserves everything in his possession. Like the madmen in *House of Wax* and *Tourist Trap*, he tries to freeze corpses in time in order to take the sting out of death, but he succeeds in doing so only for himself. It's his own obsession.

For sheriff Dan, Mr. Dobbs' antics manage to put a little extra sting *into* death. He soon discovers that Dobbs has control over the entire town, and that the entire town is, in fact, quite dead. They are zombies in the voodoo sense, and they must continually revisit Dobbs' office to have their crumbly mortician's wax retouched. Most of the town's residents need to do this every week, but Dan's wife Janet is an exception, needing a touch-up only every three weeks or so.

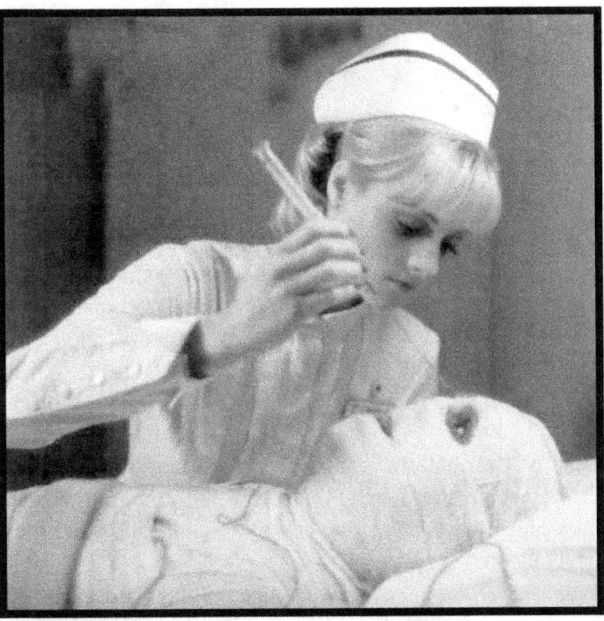

Dead and Buried has a surprise in store for anyone unlucky enough to end up in Potter's Bluff.

Dobbs tells Dan that it is Janet's durability that makes her his masterpiece, but Dobbs' *real* masterwork turns out to be Dan himself, who, like the protagonist in *The Shadow Over Innsmouth*, isn't aware (until it's too late) that the entire town is in on the conspiracy, and that he himself is much more a part of that conspiracy than he had feared possible. He's as close to a living being as it gets in Potter's Bluff, because he doesn't know (until the end) that he's dead as well. In Dan, Dobbs has created a kind of Pinocchio in reverse—a real live boy who turns into a puppet.

Dobbs' "children" not only kill to keep the town's secret and provide him with fresh specimens, but they seem to have inherited traits of the father; they meticulously film and photograph every detail of every murder, *preserving the moments*. *Dead and Buried*'s obsession with the preservation of single moments in time speaks very clearly to our fear of death. *If we can freeze time*, the fear center of our brain says, *we can stop aging, decay, and the onset of death*. Never mind that we also stop life—it's almost worth it to our primal, fearful side to avoid making that final exit. Dobbs' power over the town is certainly unsettling, reminding us of our impending helplessness as corpses under the mortician's knife. But as creepy as the notion of being a zombie, suspended in time between life and death, might be, the idea of making that final journey out of the body and into the unknown is certainly no more appealing. Being a zombie is at least somewhat comprehensible to us while we're alive; there is still some "living" in "living dead."

THE THING (1982)
Dir. John Carpenter
LET'S SCARE JESSICA TO DEATH (1971)
Dir. John Hancock

John Carpenter's remake of *The Thing* was at first trashed, and later praised, for Rob Bottin's mindbending creature effects. Bottin's work landed him in the hospital with nervous exhaustion, made him famous, and seared itself onto the brainpans of everyone who watched it. But when you look a bit closer at it, you realize that *The Thing* is a rather quiet tale of paranoia, punctuated by several of Bottin's visual exclamation points.

If the still-unsurpassed makeup effects freakouts are the flesh of Carpenter's movie, then paranoia is the skeleton. We spend so much time in dread, wondering when—and from within whom—the next transformation is going to take place, that we're a wreck by the end of it, and we immediately blame our rattled psyches on the gore.

The Thing's pervasive sense of paranoia compounded by isolation reminded me very much of *Let's Scare Jessica To Death*, the 1971 classic that most of us 30-something fanboys caught as kids on *Shock Theatre* (or whatever equivalent you grew up with), and that I will personally count among the scariest movies I've seen. Its creepiness relies on its ability to make us empathize and identify, and that depends on Zohra Lampert's performance as Jessica, which is simply wonderful.

Jessica and *The Thing* are both stories of people in self-imposed isolation. Jessica is recovering from a nervous breakdown at a tranquil house by a lake, and the men in *The Thing* are military scientists stationed in the Arctic. Though no motivations are given for the scientists' choice of locale, we get the impression that they are running

Kurt Russell can trust no one in *The Thing*.

from something back home, hiding out. The outer landscape matches the inner. In both films, the characters' sense of privacy is invaded by an outside force, suggesting that their demons have chased them into their sacred headspace. The trauma that drove them to retreat is demanding confrontation.

And also, in both *Jessica* and *The Thing*, the demon takes over the bodies of those closest to the protagonist. In a classic shot from *The Thing*, the men are standing around in the snow, trying to figure out a way to tell who isn't human. The camera pans across each of their faces, all of which are concealed by goggles and parka hoods, rendering them indistinguishable from each other and alien-looking.

Jessica can't trust her friends with her deepest paranoia—that the strange woman staying with them is a vampire—because she's mentally ill. But she knows she's right. She cannot cope with the idea that she might be deluded, so her narcissism insists that her demons are external. In Jessica's distorted narcissism, her reflection (shadow) becomes the face of a stranger, a monster.

And in the end, her perceptions prove her right. Her closest friends have become her enemies, succumbing to the influence of Jessica's monster. They infiltrate her bedroom—the most private space a person has, and the last safe place in Jessica's mind. She runs desperately until she reaches the lake, where she hightails it away from shore in a rowboat. The vampires stand at the shore, unable to pursue any further. And Jessica, with nowhere left to run, drifts in the middle of the lake, forever and ever...

The vampires and Jessica have reached a stalemate. Jessica cannot confront her shadow, and thus can no longer participate in her own life. As without, so within.

In *The Thing*, helicopter pilot R.J. MacReady (Kurt Russell) seems to be the only one up to facing down the demon. The rest of the men either succumb or get "lost in the storm" during the struggle. If indeed MacReady's landscape mirrors *his* inner, then in the end he destroys himself in order to keep his demons *to* himself. All warmth and shelter, all chance for communication with the outside world (as well as the world's chances of discovering the demon) is lost.

I *loved* the ambiguity in the endings of these films; horror films should never be cut-and-dried. That's the whole *point* of horror stories: that you can't go home again. Life has been altered irrevocably. I commend Carpenter for giving *The Thing* this kind of ending; I'm sure test audiences didn't respond too favorably to it, and the country was apparently not ready for it if its box office intake was any barometer. I personally am so goddamn sick of the typical *have-final-battle-with-the-monster-and-escape-its-lair-before-it-explodes* ending I could projectile-vomit popcorn with enough velocity to kill an usher. And while *The Thing*'s climax does have these elements in it, Carpenter brings enough of a twist to the formula in the darkness of his ending. MacReady may get off one last one-liner before blowing the monster to pieces, but he's

doomed himself in the process, so the mood of the piece never becomes too popcorn. With a handful of exceptions, many of Carpenter's heroes meet similar fates; they're like Wyatt Earp with a lot less luck on their side.

THEY LIVE (1988)
PRINCE OF DARKNESS (1987)
Dir. John Carpenter

At the time he made it, John Carpenter might have considered *They Live* to be the least horrific of his films. Under the shadow of the Bush Administration, it only grew more and more horrific each day.

They Live has aged better than it has any right to, for all its cheesy aliens and its 10-minute wrestling match. But in the wake of *They Live*'s release, the Republican stranglehold grew tighter than ever, and *They Live* has become more relevant than Carpenter had ever thought it could—or wanted it to—be. Lines like, "Racial justice and human rights are nonexistent" are horrifying in light of the amending of the Constitution to deny gays the right to marry, and the acquittal of the cops who beat Rodney King half to death.

And on the subject of Rodney King, it's important here to mention the significance of Los Angeles in both *They Live* and Carpenter's *Prince of Darkness*. Carpenter has called *The Thing*, *Prince of Darkness* and *In the Mouth of Madness* his "apocalypse trilogy," and it would be just as fitting to call *They Live*, *Prince of Darkness* and *Escape from L.A.* his "L.A. trilogy."

Aside from the subject matter and location, actors also link the films (Peter Jason and Robert Grasmere appear in both *They Live* and *Prince;* Keith David appears in *The Thing* and *They Live*). Reading between the lines, it would appear safe to assume that Carpenter believes the apocalypse will begin in L.A.

Roddy Piper and Keith David battle evil in *They Live.*

They Live comes on the heels of Carpenter's experiences making big-budget movies for the major studios. He has recalled, in an interview for the Stanley Wiater book *Dark Visions* (1992), succumbing to Hollywood hubris while shooting *Christine.* After listening to lawyers and agents who stroked his ego, telling him to put his name above the title, he realized too late, "How can I go around and show my face anymore? This is Stephen King's *Christine*, not mine!" It's safe to assume that he is not horribly fond of his big-budget days, and that they likely inspired the "L.A. trilogy" in some way.

Quoted, again, in *Dark Visions:*

> The first thing (Universal Studios) told me after I started making it was, "Can't you make these characters middle-class so the audience can identify with them?" I said, "That's the whole point: the aliens are controlling the middle-class. You're only pure if you're poor. You haven't been touched by this incredible greed." Then one of the Universal executives said, "Then what's the point of all this? We all sell out everyday. Might as well be on the winning team." And I wrote that down and used it in the movie!

I suppose if I were John Carpenter, I would have taken those words as a sign of the apocalypse, too.

There are three motifs that link *Prince* and *They Live* besides the landscape and familiar actors. First off, there are the central images of the church and homeless people. In *They Live,* both are used as symbols of purity—the hero lives in a homeless village, and the church is the secret meeting place for the revolutionaries. In *Prince,* however, the homeless are all pasty-faced murderers, and the church has been hiding not only a vast Vatican conspiracy, but also the Devil himself, for centuries. And the third motif is that of the rebel transmission, used to try to alert the films' "sleeping" heroes. In *They Live,* the transmission appears on television, whereas in *Prince*, it invades the dreams of anyone who happens to fall asleep inside the church. In both cases, the messages attempt to warn the films' heroes of a grim future that only they can prevent.

Much of the dialogue in *Prince* is metaphysical and scientific as opposed to spiritual, which is what makes its first hour so wonderful, and its last 40 minutes sort of disappointing. For much of *Prince*, we are led to believe that we might well be watching the world's first "quantum horror" film, with all the talk about the devil being the embodiment of the chaos that rules the subatomic world, and with those wonderfully enigmatic "future transmission" dreams. And let's not forget Carpenter's brilliance at building atmosphere. *Prince* is saturated with those "Carpenterisms"—throbbing music in the key of E Minor, the camera's emphasis on blurry figures in the background, and composition of shadows—that practically define the experience of watching his films.

Alas, the payoff just can't quite match the buildup here, as the climax gives us zombies and green liquid as our primary villains, and Satan turns out to be a big red guy.

The same argument could be made for the climax of *They Live*, I suppose, which sets itself up as a heavy-handed but refreshingly anti-Republican sci-fi conspiracy movie that predated *The X-Files* by years, only to become a pretty standard shoot-em-up by the climax. In fact, Carpenter usually provides little caveats in interviews, calling all his films "basically a (western/action/monster) movie with some social truth in it."

Both *They Live* and *Prince* also continue another tradition Carpenter started with *The Thing*: the self-sacrificing hero and the open ending. The most haunting self-sacrifice of these three films has to be Catherine's plunge into the mirror at the conclusion of *Prince of Darkness*. She finds herself trapped in the dark-water mirror-world as a result of her efforts to keep Satan out of the physical world. Priest Donald Pleasance smashes the mirror, destroying the gateway, and the camera cuts back one last time to Catherine's tortured face on the other side as she reaches for the dying light. It's actually one of the most effective shots Carpenter has ever committed to celluloid.

Uneven though these films might be, I'd still call them the last films of Carpenter's "golden age." There's an energy and passion to them that's still evident upon watching them, and *Prince* featured some set pieces that can be called "classic" Carpenter—particularly the opening credit sequence, the hobo attacks, and the very last scene, which is punctuated by a maddeningly teasing final shot.

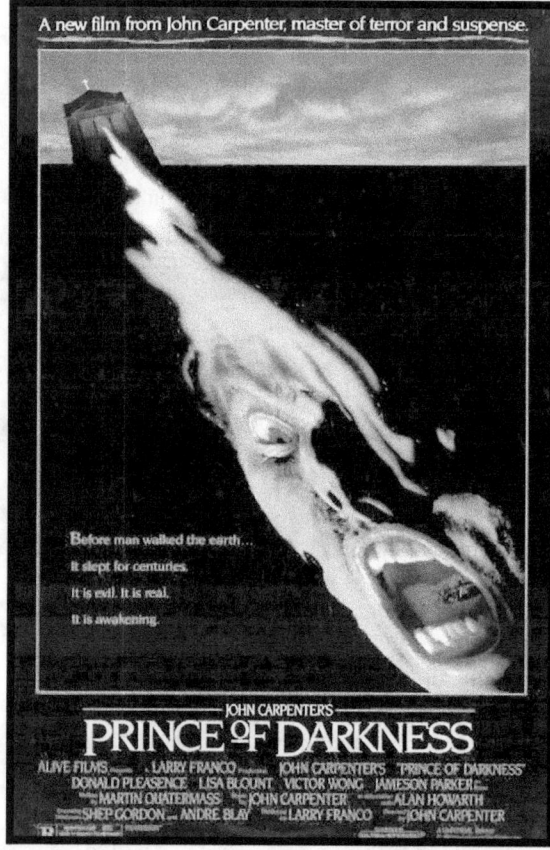

After *In the Mouth of Madness*, Carpenter's work seemed to grow less inspired and, let's face it, less coherent with each consecutive film. It all ultimately culminated in *Ghosts of Mars*, one of the most head-scratchingly pointless and uninspired movies I've ever seen. He only seemed to find new creative energy by working on the *Masters of Horror* series for cable television. Perhaps it's all a matter of perspective, and time, as with so many Carpenter films in the past, will prove *Ghosts* to be simply ahead of its time. Believe me, I'd like nothing more than to be proven wrong about this. But I believe that *Ghosts*, *Vampires* and *Village of the Damned* will become known as Carpenter's "crap trilogy."

THE LAST BROADCAST (1998)
Dir. Stefan Avalos, Lance Weiler

Modern media plays no small part in fueling the fears of any conspiracy theorist. According to the more Quixotic among us, the media is apparently always busy covering up the truth, coloring the perception of the masses, slanting the news, and serving corrupt masters. In the eyes of any given extremist group, the media is under the control of the opposing extremist group. Whether or not any of these groups are entirely correct in their paranoia, it is certain that modern media is more than capable of manipulating the truth of an image, manipulating the perception of the events it relates to the viewer. And addressing this idea much more overtly than its counterpart *The Blair Witch Project*, is *The Last Broadcast*, a faux documentary questioning the guilt of a man named Jim Seward, charged with murdering the crew of a documentary *within* the faux documentary.

There are three supposed investigations going on in *Broadcast*: there's a cable access show called *Fact Or Fiction* that journeys into the New Jersey Pine Barrens to hunt for the Jersey Devil. When the *Fact Or Fiction* crew is butchered by someone or something while filming out in the Barrens, the sole survivor becomes the sole suspect, and his prosecutors' edit of the recovered *Fact Or Fiction* footage becomes the second investigation. And last, there's the framing documentary investigating *both* investigations. This framing doc—which is supposed to be the movie that we're actually watching—is trying to establish that the prosecution wanted a scapegoat in Jim Seward, and unwittingly framed an innocent man in the process. But as we'll discover, *The Last Broadcast* has even more surprises in store for us.

In truth, the only investigation that is completely honest with its intended audience is the *Fact Or Fiction* Jersey Devil report. Numerous times the crew is heard talking about how the director wants to play it all as real as possible and not rig any of the proceedings. The poor saps are trying to do a real investigative documentary, with no idea that they are being set up by the mastermind that is behind every event in the film. By its end, *Broadcast* has drilled into our heads that we can't trust *any* of the footage we've seen. It reveals Jim Seward to indeed be innocent, and then reveals the horrible truth about its own self.

Broadcast's message is a bit heavy-handed, but the film is still quite fun, surprising and creepy. It certainly merits all the controversy it's earned; *Blair Witch* is eerily similar. But the two films are definitely different enough to warrant their existing apart from each other. *Blair* is going for a more raw, primal feel, while *Broadcast* held onto the framing structure that *Blair* abandoned—the *In Search of-* style investigative report. It's a more intellectual affair, meshing the investigation perfectly with the story that it's looking into, and wearing its opinions about the digital age on its sleeve. *Blair* used the immediacy and subjectivity of the camcorder perspective to reinforce the notion that "you are there." *Broadcast* uses the same perspective *against* the viewer, reinforcing the idea that "if you weren't there, you weren't there." It reminds us that to experience an image is not to experience the event.

The final trump card that *Broadcast* plays is a jarring one. It not only reveals that the documentarian behind *The Last Broadcast* is the killer, it breaks the rules of its narrative perspective, jumping from that of a documentary to that of bona fide cinematic fiction. It *has* to do this in order to let us see behind what the documentary camera wants us to see. All of a sudden we're viewing the events from the invisible and omniscient perspective of traditional cinema. This transition has all the subtlety of a parental slap, which is almost precisely what it is. It's the movie saying to us, "Stupid kid, the whole thing's a put-on, remember?" Of *course* we remember, but we wanted to slip into the movie and forget, and the movie was all too happy to abet us in the self-hypnosis of suspension of disbelief. Its final *coup de grace* is reminiscent of Jodorowsky's *The Holy Mountain*, pointing out its own trickery to us. Very bold, very off-putting, very refreshing.

And in the midst of all *Broadcast*'s tricks and talk, it still manages to sneak in some wonderfully creepy imagery—namely the blurry image of the aggressor in the Pine Barrens, which is slowly restored and clarified as the film reaches its climax. It's a severely evil image blurred, maybe slightly less creepy upon final reveal, but only slightly. It's still a shocking and satisfying payoff.

Both *Blair* and *Broadcast* were made at approximately the same time, *Blair* coming slightly on the heels of *Broadcast* (stirring up plenty of horror-geek debate), and *Blair* absolutely eclipsed *Broadcast* in both support and success. While *Blair* may have delivered certain pants-shitting goods that *Broadcast* did not (again, very arguably, as many audience members did not, in fact, shit their pants with *Blair* {I personally did, just to let you know where you stand with the author}), but *Broadcast* is certainly at least as well made a film as *Blair*. I finally caught *Broadcast*, some five years after it was made, on IFC. Kind of ironic, seeing as how IFC was quite instrumental in *Blair*'s grass roots hype campaign. Giving *Broadcast* its own chance at finding an audience was the least IFC could do, I suppose. Better late than never.

SESSION 9 (2002)
Dir. Brad Anderson

Sometimes in cinema, style can be so strong as to become substance. Among the myriad of examples are such films as *Rope, Suspiria, Vampyr, Un Chien Andalou,* and *Versus*. Another such film is *Session 9,* in which the film's setting *is* the story. Without the rotting behemoth that is Danvers State Hospital, the movie simply could not exist. Likewise, there's no way a filmmaker (or filmgoer) could walk inside its walls and not know that a movie would have to be made therein.

It could have been a passable exercise in horror even if no actors had stood in front of the camera. A simple hour and a half of cinematographer Uta Briesewitz's camera slowly rotating upside-down while focused on a derelict wheelchair, or patiently gliding from left to right through the walls of the decaying rooms, as it is so wont to do, would've driven the point home quite nicely. Kind of a post-modern horror version of *Koyaanisqatsi*. But, in this particular film, there are indeed characters in front of the camera, and fortunately they only serve to enhance the scenery, making us care whether or not the scenery eats them alive. *Session 9*'s subtext swelters with the

In *Session 9*, the film's setting *is* the story.

human paranoia of Carpenter's *The Thing*, as well as the inherent fear of the unseen that permeated Robert Wise's *The Haunting* (1963).

The men who toil within *Session*'s walls are asbestos removal workers. It's really a perfect character device; it gives them a perfectly plausible reason to hang out in the building; their uniforms give symbolic flesh to the armor that everyday men build around themselves (and how easily *little things* can penetrate); and they also serve the same purpose that Carpenter's snowsuits did in *The Thing '82*—they both dehumanize the characters and render them indistinguishable. Before the men don their suits, we get to know them as Gordon, the crew foreman and stressed-out family man; Mike the law-school dropout; Jeff, the mullet-headed slacker with a deep fear of the dark, Phil, the flinty hardass, and Hank, the gambling-obsessed slacker who stole Phil's girlfriend.

The building that they are cleaning out was once a sprawling mental hospital; it is now a derelict memorial to the pain and rage that once held its bricks together. It was, according to the film's characters, shut down in the '80s due to budget cuts and malpractice suits, and many of its patients were simply put out on the street. Not knowing what to do with themselves, several of these orphaned inmates keep trying to return "home", the building is haunted by ghosts that aren't even dead yet.

With the precious little good vibrations the place has going for it, it's no wonder the crew almost immediately begin to experience negative effects inside it. Soon enough, the men, wrapped to the gills in insulating uniforms, begin to simmer and stew inside their armor. The pressures that haunt them in the everyday world (losing girlfriends, fatherhood, dropping out of med school, gambling addictions, fear of the dark) seem to be magnified by the building.

Aspects of the place (vintage coins hidden in the walls, tape recordings of disturbing therapy sessions, sputtering generators that constantly threaten to throw the whole place into darkness) begin to obsess them. The building has its hooks in them. And soon enough, as in Carpenter's *The Thing*, one or more of the men may not be what he appears to be.

The pressure inexorably builds. The music (by Seattle band the Climax Golden Twins) consists largely of eerie drones and slow, dissonant piano stings. The ever-gliding-left-to-right camera helps to fully lull us into a trance. And as the film's third act reaches its crescendo, *Session* succeeds in scaring the crap out of us without ever fully showing us anything. The only visual representation of evil we are presented with is ever-encroaching darkness, as the men venture deeper into the building's basement catacombs with increasingly impotent flashlights. In the visual highpoint of the film (and one of the visual highpoints of *any* horror film, if you ask me), the main generator putters out, and nictophobic Jeff is literally chased down a corridor by darkness itself. He runs and screams while the lights successively fail, faster than he can run, until the darkness engulfs him.

Once the generator is functioning again, the "ghosts" are free to run about the corridors of the building and the minds of the men. The lights are back on, but the world is not the same as it was before the blackout. The tape player is up and running again, playing out the terrible events related in the titular session recording. It is on this tape that we are introduced to a spirit that calls itself "Simon." On the tape, and using the mouth of the girl undergoing the hypnotherapy session, he describes entering the body of the girl and persuading her to kill her family.

He tells the doctor he needs a weak host to allow him in and do his bidding, and after all this time, he has finally found his new foil in the highly volatile Gordon. Unable to cope with the pressures of fatherhood and of keeping his struggling business afloat, and ever losing sleep, Gordon surrenders to Simon and lets him in. And everyone who comes within striking distance of Gordon (including his wife and baby) pays with his or her life.

After his murder spree is complete, Gordon, like so many of the displaced souls forced out of the hospital during the Reagan years, tries to take up residence within its walls. The last we see of him, he is rocking back and forth in his cell (the same cell occupied by Simon's last host), talking to his dead wife on a broken cell phone, begging her to let him come home. If this scene is to have any actual basis in the film's logic, we could assume that he is asking her to let him come to heaven, to be "home" with her once more. And we can also assume that she refutes him; that he cannot "come home" (die) until he has paid for his crimes via life sentence.

Simon lives, so he tells us, "in the weak and the wounded." And, of course, the weak and the wounded…live *here*.

THE HOWLING (1981)
Dir. Joe Dante

Over and over in *The Howling*, references are made to "gifts." It's the title of a book written by therapy guru Dr. George Waggoner (Patrick Macnee) at first, and the subsequent references get darker and darker. More on them later.

The Howling opens up with TV static and garbled radio transmissions during the length of its opening credit sequence. Media plays no small part in the story and subtext here. There are many different aspects of predator and prey symbolized herein, and right out of the gate, we are presented with a news team using one of its female reporters, Karen White, as bait for a vicious serial killer. She's wired for sound, but the rig is faulty, and transmission is quickly lost. Her husband Bill sits with the news team in the control room, and they are all rendered utterly impotent without their technology. Thus, Karen loses her hunter's edge, and is now a damsel in distress.

It's also significant to mention, at this point, the scene in the restroom of the news station, where an anchorman stands before a mirror, practicing his broadcast in his "news voice." His real voice is a far less charismatic drawl; he uses an alter ego to "lure" viewers into his trust.

Eddie, the serial killer, has been calling and stalking Karen for weeks, and he is now offering her a chance to meet up with him. Like *Hansel and Gretel*'s breadcrumbs, she follows a trail of smiley-face stickers (his calling card) through the city's red light district. The trail leads to a porno shop, which is populated solely by men. As soon as she enters, all the men clear out in a hurry. Karen is invading the primal mind of the human male, and her presence intimidates them. It's yet another twist in the endless spiral of cat-and-mouse games being played in this movie. Men have gathered here

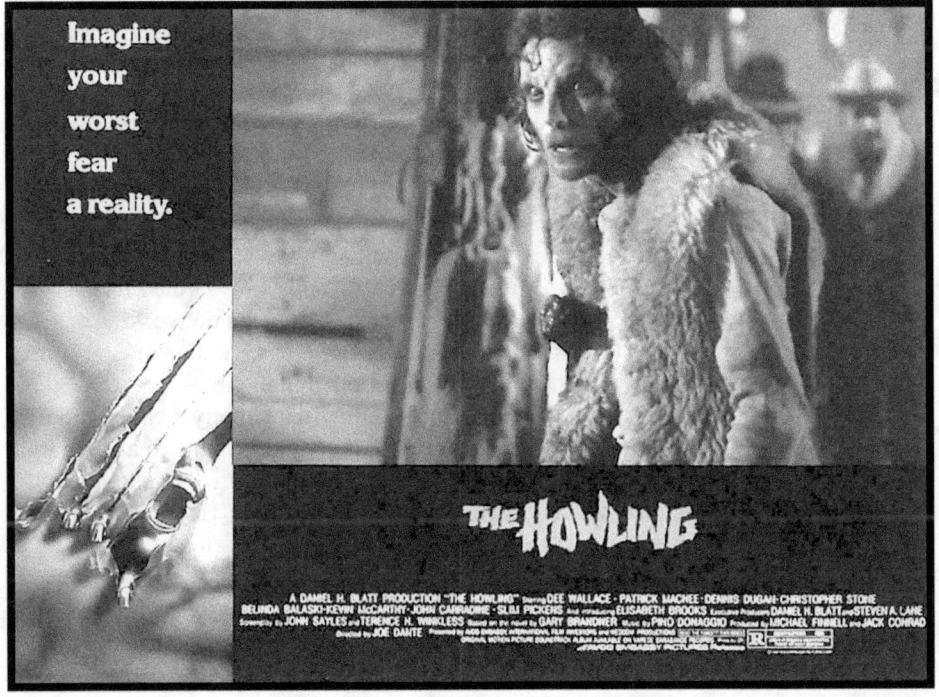

in this temple of the subconscious to objectify women—to prey on their *images*—but when a real woman walks in, the men scatter with their tails (or whatever) between their legs.

Karen follows the trail to its end—a mini-projection booth with the final smiley on the door. She opens it, and ventures beyond the façade (the smiley-face "mask" of civilization) and into Eddie's primal mind. As soon as she sits, Eddie starts the movie for her; a couple of guys in stocking masks are raping a young woman tied to a bed. *Predator-prey.*

While the movie plays, Eddie tells Karen about his last victim, saying she didn't feel anything, that normal people like her were already dead. But he feels there is something different about Karen. He believes he can make her feel, that he can "light her body up." Finally, he tells her to turn around and face him.

"I wanna give you something."

When she faces him, Eddie is silhouetted by the light of the projector, almost as if the transformation he's undergoing is, in fact, a projection itself. Eddie's real self is erupting in front of Karen's eyes, here in the black pit of his subconscious, with the rape scene droning on in the background.

The police arrive in the nick of time and take Eddie down before he can give Karen the "gift" of a predatory death. Karen is escorted outside, and in the glare of the police lights, the news cameras, and the tactless, gawking onlookers (almost all of whom are male), Karen's mind shuts down. She goes into shock, and completely represses the memory of what happened inside the booth.

All this plays out in the first reel of *The Howling*, and it is a truly riveting and inspired piece of cinema. Fortunately, the rest of it's pretty great, too. John Sayles' script is remarkably layered. God bless him for his horror scripts; they gave a desperately needed credibility to the genre in the 1980s.

After the trauma, Karen finds she is not quite ready to go back to work—she freezes under the lights of the studio. Neither can she have sex with husband Bill, who apparently would rather have nothing to do with her if she doesn't want to fuck. When she tells him she's "just not ready," he simply says, "You'll be alright," rolls over and goes to sleep.

Doc Waggoner suggests she spend a week at The Colony—his retreat deep in the woods—for group therapy and relaxation, to help her "get back to who you really are." She reluctantly agrees, and soon enough finds herself amidst a strange combination of New-Agers and rednecks. Meat is always on the menu, and always killed fresh by the men of the Colony. There is no television, no linkage to the outside world except for phones. Group therapy tries to help Karen relive her night with Eddie, but she simply cannot (or refuses to) recall what happened in the booth that night.

When it becomes apparent that something is killing the Colony's cattle, the men decide to form a wolf-hunting party, and invite Bill along. Bill claims to avoid eating meat, but is awfully quick to learn how to use a rifle. He's also quick to shoot and kill a rabbit, even though the party is supposed to be hunting wolves. "Hey, I got 'im! First shot!" he proudly declares, apparently eager to present himself as an alpha male. Later that night, he is told that it's a sin to kill what he doesn't eat, and is directed over to Marsha, the resident earth-goddess-nature-nymph, to skin and cook it for him. She tries to seduce him. He fends her off and leaves, but is attacked by a wolf-like creature on the way home.

Terry (Belinda Balaski) meets a werewolf up close and personal in *The Howling*.

And here begins act three, when the net truly begins to close on Karen. She calls her friend (and fellow investigator) Terry after Bill's attack, and she immediately joins her up at the Colony. Terry does some investigating of her own (she and her boyfriend Chris are trying to gather more information for a special about Eddie), and discovers that Eddie has spent some time at the Colony as well. Good husband Bill sneaks off at night to join Marsha in the throes of lycanthropic coitus. Indeed, he is coming right along in the program set up by the Colony—abandoning vegetarianism, technology, monogamy, civilization, and ultimately, humanity. He's adapting much better than his wife, whom the place is supposed to be helping. But the Colony has other plans for Karen.

Terry goes off exploring on her own, looking for any more Eddie evidence in an empty, foreboding cabin. Nailed to the door outside is the pelt of a wolf. Thus it becomes apparent that what we are dealing with here are not classic lycanthropes; these guys eat wolves for breakfast.

Terry discovers this soon enough when she is pursued by one of the beasts, who are not bound by the light of the moon to change. The thing is huge, certainly wolf-like, but more like a horrendous caricature of a wolf. She secludes herself in the doctor's office, where she meets Eddie the wolf face to face. And when he lifts her up into the air, puts his great gaping maw intimately close to her face while she kicks and screams, and finally goes for her throat, there is certainly some sort of primal-rape going on; some savage lust and dark surrender not entirely unlike the predatory relationships going on in the Anne Rice vampire chronicles.

Karen is next to run afoul of Eddie in the office. He's reverted back to human form, and he is ready to give her the same "gift." In fact, he adds a little more to the package this time around. "I wanna give you a piece of my mind," he says, before he removes a bullet from his skull. Then the real fun begins, as makeup artist Rob Bottin is finally allowed to strut his stuff.

Eddie's transformation is as cartoony as it is nightmarish, and rightly so, for the huge hairy goblin that he becomes is an absurd exaggeration of both human and lupine qualities. A primordial cauldron begins to boil under his skin. His mouth stretches into an impossibly wide, maniacal grin before elongating into a snout. His eyes become lunatic saucers. It's the same mood Bottin created with his "skinned rabbit" effect in *Twilight Zone: The Movie*—a Saturday morning cartoon by Heironymous Bosch.

Karen scars Eddie's face with acid and escapes…out of the frying pan and into the fire. The Colony captures her and, in the tradition of movie villains all the way back to *Dr. No*, explain their motivations to both the protagonist and the viewers. Doc Waggoner, it seems, has been trying to civilize the werewolves, weaning them off of humans and onto cattle, but they simply cannot be tamed. They do not wish to integrate themselves with humankind; they want to prey upon it, as they have always done.

In a frantic search for Karen and Terry, Chris arrives at the Colony with a rifle full of silver bullets. Almost immediately he stumbles across Eddie in the Doc's office. Eddie takes his rifle from him at first, and then throws it back at him. "Consider it a gift" (Eddie sure gives a lot in this movie), he tells him. It's either exalted arrogance or a death wish on Eddie's part.

Chris then happens upon the rest of the pack as they are planning to do away with Karen. He dispatches a number of the clan, including the doc. As the Doc dies, he mutters "thank god." It would seem that quite a few of the Colony's members are not too happy with life (Eddie's aforementioned "gift" of the rifle, John Carradine's earlier attempt at self-immolation).

In their escape, Karen is bitten and infected by her wolfish husband. Doomed to a future as a predator, she opts instead to sacrifice herself as the ultimate media object. She goes on the air one last time, preaches for a bit about the human "gift" of being able to choose between the light and dark sides of our souls, and finally allows herself to transform while the cameras roll. According to the plan they had worked out ahead of time, Chris shoots her, securing her position as civilized—and, therefore, as prey—to the end of her life. Her final moments are spent as an icon to be consumed by the viewing audience. And the audience is left dumbfounded. Half of them seem to believe it, half seem to think it's just special effects trickery. The media has become so adept at presenting itself however it likes, nobody is certain what to believe anymore. Thus, the warning goes unheeded, and the wolves once again take their place on the outskirts of society, in the wilderness, feeding on us.

There are references made throughout *The Howling* to Manson and Jim Jones, figures who were both completely given over to the dark side of their souls, and also quite charismatic, as is evident not only by the sway they had over their followers, but by the spell they've cast on popular culture in their wake. Doc Waggoner, Eddie, the anchorman with his important news voice: all of these are examples of this type of dark charisma that media embraces. They are the sly wolf that can fool a little girl into thinking he is her grandmother. Doc may be trying to encourage incorporation of the light and dark, but according to *The Howling*, this is not possible. Our animal sides want to prey upon our civilized sides, and the vicious predatory dance will seemingly go on forever.

It's quite an irony for the horror story, felt by many to be a true attempt to satiate and integrate our primal selves into our civilized lives. All attempts by *The Howling*'s characters to achieve this integration fail spectacularly, and to the soul that wishes to believe in the ability of the horror film to catharsize, this is perhaps the scariest thought imaginable. And it's also kind of ironic that so nihilistic a notion can be proposed by a film that is more dark satire than pure horror. Like its characters, *The Howling* is far creepier underneath than its surface would have us believe.

Chapter Eight:
Fear in Cinema

"HORROR VS. TERROR"

Being dramatic in films is easy enough: create a likable character and kill them off in the last reel. Being shocking, too, is easy enough if you employ a technician skilled at creating realistic intestines.

Creating fear or dread is much, much harder—possibly even harder than being funny. As ephemeral as humor is, comedy filmmakers at least have the audience on their side; people go into comedies eager to laugh.

Horror film fans, of course, are a little different. They go into a horror film *daring* it to scare them. They're jaded and cocky. Pleasing these people is oftentimes a task of Herculean proportion. Common is the horror film, as opposed to the film of terror, because horror lends itself much more readily to the objective viewpoint of cinema itself. Horror is witnessing the bloody lump under the white sheet on the side of the road as you drive to work in the morning. Horror is receiving the phone call at 3 AM that can only be bad news.

Terror, however, is *subjective.* Terror is knowing that you will soon *be* the bloody shape on the side of the road; that your wife or your roommates are going to receive that 3 AM phone call. Terror is knowing that you will soon be the object of somebody else's horror.

So it's obvious why horror is more commonplace in cinema; there's a definite detachment going on here. The perspective through which we view the film's events is that of a voyeur. The characters onscreen are entirely unaware of our presence, we can jump about instantly from setting to setting, we can fade out and come back in at a completely different point in time, almost god-like.

This is how we feed the gators, as King so rightly put it. Objective catharsis; we get to look. We've all had the urge to rubberneck car crashes and crime scenes, but social taboo keeps us a little more polite than we would probably like to be. The cinematic catharsis provides not only the satiation of this impulse, but also a freedom from guilt. We are aware that what we are watching is in essence a magic trick, and the comfort of this knowledge perhaps makes us a bit braver, enabling us to maybe look longer and harder than if we were faced with the real thing—even to cheer and laugh when the effects are extreme in either quality (or lack thereof) or quantity. Indeed, laughing at death is no small catharsis.

The film of terror is a much rarer animal. The filmmakers' obstacles are many, from the detached, "invisible man" perspective of camera and viewer, to the very fact that we know what's going on onscreen is not really happening.

Suspension of disbelief already works surprisingly well with film, a medium that is two-dimensional, larger-than-life (or smaller if you're watching at home), and often features familiar actors. But seldom does it work well enough for us to be frightened. The idea that a fictional, 2-D image can make us sleep with the lights on seems absurd and impossible. And when it *does work*, we are dumbfounded. To be subjectively scared by images on film is to more than simply suspend disbelief; it is to transcend the medium entirely. It is to establish a direct pipeline to the subconscious, which is something only the most important works of art can do.

THE EYE (2002)
Dir. Danny and Oxide Pang

The Eye will always be remembered by me as the masterpiece that could've been. Its message is that we can never trust what we see, because we may not be able to touch it.

Mun, the film's heroine, has been blind since age two, and has come to know the world by what she can touch. As the movie begins, she is preparing to undergo a cornea transplant. We're not very long into the movie before Mun is laying in post-op, blindfolded with gauze, waiting to see the world for the first time. Most of the adults in her circle tell her that the world is a horrible place that she shouldn't want to look at. The only person who tells her otherwise is Ying Ying, a little boy in her hospital, who is undergoing chemotherapy. He still has that Speilbergian perspective, seeing the beauty of the world. Mun spends her last sightless days talking with Ying Ying, performing with her all-blind string ensemble (who play loudly, boisterously, not really caring about perfect pitch—I loved the sounds they made, they seemed to be exploring the aural sense with Bacchanalian abandon), and waiting with bated breath for the big day.

Soon enough, her bandages come off, and she begins the slow process of incorporating vision into her sensory life. But Mun soon discovers that she can see a few things that others cannot.

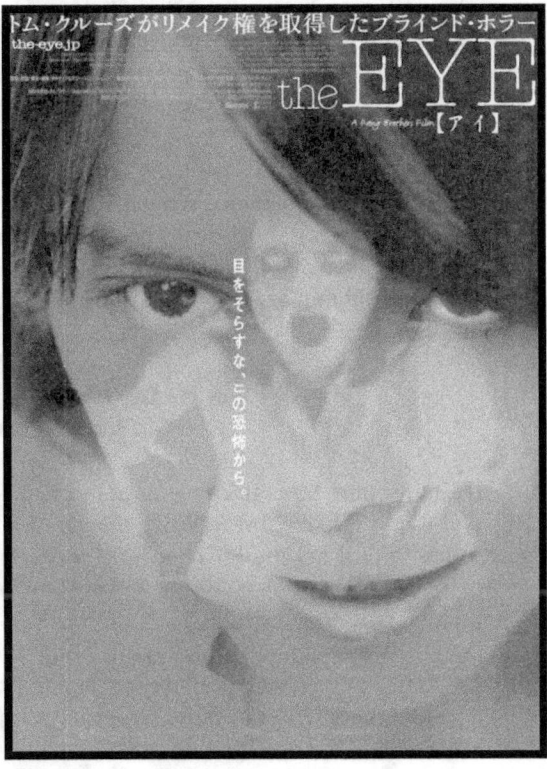

It's wonderful, the sensory games *The Eye* plays with us during its first half. The incorporation of sight actually impairs Mun's (and our own) equilibrium and sense of reality. She is seeing things that she can't touch—horrible-looking, blurred apparitions. We are given several opportunities to see through Mun's new eyes, and they are not comfortable moments. These scenes are accompanied by disorienting music and sound effects. We have no idea what is going on here, but it becomes apparent that Mun is seeing the dead.

Yes. Sounds a little familiar, does it not? And as Mun begins to track down the mystery of where her corneas came from, *The Eye* becomes more and more familiar to us. There are heavy echoes of

The Sixth Sense, as well as *The Ring*, a tiny hint of *Blair Witch*, and, oddly enough, a bit of *The Mothman Prophecies*.

The Pang Brothers have an absolutely remarkable visual flair, and they do manage to create some knockout-creepy set pieces. But as the narrative progresses, the film's scope opens up more and more broadly. This, in my opinion, is where the movie falls on its face. It begins focused tightly on Mun, on her personal world and anxieties, and how her anxieties magnify after this life-changing surgery. Its mood for this first half-hour is disorienting and claustrophobic, and the mystery that Mun's apparitions are shrouded in make them excruciatingly scary. The elevator set piece is especially remarkable, because it actually sort of ramps up the climactic scene in *Blair Witch* a little bit. When Mun enters the elevator, a wizened old man is standing in the corner with his back to her. Strong shades of Mike-in-the-corner here, of course. But in this case, the man actually turns around, very slowly, and we get to see his face, half-staved-in, for a split second. It's pretty fucking effective.

Two other set pieces in the film have that kind of impact, but as the mystery unravels, the movie loses the intimacy with Mun that made it work so well. Mun discovers that the dead people she sees pose no real threat to her or her loved ones, nor is she in danger of "seeing too much," so *The Eye*, at this point, has ceased to be a horror movie. Now it's all about tracking down the family of the tortured young seer who was cursed with these visions in the first place (hello, *Ringu*). After the false climax between Mun and the dead psychic girl's mother, we feel something else lurking on the horizon. Something tells us that the movie is not quite over.

As Mun sits in a traffic jam, she begins seeing hordes of specters walking past. And since Mun no longer fears these beings, she takes their appearance as a clue of something horrible about to happen. Indeed, they alert her to an impending gas leak that is going to wreak havoc on the stalled and waiting cars. But by this point, we really don't care. *The Eye* has opened its scope up far too wide; it is now practically a disaster film. Mun surmises that all that has befallen her since her surgery has brought her to this point, to try to save lives, and the movie can now safely add *Signs* to *The Eye*'s repertoire of influences. When the cars get gorgeously destroyed in succession, we can add *Mothman*. Mun loses her sight in the explosion, and lives happily ever after, and though we in the audience feel the need to complain a bit, we do have to keep in mind that the first half-hour of *The Eye* was one of the best horror films we've seen in years.

HALLOWEEN (1978)
Dir. John Carpenter

If I'm flipping through channels at night and I come across *Halloween*, I have to stop and watch it to the finish. When the month of October rolls around, I find myself compelled to pull out the DVD at least once. And, after at least two hundred times seeing it, the climactic chase scene still puts me on edge. After 25 years and hundreds of imitators, *Halloween* still casts as strong a spell as *Psycho*, *Jaws* and *The Exorcist*.

Its power is compelling me to write about it even in the face of the mountains of essays and theses that have been written about it over the years. Part of this is because I believe that the mindset of those who analyzed it first time around was tuned into it differently, and the collective viewpoint many fans (and detractors) had toward it is outdated. Part of it, too, is that I simply love *Halloween*, and wish to indulge myself. *Halloween* is, to me, as warm and Autumnal as a fire in the fireplace.

A great deal of the text that has been written about *Halloween* related largely to the slasher movie craze that it ignited, the debt it owes to *Psycho*, and the "rules" it established, as described by Jamie Kennedy in *Scream*. But most of this is really useless information. *Halloween* the phenomenon has little to do with *Halloween* the film, which is simple, understated, and still terrifying after all this time. Many films tried to recreate its formulas, and a few of them recreated a bit of its box office, but none recreated the magic that made it work.

Halloween not only gave us the serial killer as cinematic icon, but as literal bogeyman. Norman Bates was certainly a figurative bogeyman, but he was, after all, a mere mortal. Michael Myers was an unstoppable juggernaut with no face. His unkillability was a definite factor in *Halloween*'s scariness, but the real fundamentals of its fear factor are even more basic.

Let's take that mask, for example. In every subsequent sequel, the mask was altered in some way, and rendered quite ineffective as a result. It was a simple combination of simple elements—a William Shatner mask and some white spray-paint—that made magic in Carpenter's original. Michael's mask in *Halloween* is emotionless, which renders him faceless and mythic, but in some of the close-ups—like when he's killing Annie, for example—the mask's visage almost appears sympathetic. It's some seriously chilling shit.

And the element of the mask in general speaks to yet another factor—a factor that is present in more than one of the films mentioned in this chapter: the almost-human being, the human monster with the obscured face. Michael's mask not only terrifies by itself, but drives the viewer crazy imagining what is going on underneath. The concept of the masked killer has been done to death in all subsequent slasher flicks, of course, but it never works as well in any of the imitators. Most of the time, the mask is simply used to conceal the identity of the murderer until the last reel, but in *Halloween* we know who the killer is from the beginning. We know that Dr. Loomis barely believes Michael Myers to be human, and Loomis becomes our anchor; we take his word for it that Michael is "purely and simply: evil." And we wonder exactly what he has evolved into since we last saw him at age six; we wonder what he looks like under that mask, and we're afraid to find out. When the reveal finally comes, Michael looks as boyish as he did back when he was unmasked at the film's beginning. But for just a split-second before our eyes register, we see a monster.

The second element that makes *Halloween* the marvel that it is, is another testament to Carpenter's brilliance as a director. Carpenter asked Nick Castle to play masked Michael because he liked the way Castle walked. Carpenter's only direction to Castle throughout the film was, "Don't act, just walk." Castle never really got a chance to play Michael as a character, but we as an audience are richer for it. That walk—a casual, almost friendly amble—gives Michael diabolical grace and a subtle sense of mischief. The scene where Michael crosses the street while Laurie screams on the Doyles' front porch suggests that Michael is playful, that he never really grew up after the night he killed his sister, and that he *knows* he'll catch up with Laurie eventually, that it's only a matter of time. Its almost as if he knows something Laurie and we don't know.

The third and most important (even according to Carpenter) element of Halloween's success is the music. Carpenter is well aware of the power music has in creating mood in films, and he knows that repetition is key in making the moodiest music possible. Most of Carpenter's scores consist of throbbing bass lines in the key of E minor. The bass lines practically serve as percussion, as they rarely change rhythmically or tonally. Consistent, droning music serves to sort of hypnotize the listener—repetition is essential in evoking trance states, which is why percussion is so popular in trance-oriented religions like Voodoo. The listener grows to rely on the beat, and when s/he surrenders to it, it supports the psyche and takes it where the drummer wants it to go.

In *Halloween*, Carpenter combines repetitive rhythms with dissonance, especially during the climax: pounding bass piano, contrapuntal synth strings in the high register, and a blaring drone that kind of sounds like a car horn (perhaps a conscious reference to the car horn that Annie's corpse falls onto earlier in the film? Perhaps an *unconscious* reference to it?) The dissonance makes us tense, and the repetition informs us that we can grow to rely on it. Carpenter has stated that *Halloween* wouldn't be half the movie it is without the music, and I believe it. Mood is 90% of most of Carpenter's films, and music makes for at least half their mood.

This is not to belittle the importance of Dean Cundey's photography, which was never less than perfect. Cundey's genius with light and shadow was instrumental in establishing a unique cinematic language for *Halloween*. The opening Panaglide murder scene, the "eyes adjusting to the darkness" reveal of Michael standing behind Laurie, and the "Michael sits up" shot are hopefully used in film class somewhere in the world as positive examples of photographic technique. (If not, perhaps I should go for that teaching degree.)

Cundey's work, as well as that of a certain Ms. Curtis, was of course invaluable in making *Halloween* a classic independent film. But without the big three factors that we talked about at the outset, *Halloween* would not have been a classic and *terrifying* film. Somehow, it is still terrifying today, even to those of us who have seen it way too many times, even after decades of cultural change. There are few exploitation films that can be considered classics, and *Halloween* is perhaps the stateliest, most shining example of all. And as much as geeks like myself analyze it and pick it apart, it's not as though we can isolate a formula that can be replicated. It just happened the way it happened, and it worked beautifully.

When a critic analyzes a movie, he is of course analyzing himself, the triggers that the movie touched upon in his/her own psyche. There are little giveaways in every critic's reviews—I find it pretty amusing how many movies Roger Ebert gives 4-star reviews to in his newpaper critiques that feature lesbian sex scenes, for example. He's a great reviewer, but there'll always be a little of that Russ Meyer screenwriter in him, and God bless him for that.

Getting into horror film analysis is perhaps even more subliminally confessional. Obviously everyone's triggers are slightly different; not every horror movie has the same effect on every viewer. But there are those elite few films that seem to reach across the broadest demographics, and *Halloween* is certainly one of these. It was first since *Psycho* to mine the vein of anxiety that Ed Gein gave rise to in the American unconscious. And despite its handful of flaws, it will likely never be surpassed.

JU-ON (2004)
THE GRUDGE (2005)
Dir. Takashi Shimizu

The first time I watched *Ju-On*, I couldn't figure out how to access the subtitles on the Japanese DVD I had rented. Undaunted and eager to see the damn thing, I plowed ahead and watched it anyway. To my delight, I discovered that I was having no problems grasping the basic elements of the story. I was also getting the crap scared out of me. *Ju-On* works just that beautifully; it tells its story so well on a purely visual level that it could have been scripted in Latin or Esperanto and been just as powerful.

Afterwards, I finally figured out how to enable the subs and watched again almost immediately. The translation provided color that had been lacking for me, illuminating the relationships between all the different sets of characters, and the timelines that separated them. But all that stuff is almost unnecessary in *Ju-On*'s agenda. With the (very important) exception of the "croak" sound effect, the story *Ju-On* has to tell is practically completely visual. And though the strongest images in the film are those of Toshio and Kayako, credit must be given to the house in which they lurk, as well.

Years ago, *Poltergeist* officially brought the haunted house film to American suburbia. But I have to say that even *Poltergeist*'s house was still quite sprawling and grandiose for a tract house. There was still a Gothic element to it. And I admit that I always found the house a bit too upper-middle-class for me to identify with.

Ju-On's house feels wrong, like a low rent version of Hill House. It's a squat, depressing little thing, at least to Western eyes. It doesn't even have the squalid character of a slum; it's a sepia-toned box designed with unpleasant and claustrophobic right angles. Put any family into a box like this and it's no surprise that one of them would turn on the others, like mice cooped up for too long in a lab experiment.

But as *Ju-On*'s narrative progresses, we're made to wonder: is that in fact what happened? Did Takeo turn homicidal of his own accord? Or was something else at work? At a later point in the film, Katsuya—the house's second doomed family man—

is seemingly possessed by the spirit of Takeo, chewing on his fingers and muttering, "She deceived me. That's not my child. Not my child." This is left wonderfully unexplained: did Kayako simply have an affair? Or is this perhaps another nod to *Ringu*? (I was definitely reminded of Ryuiji stating, "I wonder if her father was even human.")

With the arrival of the *Ring* remake in the U.S., the virus finally took root in our soil. The results of the J-Horror boom were mixed. On the plus side, horror films were becoming scary again for a little while. On the less positive side, all that American studios seemed to want to do was remake the foreign ones as quickly as possible.

J-Horror was a deliberate ushering of Japan's traditional "Kwaidan" into the modern age. Staple images—ghosts with black hair, water, rage that not even death can quench—are meshed with modern devices: TV, the Internet, and the alienation of metropolitan and suburban living. And with a handful of visual nods to *Ringu, Kairo,* and *Kwaidan, Ju-On* and its American remake officially brought the traditional Japanese ghost story to the suburbs.

As with *The Ring*, *The Grudge* is at times shot-by-shot faithful to the original, and at times a fine-tuning of the original's best set pieces. Case in point: the office-building scene. The sister of the family living in the cursed house is working late, and receives a call on her cell phone, which turns out to be "the croak." In the remake, director Takashi Shimizu wisely opted to place this sequence in a darkened stairwell, as opposed to the original film's bathroom stall. It's far more tasteful, and with its *Session 9*-like shot of lights failing in rapid succession, a shitload scarier.

The Grudge's removal of the "three schoolgirls" plotline, and its addition of the "love letters" plotline, aren't conspicuous in a positive or negative way; they simply help differentiate the two films. Some might argue that the "love letters" angle might try to explain too much, taking away some of the original's Japanese flavor. I may agree—as I also agree that perhaps too much is explained in the remake of *The Ring*—but I still don't find the clarification gratuitous or hokey in either film.

The need for clarification can be seen as uniquely American, as can the "booga-booga" shock ending that *The Grudge* leaves us with. The grimness is still there, and the ghosts still kill everybody, but the American ending is decidedly quite "popcorn" in comparison to the slow, dark killing of Reka at the end of *Ju-On*.

I caught *The Grudge* twice in theatres on opening weekend, both times with the type of crowds that normally piss me off: loud, giggly and obnoxious. If the film had had a more somber tone à la *The Ring* or *The Blair Witch Project,* I would've been quite upset. But for some reason it was wonderful in this case. It was extra wonderful that in both viewings the audience was scared shitless. Lotta screaming. Any giggling going on happened only immediately after the screaming. This is the "good" kind of giggling one hears at horror movies.

Though I can see why they cut it from the American screenplay, I do admit to missing the "peek-a-boo" sub-story running through the final chapter of *Ju-On*. It emphasizes the distortion of vision necessary to see the ghosts. They are seen by mortals as filtered through shadows, security monitors, streams of water, panes of glass, spy holes, mirrors, and most obviously, the rails of the stairway banister.

It doesn't mesh logically with the mortal terror Reka must be feeling at *Ju-On*'s climax for her to step back to the mirror and stare at her reflection through her fingers, and if they had kept this sequence in the American version, I'm sure there would have been more of the "bad" giggling in the audience. But, without being hammered home by the peek-a-boo games the old man plays with Toshio in *Ju-On*, this idea is still present, if a bit more subtle. I suppose the added subtlety the remake gains from this can also count as a fine-tuning from which the movie benefits.

The most glaring inanities that remain in the remake are decidedly American, like terrified women venturing into attics all alone with nothing but a cigarette lighter. But even these lapses into typical American horror movie dumbness still made for a wonderfully interactive audience on the nights I attended the movie. The cries of "Don't go in there" seemed much more genuine than sarcastic. In fact, this was probably as frightened as I've ever seen a movie audience, and the crowds I sat with those opening nights were rowdy as hell. I had expected them to be hard to scare, but the film simply never lost its hold on them. That's how good *The Grudge* is.

ONE MISSED CALL (2003)
Dir. Takashi Miike

At his worst, Takashi Miike is merely too prolific. Occasionally his films have a cranked-out feel, good though they might still be, and that's because they *are* cranked out sometimes. But when Miike focuses and gives a film the attention it deserves, he's nothing short of brilliant.

One Missed Call is Miike at his most focused, at least since *Audition*. The high-concept pitch—*Ringu* with cell phones—is only scratching the surface. In this movie, cell phones are the new medium by which a vengeful ghost spreads its curse, but they are also much more than that.

Case in point:

In *One Missed Call* the victims received phone calls from their future selves just before they die.

During *Call*'s climax, the doomed heroine is searching for her friend in the hallways of a derelict hospital. She hears the ring tone of his cell phone and instinctively calls out his name, running off in the direction of the sound. Looking in on one of the rooms, she hallucinates her *own* cell phone lying on a gurney, cut in half and crawling with maggots, and screams in mortal terror.

The message is perhaps a bit heavy handed, but nonetheless true, and growing truer by the day. And it's as much a core fear in this film as the viral curse and the black-haired ghost: the idea that we are willing ourselves into our cell phones, identifying ourselves with them. *Becoming* them.

In *One Missed Call*, the victims receive phone calls from themselves three days in the future, at the moment of their death. Miike uses this motif wonderfully, making us wait on pins and needles for the moment when the victim's last words are uttered again in the present, letting us know that they are about to die. Likewise, Miike uses our knowledge of New Wave J-horror against us, thwarting our expectations.

There's a heavy subtext of abuse running through the film—the cycle of neglect and battery that is passed from parent to child. Miike goes so far as to make this vicious cycle the very curse/vengeful ghost itself. So we've got a couple of themes here: the very Cronenbergian merger of human souls with cell phone "memories," and the "emotional ghosts" of abuse that get passed on through generations, much like a curse. These two themes, coupled with the insane amount of plot twists in *Call*'s third act, make for a lot to digest in one movie. In fact, all of it might not hold up for some viewers on repeated viewings. But the first time watching it is nicely unnerving, and at times genuinely scary. *Call* is both a loving tribute to—and a welcome spin on—material that has become both warmly familiar and terribly cliché.

"NOTHING IS ALRIGHT"

The most concise summation of my "shadow play as therapy" theory is probably:

"Our shadows are remnants of primal urges and fears that, if not properly recognized, accepted and embraced, will manifest in ways that perpetuate the cycle of fear and negativity ad infinitum."

This theory resonates within me, and feels like the truth. But it cannot be scientifically proven, which, I suppose, makes it a faith. And if you wanted to discover my greatest fear, you would have to know this. Get to the core of someone's faith, and you get to the core of their fear.

The scariest horror tale will tell you this: Your faith is unfounded, and the rules no longer apply, if indeed they ever did.

"Everything you know is wrong."

And by analyzing the next two films with as much detail as I'm going to, perhaps I'll let you in on more than you should know about what frightens me.

THE BLAIR WITCH PROJECT (1999)
Dir. Eduardo Sanchez/Dan Myrick

BWP is a magnificent experiment with decidedly mixed results. It either worked for you or it didn't, but the idea behind *Blair*, I think, is brilliant enough to justify the film's hype and subsequent success.

BWP is an attempt to put the viewer in as subjective a position as possible, from the first-person perspective of the cameras, to the notion of working without a shooting script and subjecting the actors to hunger, the elements, and the unknown. Very thankfully, *Blair* did not inspire a cavalcade of rip-offs the way *Halloween* did, as it's an idea that can only work once. My hat is off to the Hollywood studios for not attempting to duplicate its success (the welcome exceptions of course being *Cloverfield* and the Spanish masterpiece *[REC]*).

The time couldn't have been riper for a film like *Blair*; the '90s marked the beginning of the reality TV boom. Not only does the disease known as reality TV capitalize on our fascination with seeing our fellow humans behaving badly, it also eliminates the need for writers and actors. It's as American as media can be: cheap, slothful, reeking of artistic atrophy and capitalizing on the worst in human nature. *BWP* is not only a bona fide experiment in fear; it's a—perhaps unwitting—satire of a media fad almost as scary as the Blair Witch herself.

Synopsis isn't necessary; you've seen it. Instead of analyzing the film straightaway, I'm going to share my experience of seeing *Blair* for the first time:

A local theatre was showing a sneak preview at midnight before opening day. My friends and I had waited in line for over three hours. I had heard enough about it from people who had seen it either in film school or on bootleg video, and knew that this thing had potential to live up to its hype.

The crowd was a rowdy one. By the time the film started, people were still chattering away, and being shushed by the rest of us. Those who were shushed, shushed back. This continued for about a minute and a half.

There was restlessness in the crowd that kept me from fully getting absorbed in the movie. I began to think that coming to this particular showing was a bad idea. I saw good things happening on the screen, and I wished I could watch it alone. *God, I hate people,* I thought to myself, and my girlfriend uttered these same sentiments aloud.

As Heather's performance grew more histrionic throughout the film, the crowd began to laugh at her, and though I didn't want to, I sympathized. Heather was the one element of the film that didn't convince me.

As the characters were subjected to yet another day of relentless arguing, and yet another night of spooky noises, I began to lose my patience with the film as well as the crowd. I had begun to accept the fact that I was going to be disappointed by this experience.

When Heather opened up the bundle of sticks to discover Josh's teeth, things in the theatre got a little quieter. Then Heather went back into over-the-top-drama-queen mode, and the crowd chatter was back to normal.

A brief aside, if you will permit me: I had read an interview with the makers of BWP *before I saw the movie. They were discussing the process of shooting* Blair, *and at one point they mentioned a shot of Heather, running and running and running with the camera. "Basically," they said, "it's the last thing you see in the movie." I grunted in frustration, realizing that I didn't want to have read that.*

I would now like to thank them for that bit of misdirection.

When Mike said to Heather, "Oh shit. It's a house," a wave of gasps rolled from the front of the theatre to the back. And then, miraculously, everyone became very, very quiet. I realized that, through the utter repetition of the first 80 minutes of the film, I had become frustrated and given up on it. And in doing so, I had let my guard down. I was not ready for them to find a house, and neither was anyone else in the audience. *Blair* now had our strictest attention.

The tension became worse and worse as each new facet of the house was revealed: the shambles of the interior; Josh yelling Heather's name; the runes and handprints on the walls. We, the audience, were all now in the same headspace. No one was in a laughing mood.

The terrifying house from *The Blair Witch Project*.

197

When Mike went down into the basement and got nailed, the audience made a single hivemind gasping noise. As Heather followed him down, her voice being picked up only by Mike's still running camcorder, the spatial disorientation ratcheted the tension to a height I'd never felt at a movie before. And when Heather's camera focused on Mike, standing in the corner with his back to us, I felt perhaps the closest approximation of fear it is possible to experience via the medium of film.

When the credits began rolling, the entire audience burst into applause.

It's the strangest phenomena, applauding a movie. Who exactly are we clapping for? In this case, I realized that the experience I had with *Blair* was something I'd always chased, but considered elusive and maybe impossible—being subjectively scared by a movie. I think we were applauding not only to express our amazement at this, but also to shake off any emotional residue, knowing we all had to venture outside into the October chill at 2 AM. I walked to the car simultaneously looking over my shoulder and giggling at the notion that a movie was making me do it.

Not everyone had this experience with *Blair*, of course, and everyone has his or her own reasons. A lot of people, I think, were expecting something specific, and were pissed when they didn't get it. (More than one person said to me, "I wanted so *see* the witch, I wanted to *see* those kids getting killed.") My experience happened because, in giving up on the movie as I had, I gave up any expectations I might have had of it.

Subsequent viewings (my girlfriend and I saw it six times in the theatre) allowed us to enjoy the buildup more. We were better able to hear the dialogue, as well as the noises the characters encounter at night. Heather's performance never grew on me, but I take into account that I do, in fact, know people like that in real life, and I can live with it easier.

We'll be analyzing the Mike-in-the-corner shot, and why it works so well, while we talk about another experiment in terror: *The Ring.*

THE RING (2002)
Dir. Gore Verbinski
RINGU (1998)
Dir. Hideo Nakata

A small aside: When discussing Ringu, *I will not be taking into account the novel or any of its sequels, which offer both supernatural and sci-fi explanations for* Ringu's *events. I choose to ignore them here and take* Ringu *as its own self-contained enigma. I find it scarier functioning on its own peculiar logic, and I don't want to accept explanations that ground it more in reality.*

Also: I will not be discussing the abysmal piece-o'-shit American sequel anywhere in this analysis. Thank you.

The Ring sets itself up for a tough battle with our inner skeptic within its first 10 minutes. The story concerns itself with a videotape that kills those who watch it after seven days. The movie's first victim, teenaged Katie, appears to have been frightened to death. At her funeral, Katie's aunt Rachel overhears two women whispering, "Why the closed coffin?"—implying in the ever-popular Lovecraftian copout, that Katie's corpse is *too terrifying to show, mua ha ha...*

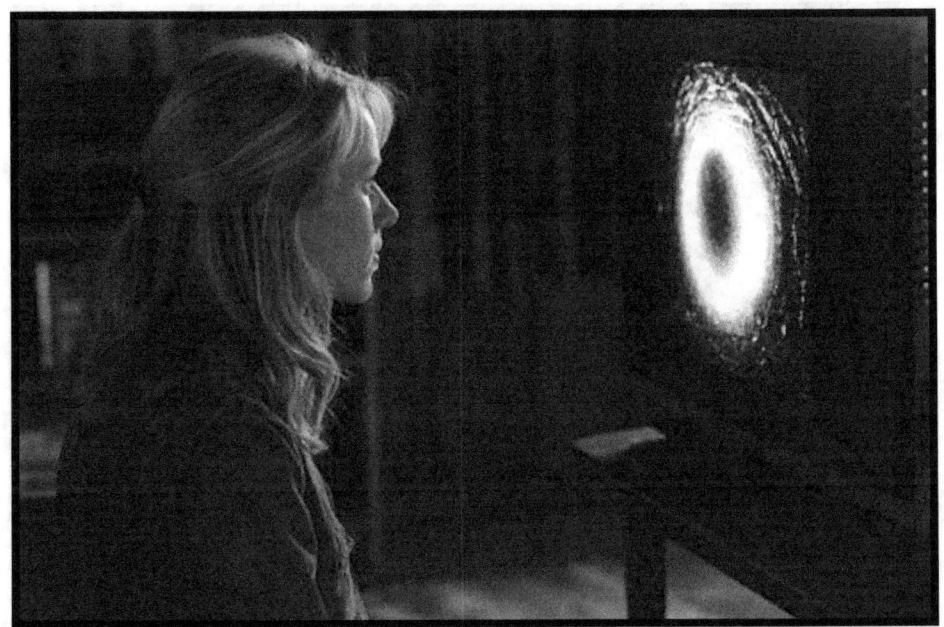

Naomi Watts as Rachel in *The Ring* (2002).

And then, not five minutes later, Katie's mom flashes back to the discovery of her dead daughter, and we get to *see* her face. And yes, it's pretty fucked up. Thus the film establishes its arrogance; it implies that its good stuff is too good to show, and then shows it. With this microcosmic setup and payoff, we are ready for the rest of the movie to unfold. *Scare me,* we think to ourselves, *I dare you.*

As Rachel tracks down the mystery of the videotape, she, her son, and her ex-boyfriend are exposed to it in the process, and each of them become convinced that they are not long for this earth. The seven-day countdown has begun, and *The Ring* has promised us that it will deliver the goods.

In leading up to the big moment, the Japanese and American versions are a bit different. *Ringu* is almost *Blair-Witch*-like in its pacing, building up tension by way of frustration. After an hour or so, you're screaming, "Will something please *happen?!*"

The first time I saw *Ringu,* I was alone at night. The execution and payoff were indeed very similar to *Blair,* and thankfully, so was its overall effect. When the reporter uncovered Sadako's corpse in the well, I had resigned myself to the fact that the film was about over, and that I was in for a disappointment. And again, as in *Blair*, I let my guard down. In fact, I had almost fallen asleep twice.

When Ryuiji's TV turned on and showed Sadako crawling out of the well, shambling toward the screen, I was no longer sleepy. My heart rate, in fact, doubled. When she crawled out of the *TV,* my heart rate doubled yet again. When the camera zoomed in on Sadako's face, revealing the one eye peering out from her shroud of black hair, I believe I made a few noises. And when Ryuiji screamed his last scream, I sympathized. *If that had been me,* I thought to myself, *my heart would've stopped too.* Sadako had crawled out of Ryuiji's TV, past my defenses and straight into my subconscious. She's still there, hanging out in the corner with Mike.

In *Ringu* a videotape seems to cause the death of anyone who has viewed it.

The American version, I think, is better at building momentum and tension. While a few scenes were recreated almost shot-by-shot, a few embellishments were made that provide very substantial scares. I was amazed that a Hollywood studio would actually take so much care to preserve, and actually enhance, the tone of the original. It certainly didn't happen with subsequent American J-horror remakes.

The sequence where Rachel descends into the well and finds Samara's corpse is much more tense than the same in *Ringu*, and the unique-to-the-American-version videotape scene of the doctor interviewing Samara is superb. It foreshadows the payoff scene by way of a simple camera trick: the first time the camera focuses on the TV on which Samara's interview is playing, we can see the edge of the TV screen, twice removing the scene from reality; we are watching an image within an image.

Toward the end of the interview, as Samara's words become more threatening, we cut back to the TV screen, and this time we are submerged in the image. We cannot see the screen's edge, and Samara is in clearer focus. This is a tiny hint of Samara's later transformation from a removed, 2-D image to a very real threat.

Though I was much more alert when I saw the remake, and though I knew what was going to happen, I still found the payoff scene remarkably effective. With one small exception:

The reveal of Samara's face in the remake is a prime testament to the phrase "less is more." In *Ringu*, all we could make out behind Sadako's veil of black hair was her eye, twisted with insane rage, and it was *just enough* to make us afraid to see her entire face. This may well actually go down with me as the scariest film image I've yet seen. The reveal in the remake is, frankly, anticlimactic. But whatever malicious insanity is not revealed by Samara's face in *The Ring*'s big scene *is* revealed in the aforementioned interview scene, and in *The Ring*'s ending. It drives home a line spoken by Samara, excised from the final cut of the film, but left intact in the trailers and on the website:

"Everyone will suffer."

If we think about the implications of Rachel and Aidan continuing the chain, we realize that not everyone can be saved. Invariably, someone's going to get stuck on the bad end of the chain, and they will die a horrible death. Their death will affect all those close to them, and those who successfully continue the chain will have to live with the guilt. Everyone will be haunted by Samara in one way or another. Everyone, indeed, will suffer.

We're talking about a shadow that cannot, and doesn't want to, be healed. We're back in Lansdale territory again: the new breed, the true evil. And unlike the serial killers seemingly born without the ethics gene in Lansdale's work, the human cancers as he calls them, Samara cannot simply be removed from existence: the only way to get rid of this virus is to spread it.

The closest we get to the color red in *The Ring* is the tree at Shelter Mountain. It's a very marked contrast to the rest of the film's color palette, for red is the color we associate with fire, and *The Ring* is a movie submerged in water. Water is everywhere because, from frame one, Samara is in the lives of Rachel's family. Katie has watched the tape. She is "in the well" as it were, surrounded by water, helpless and waiting to die. On her last night alive, the Seattle rain is pounding down, the TV screen ripples like water, and water drips and collects below the door to her bedroom.

The two bodies of water we're dealing with specifically are the ocean and the well. Samara is born a creature of unbridled imagination, and her visions surge unchecked out of her head, flooding the heads of her mother and father, and the horses they raise. In an attempt to get their daughter under control and rid their own heads of the horrible images (to "put the ocean in a well," maybe?), Samara's father keeps her in the barn, where "the horses keep her up at night." Later, of course, the horses drown themselves.

In the ocean.

And in *Ringu*, it's strongly implied that Sadako's father might actually *be* something in the ocean. Near the film's climax, Sadako's uncle tells Ryuiji the story of her mother Shizuko:

"She used to talk to the sea. She mumbled things to it. Looked like she was having fun. I hid once and listened, but it wasn't a human language."

The soundtrack on the videotape offers up the rhyme, "Frolic in brine, goblins be thine." And later on in the film, Ryuiji states, "I wonder if her father was even human."

Water and lava are a kind of Yin and Yang in *Ringu*. Water: Yielding, receptive, feminine. Water gave rise to the first primordial life on earth, but it can kill the beings that have "evolved beyond" it, if they are not respectful.

The ocean, for all intents and purposes, is a kind of outer space right here on earth. So much of it remains unexplored, and one could keep oneself up at night trying to imagine what hitherto-unseen creatures are crawling on its floor, swimming in its deepest grottos. One imagines Shizuko wading out into the ocean, calling out to something in a language that isn't human, inviting something to come to her, *courting* something...

Well, at least *I* imagine that.

And then we've got Mt. Miharayama: phallic storehouse of masculine, forceful lava, which is as malleable as water, but unable to nurture life, in fact destroying everything it touches. Men prove to be Shizuko's undoing (the reporters who refuse to believe in her psychic abilities), and she symbolically echoes this, throwing herself into Mt. Miharayama.

In *The Ring*, once Rachel watches the tape, she too is "submerged" for seven days. The rain pounds harder; her dreams are drenched in water; she must travel to Moesko

Island, surrounding herself on all sides with water, to try to uncover Samara's story; and on this trek she bears witness to the water-drenched suicides of both the horse and Richard Morgan.

But as large a part as water plays in *The Ring*, you won't find the color blue around much; the only blues in the film are heavily subdued with gray. Gray and green are the dominant colors here. The ocean isn't blue in Washington because the sky is always gray, and the film's palette is dominated by the gray of rain clouds (and TV static), and the green of foliage (and maybe stagnant well-water).

TWIN SHADOWS: COMPARING *RING* AND *BLAIR*

1

Aside from the fact that these two films have provoked the strongest reactions from me thus far in my career as a horror junkie, *Ring* and *Blair* have many similar themes that tie them together, making them kindred spirits.

Perhaps the most obvious trait the two films share is restraint. In this day and age of hardcore splatter, *The Ring* is rated PG-13, while *Blair* received its R simply for profanity. A lot of your macho alpha male type horror freaks will tell you that restrained horror films—especially supernatural ones—are "pussy," and the only truly scary movies are about "shit that could really happen": you know, serial killers and cannibals and whatnot. These people are crucially out of touch with their imaginations, and fail to understand cinema's true purpose: to make the viewer transcend reality.

No one wants to watch a movie about a guy getting up in the morning, taking a shit, brushing his teeth and going to work. And in this day and age, are serial killer flicks really any less banal? Splatter is fun, sure, but really, anybody can do it. And anyone can make a gritty, ugly film that throws viscera in your face. But *Ringu* and *Blair* not only hold back with the gore, they stretch moments of tension to pure absurdity, to the point where the entire films are mere buildup until the money shots at the end.

But even these big moments relish in restraint; it's important to mention that both these films share the central image of a human being with their face obscured. In both films the monster is given human form, and shrouded in excruciating mystery. Watching these films, I scared the crap out of myself trying to imagine what those faces looked like (until, of course, the American *Ring*'s disappointing reveal). There is, in both cases, an almost unbearable menace, and a childlike sense of mischief: Mike-in-the-corner is a dead (?) man playing a twisted game of hide-and-seek, and Samara is a dead little girl playing peek-a-boo.

Whether or not a viewer relates to these images has a lot to do, I think, with how well one remembers childhood.

2

How well connected are you to your childhood? Do you remember what it was like to not have societal rules and physical laws yet etched into your brain, and thus to believe that anything was possible? Remember what it was like to not be able to control your imagination?

Daveigh Chase as Samara in *The Ring* (U.S.)

They romanticize the crap out of the "childhood sense of wonder" in movies and books, don't they? And sure, there are times when I wish I could recapture that state of mind. But there's also a part of me that knows better. I remember what being afraid was like as a kid.

Childhood is, not coincidentally, a strong theme in both *Ring* and *Blair*. *BWP*'s child murderer Rustin Parr serves as a kind of conduit for the Blair Witch both during his life and after his death. The scariest moments in Blair all involve children: the voices outside the tent; the handprints on the walls; and the aforementioned aura of mischief in that last shot.

And of course, childhood is a much more obvious theme in *The Ring*. If *The Exorcist* explored our fear of teenagers (the children we raise and nurture transforming into masturbating, blaspheming bulimics) then *The Ring* is about our fear of childhood and children.

As children, we sleep with the lights on to avoid being subjected to our own imaginations. If we scare *ourselves* so badly as kids, it's no wonder adults look at children sideways sometimes.

Rationality is imposed upon kids, inch by inch, as they grow up, with the child kicking and screaming the whole way. As adults, we are trained to *fear* irrationality; we are told that losing our grip on how things work is a fate worse than death. Who among us, then, has not witnessed a child racing in the grips of a sugar rush, or listened to a child incessantly crying for no reason, or analyzed a particularly bothersome drawing by a child, and thought to themselves, "What the fuck is wrong with this kid?" It's been said many times that we only fear what we don't understand, and who understands children all the time? Really?

So, Samara: perhaps the very personification of what we don't understand about children. Not only does her imagination cook up strange and terrible images, but said images invade the heads of those closest to her. She doesn't ever seem to sleep. She wants to hurt people.

All the kids in *The Ring* are freaky. From Samara to the doctor's grandson on Moesko Island, to Aidan, who seems to be connected to Samara in a way the adults are not. Aidan and Samara are twins of a sort, reflections of each other. Both of them attempt to express themselves with images; both are misunderstood by the adults closest to them (and in both cases, said adults are not the parents); both have absentee father figures; and judging from the dark circles under Aidan's eyes, it's clear he doesn't sleep much either (he, in fact, watches the cursed tape in the first place because he can't sleep). It's possible Aidan sympathizes with Samara, and she might well sympathize with him, but that isn't enough to make her stop. Nothing is.

We must also note the twinning in *Ringu* at this point: Shizuko/Sadako and Ryuiji/Yoichi, psychic mother/daughter, and psychic father/son. This twinning is explored to greater effect in *Ringu 2*.

The Blair Witch has a thing for children, having kidnapped and tortured several while she was alive, and having compelled Rustin Parr to kill several more after her death. And before she kills *BWP*'s three college student protagonists, she toys with and tortures *them,* breaking down their psyches until they are little more than whimpering children. Samara toys with her victims similarly, making them understand what it's like to be her—frightened, helpless, alone, submerged in water, waiting for the end.

3

In *Blair*, Heather's obsession with recorded media is certainly the fatal flaw that strands her and her crew out in the woods. She's obsessed with capturing *something* on tape, going so far as to send her energy out into the woods in some kind of primitive séance (as Heather's journal attested to on *BWP*'s website).

The '90s ushered in the age of the Digital Amateur, making it possible to establish yourself in the entertainment industry without having to send off demo reels or head shots to Hollywood, and, sometimes, without leaving your home. Uninhibited about taking your clothes off for horny old men? Buy a webcam and quit your day job. Got a DV camera? Great! Get out there and come back with images of

Samara climbs from the well in *The Ring*.

humans acting like buffoons. If you can't get anyone else to do it, just make a Jackass out of *yourself*. Thanks to the digital revolution, we can cut out the middleman of show business and humiliate ourselves for money and fame.

Heather wants to capture evidence of the Blair Witch at any cost. She doesn't consciously put herself or her crew in danger; she just fails to consider their safety. When it becomes apparent that she has doomed herself and her crew with her recklessness, the trio's goal changes, but the mode of accomplishing it stays the same. They find that they need to keep filming, in the event that their deaths might be documented, and the document discovered in the future. The act of filming seals their fate, and becomes their only hope for post-mortem justice. Irony at its finest.

And in *The Ring*, Samara seems to know that the most expedient way to "be heard" by the world is via modern visual media. Her latest piece of art manifests itself in the form of the videotape. The tape is already an urban legend by the film's beginning, but a new master copy is made when Katie and her friends (staying in the cabin above Samara's resting place) try to record a football game.

Katie, of course, is the niece of Rachel, an investigative reporter, who has access to archives of past media (to uncover Samara's story), and modern media technology (to spread it). As an added bonus, she also has Aidan. Samara's plan is a hideously perfect one: get to Rachel by way of her niece, and force her into action by holding Aidan hostage with the seven-day countdown.

Samara's father sums it up quite nicely: "What is it with reporters? You take one person's tragedy and force the world to experience it. Spread it like sickness."

"LAST WORDS"

Horror cinema may change with the times, its archetypes may evolve with their respective cultures, and its trends may vacillate between base and sophisticated, but one thing is certain: it is not going away anytime soon.

Recently my therapist relayed a saying to me that I really took to heart: *In order to change things, you have to accept what is*. Being the overthinker that I am, I quickly expanded that idea beyond the realm of the obstacles I face in my personal life, to encompass the obstacles we collectively face. The hate and fear that inspires the whole of the atrocities in the world will not be made to go away by simply denying, or trying to forget, their existence. Likewise, attempts to censor or suppress dark art can never truly prevail. There will always be a supply as long as there is a demand, and there will always be a demand as long as there is real horror in the world.

I personally didn't *ask* to be a fan of horror films; it was more a byproduct of my experiences in childhood. Oh sure, being a fan of dark art nowadays, I get to present myself as *outré* and iconoclastic, and sure, that might get me chicks, but life certainly would have been easier for me if I had been remotely popular in school, and if my hometown hadn't tried to break my spirit and/or kill me for the first 25 years of my life. And honestly, if I could sacrifice this part of my identity that I cherish today, in exchange for a lack of real world horror, thus rendering horror films unnecessary, I'd do it in a heartbeat.

But we can't change what is until we accept and process it, and myth and allegory are among the most effective tools we have for processing real life events. Horror cinema and I are stuck with each other, and it's been one of the most positive and inspiring relationships I've ever been in. Which motivates me, once again, to draw a parallel between the world and myself.

World, listen up: We and horror cinema are also stuck with each other. The sooner we face that, the sooner we can begin to process, learn from, and evolve beyond the darkness we've been keeping ourselves in for the past several millennia. We have the tools at our fingertips, and the skills to use them. But it's time to stop being afraid of our own shadows.

ABOUT THE AUTHOR

Willy Greer is a musician, film composer and horror film scholar living in Portland, Oregon. He co-hosts *Horror Holocaust Radio*—the first and longest-running online radio show of its kind—with Jeff Dean on www.horrorholoaustradio.com. He is currently at work on the screenplay for the slasher film *Second Skin*. This is his first book.

IF YOU ENJOYED THIS BOOK
PLEASE CALL, WRITE OR E-MAIL
FOR A FREE CATALOG

MIDNIGHT MARQUEE PRESS
9721 BRITINAY LANE
BALTIMORE, MD 21234

WWW.MIDMAR.COM
410-665-1198
MMARQUEE@AOL.COM

www.ingramcontent.com/pod-product-compliance
Lightning Source LLC
Chambersburg PA
CBHW071912110526
44591CB00011B/1653